# Mimetic
# Politics

# Studies in Violence, Mimesis, and Culture

# Mimetic Politics

## DYADIC PATTERNS
## IN GLOBAL POLITICS

Roberto Farneti

Michigan State University Press · *East Lansing*

♾ The paper used in this publication meets the minimum requirements of ANSI/NISO Z39.48-1992 (R 1997) (Permanence of Paper).

 Michigan State University Press
East Lansing, Michigan 48823-5245

Printed and bound in the United States of America.

21  20  19  18  17  16  15     1  2  3  4  5  6  7  8  9  10

LIBRARY OF CONGRESS CONTROL NUMBER: 2014941653
ISBN: 978-1-61186-148-8 (pbk.)
ISBN: 978-1-60917-445-3 (ebook: PDF)
ISBN: 978-1-62895-137-0 (ebook: ePub)
ISBN: 978-1-62896-137-9 (ebook: Kindle)

Book design and composition by Charlie Sharp, Sharp Des!gns, Lansing, Michigan
Cover design by David Drummond, Salamander Design, www.salamanderhill.com
Cover image is *Tod des Konsuls L. J. Brutus im Zweikampf mit Aruns* (GG 6798),
Giambattista Tiepolo 1730, Kunsthistorisches Museum, Wien, Gemäldegalerie and is
used with permission.

green press INITIATIVE  Michigan State University Press is a member of the Green Press Initiative
and is committed to developing and encouraging ecologically responsible
publishing practices. For more information about the Green Press Initiative and the use of
recycled paper in book publishing, please visit *www.greenpressinitiative.org*.

Visit Michigan State University Press at *www.msupress.org*

*To my parents and my sister*

# Contents

# Introduction

In 1985 New York artist Jenny Holzer rented a Times Square billboard normally reserved for commercial use. She illuminated it with six words—"Protect me from what I want." The phrase—which Holzer describes as "an all-purpose admonition to self and others"—encapsulates perfectly the ambivalence about commodity culture felt by many during the 1980s.[1]

The gigantic billboard in Times Square attracted the attention of Slavoj Žižek, who argued that the truism pointed "towards the fact that in today's patriarchal society, woman's desire is radically alienated, that she desires what men expect her to desire, that she desires to be desired by men."[2] A desire is imposed on the subject by an external order, a *force* that dictates what the subject *wants* to desire.

Holzer's "admonition to self and others" could be read from another perspective, where the agent of protection, the *who* that is protecting the subject from *what* she wants, is not the order of society, or a projection of the subject's alienated self. Early human societies were well aware of the dangers represented by internal impulses and dynamics: rituals and taboos prescribed forms of protection aimed at preserving the fragile fabric of social conventions. According to a perspective that we may call "mimetic," all rituals seem to descend from a situation of jeopardy and vulnerability that resolved itself by means of a violent killing. Early human communities instituted a sort of memorial of this primal event in order to perpetuate a system of protection: *sacrifice* was this major innovation that early humans adopted in order to place a constraint on their internal dynamics. Sacrifice is indeed a protective barrier, a prosthesis used to control and ultimately ban exposure to a potentially destructive disposition: reciprocal imitation.

Mimesis refers to a universal disposition that humans share with higher primates to imitate one another, to treat one another as models and rivals at the same time, to desire and want what their neighbor wants. The kind of rivalry induced by systemic reciprocal imitation of one another's *desires* is bound to escalate until an outlet vouches for its eventual demise and restores peace and order within the community. This providential strategy allowed this diffused reciprocity to collapse into a single field of focus: it is the unanimous killing of a designated victim—of someone held responsible for unleashing the evil "animal spirits" that plagued the community—that resolves the crisis.[3] Sacrifice was therefore introduced and experimented with to channel and ritualize this dynamic, that is, "to contain and control the violence which would otherwise engulf and destroy a community";[4] sacrifice worked so long as it protected the community from drifting into the kind of conflictive reciprocity that threatened to destroy it.

Earlier human societies worked out this successful means of coping with mimetic dynamics: the violent killing of either a member of the community or, in more evolved societies, of a ritual nonhuman victim, served the strategic purpose of reconstituting the social bond after the crisis. However, sacrifice is so distant to a contemporary observer that it seems to belong to a prehistory of our social arrangements. But sacrifice has not been eliminated once and for all; it still survives in our postsacrificial societies under many disguises. This book is about politics in our (allegedly) postsacrificial times. It is about a politics that does not suppress the uncanny memories of its sacrificial beginnings.[5]

It is therefore sacrifice that protects us from what we want, where what we want does not spring from an internal locus of control, an "ego" in the meaning that the word has acquired, in Hobbes's words, in "these Western parts that have received their moral learning from Rome and Athens."[6] We *want* what our neighbor wants, and we model our wishes on the wishes of others. This dynamic of desire has dreadful implications, as there is no limit, no ultimate "satisfaction" to what we want, and the realization of the depths of this abyss brings us to ask for protection: protect me from what I want, that is, protect me from this uncontrollable escalation of "mimetic" desire, from its psychological and social consequences.

In canto 13 of *Inferno,* Dante says, "Let us turn from the sight of this abyss." It is a remarkable statement that captures the general outlook of human societies whenever a major mimetic crisis—a crisis generated by the escalation of unguarded mimetic desire—looms on the horizon. And "abyss" is a term that defines very aptly the condition of void and bottomlessness of a situation in which a fundamental human disposition (e.g., desire) is no longer directed to an external object but operates in an environment where objects no longer matter. Our desires compound themselves by feeding on the desires of our rivals.

The key phrase in Holzer's truism is "protect me," which is what politics is all about: to *protect* people.[7] Hobbes argued that when the state is dissolved by a war, "forraign, or intestine," then everyone is "at liberty to protect himself by such course as his own discretion shall suggest onto him. . . . For he that wants protection may seek it any where; and when he hath it, is obliged . . . to protect his Protection as long as he is able."[8] This book interrogates contemporary forms of protection, such as barriers, borders, norms, institutions, and the like, from the perspective of those dynamics—both psychological and political—that challenge protection. Mimetic politics is the kind of politics that has disposed of old sacrificial bounds and is no longer able to protect the life of "he that wants protection."

The French anthropologist René Girard defines "the modern world essentially as deprived of sacrificial protection, that is, more and more exposed to violence."[9] The end of ritual has brought about an intensification of mimetic rivalry; the lack of protective barriers has exposed life and politics to threats whose magnitude is difficult to estimate. Current global trends have laid bare age-old mimetic dynamics. Such words as "contagion" and "escalation" are often used by mimetic theorists to describe the scope and expansion of those dynamics, and the growth "to the extreme" of mimetic conflicts has found in the smooth space of globalization a particularly congenial terrain.[10] The challenge, for us scholars, is to contaminate the discourse of political science with other possibly untimely languages and hypotheses, and look at what Girard calls the "modern world" from the perspective of the dwindling of age-old forms of protection, like ritual and sacrifice.

A possible obstacle to a project like this is the variety of disciplines that one would want to straddle. Nothing more than the term "interdisciplinarity" suggests the split between scholarly theory and academic practice. Interdisciplinarity, to put it bluntly, is a serious liability unless it involves a number of people each working within one disciplinary niche. Interdisciplinary work by *one* scholar is always looked upon with doubt and suspicion, and the suspicion is directed at those realms that exist only in the interim between disciplines. Mimetic theory challenges disciplinary boundaries and seems to thrive in a space defined by the dialogue between scholars from different fields. However, it rarely spreads out from the interstices between disciplines to attract the interest of scholars firmly based in *one* discipline. One of the hopes of the author of this book is to prove that what I have just written is wrong, and that a mimetic perspective on politics could rise in the agenda of both political scientists and theorists.

♦ ♦ ♦

My interest in mimetic theory is indebted to both books and people. Some years ago I came across a review article of the Italian translation of René Girard's book on Shakespeare. I read the book and wrote a long article for the Italian journal *Strumenti Critici*. I found Girard's interpretation of Shakespeare impressive, its implications fascinating, and I decided to work in greater depth on the possible spillover effects of mimetic theory into *political* theory. I soon understood that mimetic theory could hardly be made into a fitting companion of political theory, that it clearly could not support some of its background premises; plus, the very tenets of mimetic theory seemed at odds with the normative foundations of political theory.

The normative subfield of political science, a subfield that focuses on the contested meanings of such notions as freedom, equality, justice, and democracy, is concerned less with facts of the world—facts that could be empirically ascertained—than with meanings and values. Humans, according to both theorists and philosophers, are eminently "social creatures whose deep aim is to live in a community with others and to share with others a conception of value."[11] This definition stresses the normative outlook of our attitude towards the world and ourselves, but it also shows how typical and context-specific is the language used by theorists.

Mimetic theory does not challenge the assumption that we are normative creatures, sensitive to reason. However, the mimetic understanding of agency and morality grants a very special status to *imitation;* it supports the claim that human behavior is gregarious and derivative, never authentic. It challenges the very notion of autonomy and its epistemological derivates, and questions the very premises of the tradition that is still dominant in both political theory and the theory of international relations, a tradition that has Kant firmly planted at its center.[12]

Speaking of the larger domain of political science, it is interesting to notice that the age-old distinction between natural sciences and the mixed domain of *Geisteswissenschaften* runs across its corpus, where two bordering subfields are separated by a deep epistemological gap: theorists and scientists speak different languages, and each language has its own outlook and agenda. To be sure, the difficulties and resistance met by mimetic theory in its attempt to find common ground for mutual exploration with the empirical concerns of political scientists indicate that the methodological distance between the two is quite big. Aside from some rare signs of interest, the contemporary agenda of political science has turned "from the sight of this abyss."

In this introduction I will try to situate mimetic theory in a budding web of debates and discussions in the social sciences, focusing on the work of those theorists and scientists who have gleaned the high potential of mimetic theory for cross-contamination.

In this book it will be argued that mimetic dynamics are not accidental but rather constitutive. The five chapters of the book highlight these dynamics and show how they *constitute* the political processes that are otherwise investigated through biased presuppositions. The Israeli-Palestinian schism and its impact on global politics is taken as a paradigm for illuminating the mimetic mechanisms of aggregation and disaggregation that characterize politics today. The first three chapters of the book consistently apply this paradigm and delve into such areas as democratic peace theory, conflict resolution, and globalization, in order to open up a new perspective on politics.

Chapter 1 expounds the basics of mimetic theory and says a bit about what we gain by adopting a mimetic perspective and how this perspective serves to illuminate and explicate political processes. The chapter previews the main cases covered.

In chapters 2 and 3 I shall turn to the conflict that "represents in miniature" global mimetic lineups.[13] The conflict "between Israel and the

Palestinian authority" is a "new" type of conflict for its ubiquity across national borders. The conflict is "mimetic" because each actor can be seen as a "model who becomes a rival, or a rival who becomes a model." The second chapter examines the implications of this conflict for the mimetic lineups that structure global politics today and shows that assumptions of nonpolarity are wrong, for the fundamental structure of global politics is bipolar. The third chapter seeks to show how this arch-conflict of our time is projecting its mimetic core onto global politics by creating divisions and cleavages that affect political lineups at several levels. This chapter revisits the left-right dichotomy and shows the mimetic implications of this fundamental dyad for understanding global politics. As left and right reach out from local to global politics and become tied up with questions of identity, some international issues appear to act as catalysts to ideological polarization, especially when the language used to address them pivots on the East/West axis. I will argue that the dyadic structure of these polarizations can be explained through the dialectic of "model" and "rival" suggested by mimetic theory.

There are many areas within the general study of politics that seem to benefit from adopting a mimetic perspective, ranging from electoral politics to the dynamics of social movements, to the interrelation of politics and religion. One area in which mimetic theory should be brought to bear is democratic peace theory, which is one of the areas in which a discussion of alternative approaches to conflict resolution may prove more fruitful. Democratic peace theorists believe that material gains, if supported by just institutions, increase the chances of "satisfaction" of states and thereby reduce their mutual hostility. The fourth chapter deconstructs this underlying notion of satisfaction and exposes the background assumptions of contemporary democratic theory.

It is at the intersection between religion and politics that mimetic phenomena seem to explode in an astonishing number of directions. It is at this intersection that we see at work the dynamics that mimetic theory considers fundamental and constitutive: the rise and mobilization of doubles, the dramatization of the image of the enemy and the escalation of religious hatred and violence, the sacrificial climax of the conflict and the eventual expulsion of the victim. Modern politics is affected by a deep-seated bias, the artificial separation of politics and religion, the state on one side and the promise of salvation on the other. To be sure, the changing relationships between authority and salvation depend on changing views of and approaches to what Harald Wydra calls "issues of political spirituality."[14] The fifth chapter explores this intersection and criticizes Girard's perspective on the Apocalypse. The chapter supports a neo-Hobbesian perspective in the attempt to understand the return of the sacred in current politics, and presents a case for a novel perspective, a political-theology of the empty tomb, a different understanding of the relationship between religion and politics that could work as an antidote against contemporary resurgences of both the sacred and sacrifice.

Chapters 2, 3, 4, and 5 have already appeared in print. An earlier version of chapter 2 was presented at the conference "Understanding New Wars" at the Centre for Research in the Arts, Social Sciences and Humanities (CRASSH) in Cambridge, on February 12 and 13, 2010. It appeared in 2013 as a journal article in a special issue of the *Cambridge Review of International Affairs*, "New Wars and Victimhood."

A version of chapter 3 was presented at the Second Obergurgl Governance Symposium organized by the Department of Political Science of the University of Innsbruck, in November 2008. It appeared in print in the *Journal of Political Ideologies*.

An earlier version of chapter 4 was presented as a conference paper at the Amsterdam Colloquium on Violence and Reconciliation (COV&R) in July 2007. An expanded version of the paper was published in *Polity* in 2009.

An earlier version of chapter 5 was presented as a conference paper in Falconara on March 10, 2006. A later version was published in *Theoria: A Journal of Social and Political Theory*.

I wish to thank the institutions that supported me financially. First, the Free University of Bozen/Bolzano, which generously financed a research project titled "Mimetic Politics" (through an ad hoc research fund, the Cost Center WW5095), and then the Alexander von Humboldt Foundation, which granted me a fellowship for three consecutive fall semesters in the Exzellenzcluster "Normative Orders" of the J. W. Goethe Universität in Frankfurt am Main.

As I said, there were the books—notably Girard's books—and then there were the people. Some of these people have been a steady source of insight and inspiration for my thoughts on mimetic theory and the range of, and potential for, its application in a number of fields. Harald Wydra has been indeed an inspiring interlocutor for many years, and yet, strangely enough, I can't help thinking of things we disagree on, instead of the myriad things we agree about. I present an account of mimesis in politics that overstresses dynamics of disintegration and conflict, whereas mimetic desire does sustain education, institutions, cooperation, and so on. Altruism is also an important phenomenon that could be explained in mimetic terms. Harald may be disappointed with my rather exclusive focus on conflict and disaggregation, but mimetic aggregation, in order to secure its merits and benefits, needs to forestall any further mimetic drift, the stage in which the mimetic twins start repelling each other. Sadly enough, this difficult balance turns out to be more and more precarious and the mimetic lineups that we observe in global politics are ever more menacing and ominous.

Special thanks go to Anthony Pagden, whose thoughts on East and West (and much else) have been a constant source of inspiration in the making of this volume (and not only this volume). The epilogue of the book comprises a section that, in a tentative form, was presented as a paper at the Political Theory Workshop of the UCLA Department of Political Science in February 2011. On that occasion I benefited from insights and critiques from Anthony Pagden and from other attendees. On that occasion Barbara Fuchs offered important insights: we agreed that one should be wary of absolute "originals" in historical processes.

I owe a great deal to the patience, generosity and insight of my academic host in Frankfurt, Christoph Menke. Other people have contributed over the years to my understanding of the specifics and complexities of mimetic theory. For their thoughtful comments on earlier drafts of the papers that have become the chapters of this book, as well as for informal conversations on topics related to mimesis and politics, I wish to thank Mark Anspach, Pierpaolo Antonello, Mia Bloom, Giuseppe Fornari, Wolfgang Palaver, Alan Scott, Simon Simonse, Giulia Sissa, Arpad Szakolczai, Aaron Thomas, and George Wright. I wish to thank also the directors of the journals where my work had been previously published, and the several anonymous readers who helped in one way or another to clarify my thoughts on mimetic theory.

# A New (Mimetic) Paradigm for Our Postsacrificial Times

This book contends that the analyses and predictions of political science are biased by a series of *anthropological* presuppositions. The book follows a clue from René Girard, that "we have entered an era in which anthropology will become a more suitable tool than political science."[1] The book, though, doesn't aim to replace political science—its methods and mores—with anthropology. Rather, the purpose of the book is to provide the study of politics with a different perspective, and see whether the *new* field of interest that may result from this change in perspective could be more sensitive and perceptive to current challenges.

In a nutshell one could argue that political science, in its numerous subfields, is constituted by a number of specific presuppositions that warrant the consistency and general reliability of its findings. To be sure, these presuppositions appear to clash with the tenets of mimetic theory, which sees dyadic patterns and mimetic attitudes wherever mainstream political science sees individual actors driven by a focused capacity for agency.

The book brings "mimetic theory" to bear on the study of politics. Mimetic theory constitutes a new approach to a number of old questions in the study of human behavior. It has a strong potential to contribute to developing a new framework in which issues related to human cognition, morality, sociability, and conflict could be analyzed.

Mimetic theory is normally associated with the name of Girard. However, Girard himself has tracked countless clues to a general mimetic explanation of human behavior in literature and ancient myth, so that the theory he proposed is less an entirely novel and original theoretical development than an attempt to formalize a number of age-old insights into human rationality and sociability. In particular, mimetic theory challenges a number of treasured assumptions about people's autonomy and capacity for agency and argues that the most fundamental human disposition is *imitation*. I believe this is an extremely important insight and I will proceed from the assumption that this focus on imitation opens up otherwise indiscernible patterns in human collective behavior.

Mimetic theory, to be sure, owes its general framing and agenda to the work of Girard, and mimetic theorists are in one way or another indebted to his important work across disciplines. But I very much believe that mimetic theory is an unfinished project, and work within this field must go beyond Girard's systematization. At the time of writing, what counts as mimetic theory seems to be an extension of insights that found in Girard's oeuvre a powerful means of theoretical unification but not an absolutely original enunciation. In the following I shall consider imitation a fundamental fact about human psychology but hardly a comprehensive and rather exclusive underpinning of human behavior. The absolutization of imitation as the fundamental psychological disposition downplays other psychological facts and phenomena, like the search for, and attribution of, status, and the pursuit of power and domination, that, according to Girard, are not fundamental but derivative. Girard overestimates the disappearance of the sacred as the principal effect of Christianity and possibly underestimates the persistence of scapegoats, and the ability of persecutors to build highly sophisticated rationalizations. The phenomenon of power, the central focus of a tradition of political thinking that goes from Machiavelli to Foucault, is marginal in Girard, according to whom power is normally exercised within a framework of stipulations (the "degree") designed to contain mimetic exposure and escalation. Violence is the central piece in Girard's oeuvre and violence is never, as in Canetti and Foucault, a kind of radicalization of power. Violence is rather the *opposite* of power; it is the disruptive force that threatens the "degree" from within. Neither is Girard concerned with the issue of justice, a major preoccupation in the intellectual tradition that goes from Plato to Rawls.

However, I am not proposing my own version of mimetic theory. I am just trying to integrate further knowledge into a project that has Girard as its principal inspiration. I will not challenge the tenets of the theory (e.g., "humans are fundamentally mimetic creatures") but will try to connect the theory with other disciplines and subdisciplines, and will try to adapt it to the concerns and protocols of those disciplines and subdisciplines.

My claim is that this emphasis on imitation has distinctive epistemic advantages. It threatens a number of stipulations that define the core practices and self-understanding of the scientific study of politics, and it challenges a number of epistemic constraints that kept the study of human sociability from evolving in directions proscribed by the classical individuationist model. This new emphasis opens up vast possibilities as regards our ability to picture ourselves as social creatures, in a world in which the canonical distinction between rational cooperation and irrational conflict is threatened by a different vision, dominated by a human disposition that is irrational yet still supports all the premises of our capacity for rationality.

Imitation challenges the dogma of autonomy and disintegrates the general assumptions of a principled and rational individualism. Not so much imitation per se, but the kind of fundamentally pervasive attitude described by Girard is hard to accommodate within the broader picture of the discipline. This preeminence of imitation not only threatens stipulations concerning the status of agency within political science but also challenges the core organization of a field structured by subdisciplines. Mimetic theory straddles boundaries and prompts closer contacts between different methods and outlooks in the social sciences.

In order to show the relevance of mimetic theory and the variety of stipulations that resist its influence I will try to describe its significance across a vast disciplinary spectrum, drafting a broad map in which a number of realms ranging from anthropology, evolutionary psychology, and the social sciences writ large, react when exposed to knowledge, insights, and findings from mimetic theory.

## Mimetic Theory in Context

There is, to be sure, a growing interest for mimetic theory in such fields as literary criticism, religious studies, anthropology, and, most recently, the neurosciences. The encounter between Girard and Vittorio Gallese—one of the discoverers of mirror neurons—seems to prefigure an entirely new horizon (Gallese stated in a recent paper that "Girard's mimesis of appropriation curiously appears to have foreshadowed, at a theoretical level, some recent results of empirical research in comparative psychology").[2]

All disciplines engaged in dialogue with the mimetic approach have been challenged to reassess their individuationist assumptions, the idea of an agent driven by desires reflecting the structure of its own authentic ego. The disciplines normally resist, shielding these assumptions from mimetic critique, and the response that they normally provide is that mimesis and imitation are not constitutive of agency, but are mere epiphenomena that can be easily dismissed as barely rational.

Mimetic theorists believe that mimesis is the inherent rationality of agency, that social dynamics are inherently dyadic, and that the ultimate realities in the study of society and politics are neither individuals nor collectives, but doubles. Mimetic theory also considers the kind of individualism (both ontological and methodological) supported by traditional, nonmimetic approaches as a form of "cult" that has dire effects on our ability to grasp the real dynamics at work in politics. In Girard's words, "the more desperately we seek to worship ourselves and to be good 'individualists,' the more compelled we are to worship our rivals in a cult that turns to hatred."[3] This mimetic version of the "dialectic of Enlightenment" (e.g., a dialectic of enlightened individualism) means to expose the nexus between individualism and myth in our culture, a nexus that Girard has been trying to unveil ever since.

Political science is an interesting case of a difficult dialogue with mimetic theory (with the exception of a few people who seem to have discovered the advantages of the mimetic approach and the somewhat mythical nature of political science's attendant individualism). Here the individual, occasionally aggregated in groups, is the ultimate epistemic authority, and the "tragic struggle of the doubles," in Girard's own words the most fundamental fact of politics, would sound as a highly evocative and purely rhetorical terminology. But mimetic theory brings to the fore a number of concerns that political scientists have consistently failed to notice: reciprocal imitation as the fundamental cause of human discord, the mechanisms of spontaneous polarization in human conflicts (i.e., the emergence of dyads or doubles), and the strange and ever-growing resemblance of the mimetic rivals.

Mimesis and imitation are not unknown phenomena in either political science or any of its different subfields. However, the idea of imitation as a leading or major factor in aggregating political actors seems at odds with the presumption of an individualistic capacity for agency of the actors:[4]

> much of the discussion of comparative politics is based on the analysis of individual countries, or components of countries. This approach remains valuable and important. That said, it is increasingly evident that those individual countries are functioning in a globalized environment and it is difficult if not impossible to understand one system in isolation. To some extent the shifts in national patterns are mimetic, with one system copying patterns in another that appear effective and efficient.[5]

However, the explanation of political phenomena offered by mimetic narratives is resisted by what I shall call the "individuationist model" in the social sciences, according to which all facts of politics are brought about by the agency of either individual or aggregated individual actors. Interestingly, the two outlooks coexisted for a long time before a major epistemological split-up doomed the mimetic outlook to a kind of theoretical nonexistence until its eventual recovery in a marginal turf where theoretical anthropology and literary criticism seemed to intersect. Hobbes, in chapter 13 of his *Leviathan*, argued that "in all times, Kings, and Persons of Soveraigne authority, because of their Independency, are in continuall jealousies . . . having their weapons pointing, and their eyes fixed on one another; . . . which is a posture of war." Hobbes here established the same nexus between reciprocal imitation and rivalry that constitutes the central tenet of mimetic theory. A powerful "Jealousy of State," together with a more intrinsic impulse to provide for the welfare of its subjects, was the driving force in the continual warfare that characterized international politics in the early modern age.

However, as I said, this emphasis on imitation remained ineffective, and in modern political thinking the state remained the single "nonjealous" locus of agency that determined whether and when to engage in either trade or warfare with neighboring states. It is the recent resurgence of mimetic theory in other fields, and its still embryonic spillover effects in the social sciences, that brought to the fore a number of (still limited) discussions on the immense importance of both "jealousy" and imitation in politics.

In order to understand the potential for innovation of mimetic theory one needs to locate it within the broader spectrum of the social sciences, and see at what level—and in proximity of which cognate fields—the theory appears to engage with the facts and phenomena of politics.

Mimetic theory challenges and even subverts a number of epistemological stipulations that constitute the fabric of *political* science. Its causal story, its methods, and its background anthropological presuppositions are so different from those that dominate in the social sciences that it is hard to find a platform for mutual exploration. Political scientist Mark Juergensmeyer has acknowledged the high epistemological impact of mimetic theory but refused to consider either mimesis or sacrifice as universally pervasive. To Juergensmeyer "war is the context for sacrifice rather than the other way around," a statement that discloses a powerful anthropological presupposition, namely, the idea that violence is universally pervasive; it is a biological fact that helps to explain the rise and rationale of sacrifice.[6] To Girard, instead, violence is *not* biological, or at least a purely biological explanation does not fully account for the complexities of violent behavior. The causal story implied by Girard begins with reciprocal imitation, not from an impulse to harm.[7] Imitation is a biological fact about humans, and brings the community to the verge of a deadlock whose only possible way out is sacrifice. By spilling the blood of the victim, society pulls itself together and solves the tensions brought about by this escalation "to the extreme," and into the abyss, of mimetic desire.

Scholars interested in mimetic theory have variously interpreted the kind of original sequence that explains the direction of causation in a process that seems to start with reciprocal imitation and ends with the sacrificial resolution of the crisis. If, according to Girard, the sequence details the following order: (1) imitation, (2) small-scale conflict, (3) contagion, (4) large-scale conflict, (5) sacrifice, and (6) resolution, Juergensmeyer challenges the sequence by posing "organized conflict" at the very outset. He points out that "the social activity of organized conflict, whether against an animal in a hunt or against other people in battle, is a primal form of human activity."

"Primal" here is obviously a synonym for "biological," meaning that the kind of conflict that is being structured and contained through elementary social practices comes *before* imitation. The pervasive conflictuality that one can detect in all human societies, a conflictuality that Juergensmeyer names "cosmic war," is therefore the only context in which sacrifice is argued to make sense. War comes *first,* whereas sacrifice, let alone mimesis, follows suit. This is, in a way, the solution favored by political scientists of a realist persuasion, who believe that either selfish behavior or even aggressive behavior is a fundamental biological trait. This "solution," though, fails to acknowledge the mimetic clause that "most human conflicts are reciprocal affairs," so that it is mimesis that features as the irreducible biological fact about humans.[8]

It is interesting how political theorist John Keane denies this aspect of mimetic theory and argues that Girard is just the most radical among a number of "proponents of violence"[9] who have joined forces in the attempt to propagate the antidemocratic belief that violence is universal and ineradicable and that "all political orders naturally rest upon violence, whose 'real' or 'ultimate' purpose is to contain the violent capacities of others."[10] "In emphasizing the *contingent* and *erasable* character of violence," Keane's book takes issue with Girard's attempt to demonstrate that violence is generative of the body politic and therefore at odds with the democratic idea that it is consensus and dialogue that generate and strengthen social bonds. Mimetic theory is framed as a potentially undemocratic approach to the study of society and politics.[11]

Another attempt to harness the disruptive effects of mimetic theory and turn it into an effective companion of either political theory or the theory of international relations comes from Harald Wydra. He accepts, *pace* Juergensmeyer, the fundamental structure of the sequence and grants to imitation its primary function: "the mimetic hypothesis . . . does not assume man's innately dangerous nature but conjectures that mimetic behavior is the anthropological constant in human relations."[12] However, Wydra believes that this anthropological presupposition is consistent, and not at odds, with the tenets of political *theory.* To him, "mimetic theory is congruous with the central idea of modern political theory that violence and the fear of violence are generative of order."[13] This is a contentious allegation, as "modern political theory" is a comprehensive theory of human agency that grants the individual the mental ability to stipulate conditions of sociability, whereas mimetic theory highlights nonconscious psychological processes, and implies nonagentic behavior on the side of the actors. The reach of Wydra's work, however, extends beyond its occasional engagement with mimetic theory. His recent work takes issue with the tenets of mimetic theory and explores the implication of sacrifice and the sacred for politics. Wydra has ventured into a radical attempt to reframe the study of politics so as to include a number of elements and implications that have been repressed through the process of canon-making that led to the current outlook and agenda of canonical political theory.

Two writers who have engaged directly with Girard's oeuvre, marking significant departures from the original framing of mimetic theory, are Jean-Pierre Dupuy and Paul Dumouchel, who published, in French, a book that took Girard to task: *L'enfer des choses*.[14] Here they pushed the methodological implications of mimetic theory "to the extreme" and dissolved the boundaries and stipulations among disciplines that structure the (nonmimetic) knowledge of social systems and phenomena. This book straddles discourses and disciplines and engages with the very same phenomenon that inspired the present volume: postsacrificial societies no longer avail themselves of an easy and handy way to dispose of human violence and need to work out alternative means in a world in which mimetic dynamics are being pushed to the extreme. To Dupuy and Dumouchel, the world-scale economy—with its all-permeating logic and its founding myths—is the new *katechon* that keeps the world from imploding into apocalypse.

In the following I will make a case for the advantages of engaging in a profitable dialogue with mimetic theory, but I will not deny that this may imply a diminution of the epistemological claims that political scientists feel entitled to make. One important aspect of the mimetic understanding of politics concerns precisely the nonagentic outlook and perspective of this alternative theory. Genetic stories of how political systems come into being support nonmimetic and endogenous dynamics. The making, or emergence, of political systems is normally explained as an endogenous process of expansion and conquest directed by mindful elites concerned with the acquisition of power, natural resources, and international influence. One of the very few scholars who have challenged the individuation model in explaining the rise and growth of polities is the historian Barbara Fuchs. In her book *Mimesis and Empire* she explains how

> mimetic mirrorings among emerging early modern nations challenge the process of individuation by which those nations attempt to become fully consolidated with an exceptional claim to an imperial destiny. Imitation compromises the narratives of national distinction by emphasizing inconvenient similarities and shared heritages.[15]

Fuchs's book challenges the canonical idea that a single process of individuation would explain the rise of polities. But the book does not consider the narratives and cultural practices of reciprocal imitation that are the real medium of the mimetic mirrorings among early modern nations. I propose a more general model in which polities are capable of imitation even outside the bounds of the literary media scrutinized by Fuchs. So, unlike Fuchs's, my study owes more to Girard than to Auerbach and focuses on actual, immediate mimetic dealings between polities. And while Fuchs seeks "to read the state and its intentions into early modern representations,"[16] this book challenges her view that imitation is "state-sponsored." The state does not mandate imitation through the poet, or the artist, or such supra-individual agencies as "culture." It is indeed *the state itself that imitates.*

The historical rationales used to explain the rise and agency of empires are biased by the assumption of the *originality* of the intentions that spur historical events. I will show how polities, unfailingly, arise out of a process of harsh polarization in which *two* rival political entities set out to grow in size and political ambition by modulating one's own patterns of agency on the patterns exhibited by the rival. It is a reciprocal dynamic, in which it is difficult to track a beginning, a primal spur of the pattern. I follow Girard's sequence that *ex imitatio oritur bellum,* and not the other way around. Imitation comes first; it is a biological trait that plays a critical role in the process of hominization and that has expanded into a distinctively human capacity. And it is precisely this emphasis on the imitation/rivalry complex that sets mimetic theory apart from the narratives that structured the modern understanding of human sociability.

## Mimetic Doubles

To Girard "once his basic needs are satisfied (indeed sometimes even before), man is subject to intense desires, though he may not know precisely for what."[17] These desires are considered mimetic inasmuch as the subject turns to another person "to inform him of what he should desire." Mimetic desire is not egocentric and humans did not develop mimetic dispositions in isolation from one another. In evolutionary terms, mimesis is the residue of a stage of poor differentiation, a reminiscence that stuck in our genes for its evolutionary advantages. But the powerful combination of mimetic attitudes and poor introspection turns this "suggested desire," or "emulous desire," into the catalyst of a type of conflict that does not necessarily occur in conditions of scarcity. In Girard's words: "The rival desires the same object as the subject, and to assert the primacy of the rival can lead only to one conclusion: rivalry doesn't arise because of the fortuitous convergence of two desires on a single object; rather, *the subject desires the object because the rival desires it.*"[18]

Mimetic theory identifies imitation as the driving force in human relationships and argues that by imitating each other's desires people engage in endless contests for the same objects, unaware of the actual psychological drives that propel them.

It is important to focus on this stage, in which by obsessively imitating each other the rivals become increasingly similar. They end up stealing attitudes and desires from one another in the attempt to remodel their attitude and outlook. Eventually they lose their chance of autonomy and become "mimetic doubles." It is precisely when polarization and mimetic antagonism escalate that the rivals begin to perceive one another as one of a kind: "as the crisis grows more acute, the community members are transformed into 'twins,' matching images of violence. I would be tempted to say that they are each *doubles* of the other."[19] This is the peak of the mimetic conflict, when the story of reciprocal imitation has escalated to the point that every difference has been erased and the rivals stand in front of each other as matching images. What we get here, in Girard's words, is "a merciless battle between twins."[20]

Girard gives a detailed description of the dynamics of how the rivals turn into mimetic twins. They will become more and more similar as they observe each other, and their "hostile feeling" will grow. . . . One thing is thus sure: there will be a clash, and it will occur when the lack of differentiation between the two adversaries reaches a point of no return. Reciprocity and the loss of differences are one and the same thing.[21]

Girard maintains that imitation and rivalry are *unum et idem*—they are the two sides of the same coin. "The principal source of violence between human beings is mimetic rivalry, the rivalry resulting from imitation of a model who becomes a rival, or of a rival who becomes a model."[22]

It is important to bear in mind that this animosity is contagious, and mimetic desire spreads and compounds itself until it reaches a level of saturation that the community can hardly bear. Girard has a compelling explanation of how this violence is eventually discharged and dispersed. To Girard the classical way to resolve the problem of this mimetic escalation of violence (although the members of the group remain unaware of the mimetic drive of their hostility) is to identify someone responsible for the evils that plague the community. A new type of polarization sets in and a "scapegoat" is identified and put to death. The cycle of violence is broken and order restored.

There is another crucial element that we need here in order to get the sense of how this mimetic predicament is a sort of inescapable deadlock. Girard hastens to tell us that "mimetic violence grows behind the back of those involved."[23] In other words, it can be perceived only "by someone who is outside the conflict because *from the inside you must always believe in your difference.* . . . From the outside, the adversaries look like what they are: simple doubles."[24] Here the parties would never acknowledge that the force that drives them into conflict is not a mark of their agency but rather a shortcoming, a *deficit* in agency, a mere act of imitation. To Girard "having a scapegoat means not knowing that we have one," and the members of the group are so steeped in this mimetic predicament that in no way can they pin down the causal drive of their actions.[25]

Mimetic theory teases out the mechanism of "sacrificial violence," the unanimous polarization of a group against "the scapegoat chosen unconsciously by the mimetism of the lynchers."[26] Curiously enough, Girard himself has argued a number of times that this mechanism is no longer a viable blueprint for social dynamics, for it has been superseded by new post-sacrificial configurations.

The violence against the scapegoat is "sacrificial violence" because the unanimous killing of the victim is the origin of the "sacred." The members of the group have a faint grasp of what they perceive as a causal nexus between the killing and the resolution of all conflicts. Because of its resolutive effects, the killing is endowed with special powers; mindful of its peacemaking effects, the group becomes cautious and predictive, and in order to avoid, contain, and control mimetic violence its members reiterate and ritualize the sacred origins.[27]

It is important now to expand upon this crucial notion of the sacred, for "sacred" refers to a content that describes a variety of practices and attitudes. Although contemporary political science pays little attention to it, the sacred has undeniably returned in many ways and it plays a huge role in contemporary politics. While according to a classical view the sacred is a *remnant* of a religious understanding of the universe, to Girard the sacred is less a cultural phenomenon than a universal *psychological* fact. The cultural phenomenology of the sacred is thus reduced to an underlying psychological factor and the sacred itself to a psychological attitude by which the "natural, distant, and inaccessible causes" of events are replaced by *human* causes, and human scapegoats are held responsible for the evils befalling humankind.[28]

To Girard, the nexus sacred/violence feeds on dynamics of scapegoating vindicated by a form of "collective delusion."[29] The sacred is the *psychological* element that prompts this delusion. This psychological aspect of Girard's theory is crucial, for it is this particular aspect that vindicates Girard's famous claims as to the emancipatory thrust of the Gospels, that Christianity is less the receptacle of the sacred than its more powerful antidote, the *pharmakon,* that dissipates the delusion responsible for strengthening the nexus sacred/violence.

Girard's theory of the origins of religion was not conceived in a vacuum: other scholars, more or less all tributaries of Freud's theory about the origins of culture in *Totem and Taboo,* have argued that ritual, religion, and culture derive from mechanisms of collective aggression.[30] What is specific in Girard's theoretical construction is, first, the role played by reciprocal imitation in triggering the violence, and second, the mechanism of eventual revelation of the collective mistake that promotes the unreflective iteration of the mechanism. It is Christianity, according to Girard, that made the old sacrificial outlets useless. Christianity destroyed the only expedient device that allowed the group to reharmonize its members after a flare-up of mimetic rivalry.

Christianity did not bring peace to the world. After Christianity, that is, after the recognition that victimization is instrumental to preserving and reinstating the archaic order, the escalation does not stop, it keeps rising "to the extreme" and is mildly and only spasmodically contained by pseudo-sacrificial devices and "minor" sacrifices that ultimately fail to keep it at bay. Here, the mimetic escalation that generates doubles no longer relies on the specious identification of a victim that attracts all the animosity and allows the community to reconcile.

This is the point at which mimetic theory comes into close contact with the notion of "sacred violence" used by American legal theorist Paul Kahn. According to Kahn, Girard's account "is too totalizing and mechanical" and fails to acknowledge the "sacrificial character" of current practices of popular sovereignty in the United States.[31] Kahn details the survival of sacrifice, under the modern species of torture and terror, that the contemporary democratic framework of Western nations—notably the United States—fails to acknowledge, let alone suppress. Resurgent forms of sacrifice escape the tight-knit frame of "law" and operate in our world relatively unbound.[32]

But why is the "sacrificial" solution no longer viable according to Girard?

The transformation from an expedient and fundamentally sacrificial neutralization of mimetic violence into the nonsacrificial reciprocal opposition of two rivals is an effect of Christianity. The narrative of Christ's crucifixion and final resurrection revealed that the victims that used to attract all the violence were expedient devices used by communities strangled by violent mimetic divisions. Christianity revealed that the victims of mimetic rage were innocent and could no longer be used as the sacrificial foci of a polarization of all against one. Christianity deflated a pleasing story of guilt (of the designated victims) and innocence (of the perpetrators) that absolved the crowd and incriminated the target of its rage as the sole carrier of all culpability.[33]

We now live in a post-Christian world in which violence is denied its age-old sacrificial outlet and therefore is bound "to grow to the extreme." Girard is very clear on the process that led to the eventual overcoming of sacrifices: the archaic polarization "focused on a victim whose destruction made a return to order possible. Today, it is of a piece with the escalation to extremes because there can no longer be unanimity about the guilt of victims."[34] The more difficult it became to rationalize the killing of innocent victims as an irrational and nonetheless expedient solution to the accumulation of mimetic animosity, the easier and faster this diffused animosity escalated into a dyadic pattern that culminates in the eventual confrontation of the two members of a mimetic dyad.[35]

Think of an ancient myth illustrated by Girard in *Violence and the Sacred*. It tells the story of two cousins, a man and a woman, where each demands that the other prove his or her love by self-disfiguration. It is interesting to observe that over the process

> differences cancel each other out; a symmetry is constantly generated, invisible in each synchronic moment taken separately but visible in the accumulation of successive moments. This is what constitutes the non-difference of the sacrificial crisis, a truth forever inaccessible to the two partners who live out the relationship in the form of alternating differences."[36]

Here something like a "sacrificial crisis" is the natural outlet of this compounding of mimetic rivalry. Before the advent of Christianity—before the upsetting revelation that mimetic violence operates "without a reason"— the process was bound to terminate *before* it could escalate to the extreme. A scapegoat displaces all the animosity from its bipolar axis and concentrates it onto itself, until "the symmetry of the overall picture" disintegrates in the total asymmetry of "the entire community on one side, and on the other, the victim."[37]

Girard has drafted a powerful genealogy to explain how reciprocal polarization has come about. To Girard what is remarkable about it is that it is a relatively new phenomenon, a by-product of the revelatory power of Christianity. By revealing that scapegoats are innocent, Christianity deprived violence of its "natural" outlet. Mimetic violence is therefore bound to escalate to a breaking point, and there is no sacrificial device at hand to channel it and drive it towards a workable scapegoat.[38]

The plight of the community is precisely this growth to the extreme of mimetic polarization, which is not contained by any effective sacrificial measures. In Girard's words,

The escalation to extremes is a completely irrational phenomenon that only Christianity explains because over 2000 years ago it revealed the inanity of sacrifice, and regardless of those who still like to believe in its usefulness. Christ took away humanity's sacrificial crutches and left us before a terrible choice: either believe in violence, or not; Christianity is non-belief.[39]

To be sure, *unanimous* polarization against a victim (as opposed to *reciprocal* polarization) has not disappeared from the world. And we know that this phenomenon is not only archaic but also highly regressive; it is a sort of a cultural atavism engaging groups that fail to see that their victims are innocent. Violence *between* groups, instead (especially the type of intergroup warfare described by Clausewitz, which escalates with no seeming end), is the result of the process of symmetrization prompted by the dwindling of the sacrificial outlet. The kind of mimesis that operates mostly unacknowledged in politics is now exploding in an astonishing number of directions, with no possibility of redirection towards a workable scapegoat. And if no outlet is available, the ensuing violence is bound to grow to the extreme.

In the following I shall present the epistemic credentials of mimetic theory to contribute to such fields as political science and political theory. I will try to find a possible locus for mimetic theory on the contemporary map, and see if the theory has a chance to engage with a number of cognate disciplines. The problem, I shall maintain, lies at the core of the epistemological stipulations that structure those disciplines.

## Mimesis and Autonomy

Speaking of the epistemological stipulations that structure the methods and practices of political science, one important fact is the attendant ontology of the discipline. If one looks at the schools and trends that inform our theoretical orientations as political scientists there are two very general approaches, each defined by what items are considered to have ontological preeminence. The first approach considers the *individual* as the ultimate reality in political processes. The other approach considers *groups* as the decisive realities. Mimetic theory challenges treasured views by targeting their underlying ontology. The mimetic perspective highlights neither individuals nor groups, but "doubles," or "mimetic twins."

According to this perspective, in order to grasp the fundamental rationales of political processes we need to concentrate on the distinctive propensity of either individuals or groups to engage in mimetic contests resulting from their unreflective disposition to imitate each other's *desire*. But this specifically mimetic desire is not egocentric, or based on the psychology of the individual taken in isolation from society, and its target and intensity cannot be measured by simply surveying the psychological outlook of the subject. Mimetic theory in fact focuses on the mimetic contest itself, on the dynamic whereby the rivals lose their *autonomy* and become mimetic doubles.

So the crisis of the concept of autonomy is a result of the specific ontological commitment made by mimetic theory. Reasoning in terms of doubles—*mimetic* doubles—rules out the overall capacity for free agency of the actors involved. Doubles are, by definition, not autonomous, for their capacity for agency is split in two; they each turn to the other to "know precisely" what to desire.

This is arguably a major breach of a set of epistemological conventions that lie at the core of normative political theory. Especially after John Rawls's *A Theory of Justice* was published in 1971, political philosophy took a dramatic normative turn that helped relaunch the whole subfield within the broader field of political science, where empirical and theoretical approaches were dominant. The ambition of political philosophers ever since was to demarcate their field from other nonnormative and nonphilosophical speculations about political decisions. The questions they asked found a new framework in which people inspired by Rawls's book (including his critics) engaged in a number of debates on the vast normative possibilities of political theory. But this framework was built on a fundamental assumption about human psychology, that people were normatively capable and therefore sensitive to reasons. Their actions were free and intentional in a way that the mere notion of behavior could not fully articulate.

Emphasis on imitation and unconscious processes suggested a commonality of intent and a degree of mutual understanding with such fields as neurophysiology, anthropology, and evolutionary psychology. The emphasis was ultimately on the mechanisms and logics of human agency, over and beyond the contingencies of human motivation and thought. Altruism, for one thing, could be understood in terms of genetic benefit, just like other attitudes and psychological outlooks that philosophers attribute to the human capacity for thoughtful deliberation. Theorists and philosophers stress the distinctions between actions and behavior, where actions "differ from performances that are merely behavior . . . in that *reasons* can be given for them."[40] And reasons entail a freedom of the will; they are *forces* amenable to the contingencies of volition and deliberation.

Mindful of this gap in the meaning of simple terms—a gap that is reflected in our everyday use of language—Steven Pinker has distinguished two different meanings of "altruism." In the evolutionary biologists' sense altruism "is defined in terms of behavior," whereas "in the psychological sense" (but we may also call it the "philosophical sense") it is defined "in terms of motives."[41] Here the discriminating element is the altruist's awareness of the attendant benefits of its behavior, namely, her ability to consciously will the welfare of another individual. Interestingly the divide between the two forms of altruism is the same divide between two realms that hardly communicate with one another. On the one side we have the scientists who explain altruism, again, in terms of genetic benefit; on the other we have theorists who explain altruism in terms of deliberation and choices.

If a discipline is geared towards behavior, and is little sensitive to the complexities of human motivation, its chances to dialogue in a mutually fruitful way with normative realms are very small, and very little effort has been made to put mimetic theory at the intersection between realms. Political *theory*, after the strong normative turn it took in the early 1970s, considered all explanations of political behavior that were not grounded on the capacity for deliberation as anomalous. Being reborn under the philosophical species of normative political philosophy, this age-old philosophical discourse—with origins in the writings of Plato and Aristotle—has set new standards of normative propriety, thereby demarcating its realm as a space in which philosophical talk is focused almost exclusively on topics that possess some sort of normative purchase. Accordingly, justice and justification were pushed to the top of the agenda of discussion, and even the attempts to identify items over and beyond justification (such as the "good" of the early communitarians) was seen by philosophers as exceeding the bounds of their discipline.

Agency differs from behavior as it implicates (1) the capacity to give and acknowledge reasons and (2) a sense of awareness on the part of the agent, that is, the knowledge of the internal states that caused the action. So the two fundamental assumptions behind this conception of agency are the following:

1. The *classical* belief that "we cannot have a desire except for a reason"[42]
2. The idea that "[s]elf-knowledge is a necessary condition for agency; and intentionality as it figures in agency therefore must be transparent"[43]

Autonomy is neither a psychological fact about agency, nor a mere attribute of rationality; it is a complex notion entailing the ability to give oneself the rule whereby we act. But the determination of the rule is a complex operation of the mind that cannot be explained, according to the proponents of the autonomy thesis, in purely epistemological terms. The considerations we make when we opt for a given course of action are *normative,* so long as we commit ourselves to *this* course of action and are responsible for it, and so long as we have a special knowledge of the states of mind that accompanied the action.

According to this classical account, a motive or reason can be used to explain the action it is a reason for. And this explanation resonates with normative notions such as duty, opportunity, and obligation. Desires are the spurs of our actions, but "we cannot have a desire except for a reason," in the sense that we can explain the action as our own action, as something deliberate and consistent, where the desire that prompted us to act in a certain way (including ways we would not want to confess) can be explained as serving a sense of purpose we have, or, alternatively, as a failure in our conscious attempt at directing ourselves.

Proponents of the autonomy thesis are also keen on attaching to the notion of autonomy a special knowledge of one's mental states. We attribute responsibility to agents that supposedly knew what they were doing. Actions for which we disclaim agency are not imputable to us, for we acted in a state of ignorance, a kind of somnambulistic condition that undermines our capacity for assuming responsibility.

The autonomy thesis finds little space in the psychology of mimetic agents, and for this reason the kind of mimetic behavior described by mimetic theorists would be considered irrational and therefore normatively irrelevant by most political philosophers. *Mimetic* agents are, admittedly, poor introspectors; they can either give or acknowledge reasons, but their knowledge of reasons is not genuine. They inhabit a world of expedient rationalizations that shelter and suppress their mimetic psychologies. Mimetic agents fail to give an account of themselves, for they have little access to the reflective sources of their judgment. The structure of their agency challenges the two fundamental underpinnings of the autonomy thesis and shows that the normative qualifications that define agency are somehow suspended.

The rejection of some established epistemological stipulations sets mimetic theory apart from the mainstream philosophical discourse of political theory. The purpose of this study is therefore to provide a fresh look into a number of phenomena by dispensing with the venerable notion of autonomy.

Now I want to draw attention to a different set of epistemological presuppositions, those we find in some areas of the broad field of political science. It is interesting to see how people working in cognate fields appeal to opposite epistemological stipulations. Political philosophers have strived to find a place for free agency and intentionality in a mechanistically understood social world, whereas political scientists have tried to dispense with these notions, and sought to work out an empirical framework untroubled by normative considerations or puzzles. In their seminal book *Theory of Games and Economic Behavior* John von Neumann and Oskar Morgenstern had reached a point of formal elucidation of game theoretical models "beyond which it is difficult to go . . . without auxiliary concepts such as 'agreements,' 'understandings,' etc."[44] This caveat indicated that game theory fell a bit short of a comprehensive and definitive characterization of all social interactions. It is indeed the very nature of coalitions to require a meta-theory that accommodates mutual "understandings" before the actual stipulations among the actors.

## Pelopidas's Paradox

One ruling assumption in the social sciences is that egoistic behavior and prosocial behavior are mutually exclusive. It is either-or. Rational-choice approaches have multiple applications in experimental economics, theoretical anthropology, evolutionary psychology, and the social sciences; they hold onto this either-or type of assumption and look at social phenomena in these mutually exclusive terms. The story of the prisoner's dilemma in particular "has entered popular culture as a crucial example of the interplay between competition and cooperation."[45] But the interplay consists in either-or types of choices made by the actors in the game. I want to show that this epistemological deadlock is the effect of the individuationist model, and it disappears as soon as we take a different approach, one that considers the individual the *penultimate* reality in the study of social phenomena.

A powerful innovation for this field acknowledging that the "interplay" between the actors could actually consist in something escaping an either/or type of characterization—either cooperation or failure to cooperate—was effected by John Nash's theory of noncooperative behavior. "Nash had the critical insight that most social interactions involve neither pure competition nor pure cooperation but rather a mix of both."[46]

I do not intend to engage with mathematical models or experimental economics. My point is to reveal the great potential of mimetic theory for innovation in the study of politics. Here the general epistemological model used in social interactions analysis is the classical one according to which competition and cooperation are mutually exclusive facts, and there is no "mix" of the two in actual games.

It is interesting to notice the extent to which the language changes along the spectrum of the disciplines, depending on the perspective on the psychology of the agents, so that game theorists speak of antagonistic behavior where theoretical anthropologists prefer the less neutral definition of "selfish behavior." But all in all the alternative remains; the distinction between cooperative and selfish as mutually exclusive is never dissolved in a higher configuration.

However, this rigid characterization of human sociality does not capture the realities and complexities of social behavior, and one can see that all societies present a conspicuous string of behavior in which people's prosocial attitudes are largely consistent with their egoistic impulses. The purpose of the following pages is to clear the ground and expose the biases and inconsistencies caused by a number of orthodoxies. Mimetic theory offers an alternative perspective as it challenges the very notion of autonomy, the idea of a core ego, a quintessential nucleus of identity that directs our choices and frames our dispositions, a psychological agency that makes us selfish and self-interested. This model argues that the subject executes the will and directions of a locus of agency that lies within itself. The mimetic model, instead, places this locus of agency and control *outside* the subject, in the attitudes and desires of someone that Girard calls "the rival." There is no internal blueprint that the ego could look into in order to find clues on how to act, for the blueprint is situated outside; it is provided by the desires of the subject's neighbor, its mimetic alter ego, its model.

Rival and subject, though, are not two distinct agencies, inasmuch as they are engaged in a reciprocal activity in which the contours of each appear faint and fuzzy. They act as individuals; they express their wishes and orientations; they abide by social norms of conduct; but they appear to be involved in a drama of reciprocal imitation that they typically tend to minimize. They treasure the tale of autonomy and individual agency supported by the kind of Platonic humanism that permeates their "culture." Interestingly, social scientists have taken for granted this tale of autonomy and agency and consistently describe and analyze social phenomena *as if* the ultimate agentic authority rested in the individual alone.

So the focus of mimetic theory rests not so much in the subject, in its psychological outlook and dispositions, but rather in the mimetic interplay between the subject and the rival, the gray area of mutual concern in which it is difficult to track the actual, *original* source of the desires leading to actions.

To be sure, the notion of the subject being *selfish* becomes problematic if we take this mimetic perspective. It is in fact not the *subject*'s self that is served up by his resolution to act in a certain way, to pursue desires that he always considers his own. The kind of subjectivity that figures in descriptions and experiments of social scientists, theoretical anthropologists, and game theorists is actually, on closer scrutiny, *selfless,* for its "self" is constituted by the acts and attitudes of the rival. It is indeed the rival's *desires* that are duly emulated by the subject, and eventually reported as *his own* desires, namely, as authentic emanations of his core genuine dispositions. The rival is the template for the subject's desires. But still it is difficult to determine who's who, for there is no determining attribute that tells the two apart, for they are both trapped in the same psychological predicament, and the selfishness of each feeds on the attitude of the other.

Let us go back for a second to the paradigm currently dominant in the social sciences, the paradigm including rational choice approaches and explanations based on people's rational capacity for autonomous agency. Theoretical anthropology is an interesting case in our discussion of mimetic theory, for a major strand of work in anthropology seems committed to what a number of theoretical anthropologists have called the "selfishness axiom," the idea that people are driven by their own views and dispositions, and thereby act in light of their self-interested appreciation of facts of the world.[47]

Although the selfishness axiom has been challenged over the last three decades, it remains, to be sure, the guiding principle in the ways theoretical anthropologists figure out patterns of social behavior. This axiom is grounded on the assumption that individuals seek to maximize their own material gains when interacting with one another in society. The authors of the collective volume *Foundations of Human Sociality* allege that the last two decades have seen an important shift in the model of human motives, making room for alternative approaches, more focused on altruistic impulses. However, according to these authors the old axiom still holds and the two principal outlooks in the rational disposition of the agent—that is, egoism and altruism—are treated as mutually exclusive.

To be sure, the idea that human actions have an exclusively selfish rationale has been challenged by several scholars, both in philosophy and in the social sciences. Bernard Williams, for one, wondered in a seminal paper, "can we define notions of rationality which are not purely egoistic?" and his answer was yes.[48] Other scholars from different disciplines have stressed the limits of any account of human agency that rules out altruistic attitudes. Steven Pinker has identified a "sympathy-altruism hypothesis" as a viable alternative to forms of psychological hedonism and egoism (what he calls the "cynical alternatives" to the hypothesis). He has provided empirical evidence in support of the autonomy and objectivity of the hypothesis and has explained altruism as an attitude supported by the practical (genetic) benefits of the "altruist's genes."[49]

Interestingly, if we take the mimetic approach as far as it goes—if we try to make sense of the psychological dynamics described by both cynics and optimists in terms of a dramatic alternative in different terms, that is, in the terms of mimetic theory—we see that the experimental reality of the evidence for "altruistic behavior" depends on assumptions and stipulations that the authors of the experiments never challenge. And this, admittedly, is a case in which the premise distorts the issue, where the premise is that there is such a *real* thing as purely egoistic behavior, and this behavior is, by definition, asocial or even antisocial.

Objections to the approach supported by *Foundations of Human Sociality* are committed to making available a different kind of framework, one where the goods chosen for the anthropologist's experiments and social games are not amenable to the alternative selfish/prosocial and do not serve the theoretical premises of the experiments. To be sure, the kind of physical goods used as the standard currency in these experiments constitute only a small subset of the overall amount of goods that circulate in human societies and that people receive in recognition of their efforts and services. A different set of goods may turn out more recalcitrant to the theoretical framework that underlies the experiments reported by *Foundations of Human Sociality*. So we should imagine practical situations in which the behavior of the actors challenges the rigid alternative between selfish and prosocial, situations in which the mimetic attitudes of the actors prove that the description of their choices in the game is biased by false or limited assumptions about their psychologies. The next step would be to see if the mimetic explanation describes in a more comprehensive manner the "interplay" of the actors by framing it in a dialectic subject/rival that downplays the status of the "object" in the game.

The counter case I have in mind could be drawn from Plutarch's account of the bond of friendship and cooperation that holds together a group of Theban men (in his *Life of Pelopidas*) during the Spartan occupation: Plutarch writes that each of these men "were attached to each other by the closest ties of friendship and were rivals only in the pursuit of valour and reputation."[50] Valor and reputation, as well as honor and glory (Machiavelli comes to mind), are *social* goods; namely, their value is encoded in a thick network of arrangements that predate the Thebans' commitment to those values. In other words the appeal of such goods as valor and reputation to the agent's selfish initiative *is consistent with* the agent's endorsement of a set of social codes that makes those goods socially valuable. Hence, any commitment to the selfish satisfaction of one's longing for such goods as "valor and reputation" doesn't preempt the bond of cooperation that ties the subject to the group. One could say that, under certain conditions, the selfish pursuit of valor may even *strengthen* the social bond, for it is a prosocial endeavor treasured by all members of the group.

Pelopidas's behavior seems to defy the categorization suggested in *Foundations of Human Sociality,* inasmuch as the Theban hero's egoism *is consistent with* his cooperative vocation. Let us now try to picture this situation in the book's own terms. If we are to label the behavior of the players involved in the experiments, they appear to be either "selfish" or "cooperative." In Pelopidas's case, *both* labels suit his behavior. In other words, Pelopidas's attitude neither violates nor validates the selfishness axiom. This doesn't mean that Pelopidas's case constitutes a freak deviation from any agreed-upon standard of what it is to be "human." It rather shows the inefficacy of the premise, in the sense that it challenges not so much the existence of selfishness as the existence of the self.

The logic of the experiments aimed to prove the "cynical" hypothesis can be repaired if we take a different perspective, one that dispenses with the idea of the locus, or of the nucleus of our intentions and desires, and displaces the sources of agency in that *infra* between the ego and the *alter* where mimetic interactions take place. "Valor and reputation" are mimetic virtues, for they embody the human aspiration to be imitated and become the model of our rival.

Political philosopher Charles Larmore has argued that a different understanding of the self could be gleaned from the works of such noncanonical writers as Sartre and Girard, an understanding that exposes the limits of a notion of subjectivity tied up with the idea, with origins in the writings of Stendhal, of the *naturel,* of some sort of inner substance that defines our character and thoughts and makes them unique. As to Girard, Larmore believes that "no other thinkers had ever dealt such a devastating and successful critique in order to demonstrate *the imposture of authenticity.*"[51]

◆   ◆   ◆

The new perspective on social phenomena granted by mimetic theory allows us to detect dynamics and facts otherwise unavailable. Emphasis on such social virtues as valor and reputation allows us to see how those dynamics generate a thick ontology of items "for which to strive." The rivals, coupled in little teams of two, are the ultimate social realities in this scenario. They strive to become full-fledged individuals, but their selves are still lacking focus and character. In order to make up for this lack they turn to each other with a metaphysical request: not "Who are you?" but "What do you want?" Rivals are nonagentic twin-sets to which we can hardly trace the burden of moral responsibilities. The coming-to-being of subjectivity is a much less obvious process than we have always believed it was. In the following pages I shall detail the different stages of this process, beginning with a discussion of the ultimate structure of social realities, a discussion of bipolarity.

# CHAPTER 2

# The Mimetic Context
# of the "New Wars"

A ccording to a widely accepted view the principal characteristic of twenty-first-century international relations is "nonpolarity." New conflicts and emergencies are explained by appealing to the collapse of bipolarity and the attendant mobilization of multiple actors: "a world dominated not by one or two or even several states but rather by dozens of actors possessing and exercising various kinds of power."[1] Deterritorialized warfare (e.g., civil conflicts and insurgencies that spill across national boundaries, blurring the distinction between "internal" and "external" in international relations) is seen as an "aggressive response to the depolarization of the post–Cold War period," now made chronic by globalization.[2]

A major challenge to the theory of nonpolarity comes from mimetic theory, a general explanation of human behavior and conflict with great potential to recast perspectives in the theory of international relations. Its focus on dynamics of polarization and victimization challenges treasured paradigms and places strain on received views.

Mimetic theory challenges one of the most treasured assumptions in the theory of international relations, that is, the epistemological individualism according to which individuals, states, and organizations possess a distinct locus of agency and a capacity to act in isolation from other actors. A whole

strand in the discipline has adapted this individuationist model to the complex reality of systemic processes, but individuals and groups are treated
quasi-consistently as intelligent agents driven by strategic concerns.[3] Mimetic
theory challenges this individuationist outlook by focusing on the coupling
of political actors and on their mimetic interactions. Put differently, mimetic
theorists are keen to aggregate the processes detailed by the individuationist
model in *dyads,* and to claim that each member of these dyadic compounds
engages in dynamics of reciprocal imitation. Thus *nonpolarity* is always a
distorted visual effect, or at most a brief and insignificant interim situation,
for *bipolarity* remains the dominant mode of aggregation in politics.

"Dyads" and "dyadic patterns" are not new concepts in political science.
Scholars have long been aware of advantages and biases in sampling pairs of
states in order to measure the risk of interstate conflict. The problem is how
to sample *relevant* (nonrandom) dyads in order to produce valid and not
biased inference.[4] In the following, sampling is limited to a case in which
there is strong evidence of reciprocal mimesis (e.g., Israelis and Palestinians).
Mimetic theory will be applied to see the extent to which a *growing similarity* between the two members of the dyad increases the risk of conflict.

States or groups are eligible for pairing in mimetic dyads only if there is
evidence of a number of contingent aspects, such as a growing similarity in
the attitude and outlooks of the two members combined with an accompa-
nying "rivalry." Mimetic dyads are therefore more specific than dyads where
members are *just* rivals: if rivalry is typically characterized by "a sustained
mutually contingent hostile interaction," *mimetic* rivalry is defined by a
tendency of the rivals to reciprocally imitate one another.[5] The rivals do not
engage in mutual conflict because they *are* equals,[6] but because they have
*become* very similar.[7]

Once we have secured a different vantage point on political processes
and conflicts, one focused on "doubles" and (mimetically relevant) "dyads"
and not on individual actors, we can see how these dynamics of reciprocal
imitation are in fact constitutive of the processes at hand. The processes of
mimetic aggregation and disaggregation that occur at the level of global politics explain the virulence of the "New Wars" (NWs), the attendant dynamics
of victimization (of groups and minorities), and the difficulty in finding
effective political solutions. This chapter engages with a broad segment of
the literature on NWs in the attempt to slightly amend its core assumption.

Rather than viewing NWs as the result of the mobilization of individual actors no longer constrained in larger patterns, the chapter will look at these new types of war as resulting from the proliferation of mimetic dyads.

The application of mimetic theory to the theory of IR has vast possibilities, and this chapter has two main purposes, one general and one particular. The general aim is to show that mimetic theory generates a new set of research problems by presenting political realities in a new, nonindividuationist perspective. The general aim consists therefore in bringing mimetic theory to bear, and proposing a new paradigm centered on the dyadic outlook of the structures and processes of international politics. The particular aim is to intervene into the specific discourse of NWs theory and amend its individuationist logic. In pursuing both aims, I shall explore the possibilities of mimetic theory in areas where Girard has ventured only tentatively with descriptions and arguments that are highly suggestive, but at times erratic and impractical.[8]

I shall introduce the basics of mimetic theory in the first section, where I explain why the theory challenges the tenets of nonpolarity. Mimetic theory argues that the dynamics of polarization, in which two political actors dissolve previous allegiances and push the system into a new equilibrium, are a major strategic innovation compared to the kind of ubiquitous conflictuality that occurs in conditions of nonpolarity. Reciprocal polarization aggregates the actors in two specular scenes in which all violence "operates without a reason."[9]

"New wars theory" supports the paradigm of nonpolarity, arguing that new conflicts occur in chaotic patterns punctuated with eruptions of violence over which the state has lost its monopoly. Herfried Münkler has shown that "asymmetrization" (*Asymmetrisierung*) in politics and warfare is the principal characteristic of the global age, whereas Kalevi Holsti uses the notion of "wars of a non Clausewitzian type" to describe precisely the same type of conflicts, namely, wars that defy *symmetric dyads*.[10] "Asymmetrization" describes, then, the process of progressive deterioration of nexuses (e.g., the nexus borders-sovereignty) and practices (of warfare and negotiation) that were obvious within the Clausewitzian paradigm. These conflicts are no longer duel-like contests between actors belonging to the same ontological sets (e.g., "states"), but they are inherently ubiquitous and "asymmetrical" new wars.[11]

After the end of state-centered politics and warfare, NWs erupt in the empty space that separates the dwindling normative arrangements mandated by both the state and its international delegates, from normative and ideological configurations yet to come. No longer states or coalitions of states versus other states and other coalitions of states, but a disordered series of eruptions and "minor" conflicts in which identity, not territory, plays the pivotal justificatory role (as I will show in the third section). I will argue that mimetic theory helps amending the logic of NWs by replacing "asymmetrization" with mimetic reciprocity, that is, the progressive transformation of symmetric contenders into mimetic twins. The symmetry between the twins is so radical in the end that it becomes difficult to distinguish them from one another: this process leads to a level of "undifferentiation" that needs to be compensated by claims of civilizational status. Identity rationalizes this loss of difference, as I shall explain.

Girard is very specific about this mimetic dialectic of mutual reciprocity and the loss of differences, "Simultaneity in action, the trend to extremes at the heart of the alternation of victories and defeats, the reciprocity at the heart of every kind of exchange."[12] One page earlier Girard had stated that "reciprocal action" is always at work,

> even when combat has not yet occurred: the two adversaries, the attacker and the defender, will become more and more similar as they observe each other, and their "hostile feeling" will grow. If they both withdraw, it will only be to attack each other more fiercely later; if one withdraws, that withdrawal could be a sign for the other to attack. One thing is thus sure: there will be a clash, and it will occur when the lack of differentiation between the two adversaries reaches a point of no return. Reciprocity and the loss of differences are one and the same thing.[13]

Framing canonical issues in mimetic terms may sound peculiar or fanciful, but mimetic theory has the power to disclose dynamics that conventional wisdom has left unaddressed. In the following I shall provide a good deal of theory and will present a case against contemporary NWs theories. The Israel/Palestine schism will be considered as an example of the mimetic structuring of political phenomena at the global level. This schism reveals the hidden structure of a scheme that underlies postmodern conflictuality and acts as a consistent reminder of the dyadic pattern in (global) politics. As Herfried Münkler argues:

> The conflict between Israel and the Palestinian authority represents in miniature a regionally limited copy of the global political line-ups.[14]

The conflict between Israelis and Palestinians can be seen as the "first new war," for it exploded in 1948 when conventional warfare was still the rule. As Kaldor has pointed out, "since Israel made peace with the neighboring states, the conflict is no longer expressed in terms of interstate war and has begun to exhibit some of the characteristics of the new types of conflict."[15] What makes this war "new" is the global setting, which has changed the perception of the stakes involved and made difficult a coherent understanding of the profiles and outlooks of the actors involved. The course of this conflict is deterritorialized inasmuch as "Palestine" is only one of its several fronts.

Tensions in Middle Eastern politics resonate globally, and the Israeli/Palestinian schism has often been described as arising from a deep-seated East/West fault line, a deep cleavage that is being displaced from its original setting between Asia and Europe and has exploded now in major "global political line-ups." The following chapter examines precisely the effect of this resonance and the impact of this miniature conflict on a number of cleavage lines, deeply mimetic in nature, that are opening up in global politics.

In the first section of this chapter I introduce the basics of mimetic theory. In the second section I present a tentative analysis of the similarities between Israeli and Palestinians. Here one of the tenets of mimetic theory—the idea that the more similar the actors engaged in mimetic disputes become, the more aggressively they resort to markers of identity to show off their differences—can only be approached perspectivally and tentatively. In the third section I will argue that NWs arise out of polar and highly symmetrical mimetic confrontations between rival actors that shape and model their behavior and outlook by imitating each other. In the fourth section the chapter concludes with a restatement of the case for mimetic theory in order to affirm its epistemic strength in the broader theory of international relations. In particular, this last section examines the implications of mimetic theory for the *ethics* of the international relations and shows how the theory dissolves the concept and discourse of victimhood.

## Mimetic Doubles

The notion of rivalry is fraught with ambiguity, its use in the theory of international relations is often vague and unspecific, and it seems still true that "there has been little reflection and no research on how and why states become rivals."[16]

Scholars who have investigated the sources of rivalry between states agree that alliances and military buildups compound the power status of a state and escalate the rivalry.[17] According to Brandon Valeriano, this is the very origin of "proto-rival" status, in the sense that alliances and buildups turn a situation of nonrivalry into a proto-rivalry. However, this genetic story of rivalry fails to acknowledge a penumbra of psychological factors (including a possibly existing record of mimetic exchanges) before the *tactical* escalation of rivalry.

Mimetic theory is concerned with a variety of phenomena that occur in the interim between the nonrivalry condition and proto-rivalry status. From this perspective—from the perspective of mimetic theory—I still believe that there has been little reflection on how and why states become rivals. And there has been little reflection because canonical wisdom on this topic is considered unproblematic, and this explains the fringe status of subversive theories in general. Mimetic theory, for one thing, is not tackling an exhausted paradigm (in which case it would be greeted as a welcome contribution); it rather seeks to repair or even replace a paradigm that almost nobody considers problematic.[18] As in the case of dyads, the research agenda has been focused on biases and constraints in sampling and collection strategies, and not on the genetic story of rivalry, namely, on "why states become rivals."[19]

Mimetic theory constitutes a new approach to a number of old problems in the study of human behavior. It has a strong potential to contribute to developing a new framework in which issues related to human cognition, morality, sociability, and conflict could be analyzed. René Girard has investigated the pattern whereby polar opposites grow out of so-called mimetic antagonism. His lifelong speculation on patterns of mimetic violence in myth and literature has yielded insights into the nature of human agency and rationality. Girard himself has traced countless clues for a general mimetic explanation of human behavior to ancient myth and rituals, and the theory he proposed seems less an entirely novel and original theoretical development than an attempt to formalize a number of age-old assumptions about human rationality and sociability.

In chapter 1 I argued that reciprocal imitation is not an innocent pursuit with no real impact on the dynamics of sociability. On the contrary, by imitating their own desires human beings are bound to desire the very same objects and thus become rivals. Rivalry is therefore an immediate fallout of this fundamental disposition to imitate, and what matters most is that the rivals remain unaware of the actual psychological drives that push them.

In a series of conversations with Pierpaolo Antonello and João Cezar de Castro Rocha, Girard rehearsed his argument and presented it in a very sharp fashion, explaining the genesis of this "doubling" out of the mimetic predicament:

> the subject will tend to imitate his model as much as his model imitates him. Eventually, the subject will become the model of his model, just as the imitator will become the imitator of his imitator. One is always moving towards more symmetry, and thus always towards more conflict, for symmetry cannot but produce *doubles,* as I call them at this moment of intense rivalry. Doubling occurs as soon as the object has disappeared in the heat of the rivalry: the two rivals become more and more concerned with defeating the opponent for the sake of it, rather than obtaining the object, which eventually becomes irrelevant, as it only exists as an excuse for the escalation of the dispute. Thus, the rivals become more and more undifferentiated, identical: doubles. A mimetic crisis is always a crisis of undifferentiation that erupts when the roles of subject and model are reduced to that of rivals. It's the disappearance of the object which makes it possible. This crisis not only escalates between the contenders, but it becomes contagious with bystanders.[20]

In chapter 1 I explained how the progression of this contagion leads to a saturation of violence that explodes eventually in one specific direction: the scapegoat.[21] The mechanism of "sacrificial violence" always operates unacknowledged by the lynchers, until an eventual revelation of the innocence of the victims upsets the pattern and makes the sacrificial solution ineffective. Our epoch is concerned with a new, postsacrificial form of polarization, not between the group and the victim but rather between *two* groups, as if the growing mimetic escalation that generates doubles no longer relied on the age-old "sacrificial" outlet, namely, the specious identification of a victim that attracts all the animosity and allows the community to reconcile.

Christianity, to be sure, is instrumental to Girard's genealogy, but the Christian understanding of human history supported by Girard doesn't offer per se normative clues on how to address the issue of polarizations "to the extreme." The applicability of mimetic theory, in other words, is not subject to, and warranted by, the adoption of a Christian perspective. Indeed, the psychological premises of the theory can be isolated and brought to bear, and the following is a tentative exploration of how these premises could be tied up with *actual* demands for peace and reconciliation made by *real* people and not potential candidates for final citizenship in the forthcoming Kingdom.

Girard argues that Christianity highlights the predicament of the victim and at the same time deflates the narratives of oppression of the perpetrators. The escalation of mimetic rivalry, as we saw, is also an effect of the Christian revelation. But it is not by introducing a "supplement" of Christianity, however one may want to define this, that the escalation could be stopped. Christianity, in fact, is not the cure; it is rather what triggered the predicament (e.g., the rise and eventual explosion of *all* mimetic rivalries) by depriving human societies of their pleasing rationale for univocal victimization. So, if Girard's *genealogy* of violence remains contingent on a Christian perspective, the *psychology* of mimesis bears on different epistemic grounds.

Once exposed, the mimetic context of the NWs emerges as ultimately responsible for breeding the formation of a number of "Siamese twins," para-states and transnational actors that operate outside the bounds of age-old juridical ties. In the following I shall turn to the conflict that "represents in miniature" the global mimetic lineups detailed above. The conflict "between Israel and the Palestinian authority" is a "new" type of conflict for its ubiquity across national borders. The conflict is also "mimetic" because each actor can be seen as a "model who becomes a rival, or of a rival who becomes a model."

## Pepsi Does Not Hate Seven Up, It Hates Coca-Cola

In his book *Israel and Palestine: Why They Fight and Can They Stop?* Bernard Wasserstein maintained that Israelis and Palestinians are living today as "Siamese twin societies"; however much they may wish to, neither side can escape the impinging presence and influence of the other. Think of the opening words of his book:

> *Mon frère, mon semblable!* Zionism and Palestinian nationalism, arising from different roots, drawing on profoundly different political cultures, and aiming at mutually antagonistic objectives, have strangely imitated each other down the decades.[22]

In a similar vein, in his touching monologue *Via Dolorosa*, David Hare wrote that "you cannot visit Israel unless you also visit its twin, its underside. What is the point of going unless you walk through the mirror into the occupied land?"[23]

Benny Morris, in his book on the history on the "Zionist-Arab" conflict, has used the same metaphor of the "twins" to stress the symmetry of the polarization. In discussing the nature of the terrorist wave that led, in the mid-1990s, to the assassination of Yitzhak Rabin, Morris states that "the Muslim enemies of peace nurtured and activated their Israeli twins."[24]

Elements of mimetic violence can be gleaned in what could be seen as the arch-conflict of our time, the war between Israelis and Palestinians, and many observers have stressed the striking, twin-like similarities between the two rivals. Interestingly the same dynamic of polarization can be observed within each of the two fields, where structures of internal mimetic polarization plague the political discourse of both Palestinians and Israelis. Morris has described the polarization effect of the first Gulf War on the Palestinian side of the cleavage: "Tension and conflict between various groups of Palestinians—secularists and fundamentalists, Left and Right—also increased considerably."[25]

In this chapter and in the following one, the Israeli-Palestinian schism will be taken as a paradigm for illuminating the mimetic mechanisms of aggregation and disaggregation that plague global politics today.[26] And mimetic theory, in turn, will be marshaled to illuminate a number of phenomena that political scientists have consistently failed to notice: reciprocal imitation as the fundamental cause of human discord, the mechanisms of spontaneous polarization in human conflicts, and the strange and ever-growing resemblance between the "mimetic rivals." It is precisely a mimetic strain of this kind, so I am tempted to argue, that comes into view in Morris's statement about the "Muslim enemies of peace." But if this is so, then we should wonder in what sense Israelis and Palestinians are mimetic twins.

The argument about the similarities between the two cultures is old; the peace movement, among others, invokes it regularly. Some years ago, the weekly bulletin of CERN, the European Organization for Nuclear Research, reported that one of the closing events of its Summer Students Programme was the Israeli-Palestinian party. The event, described as "an enormous success," was also an opportunity for the organizers "to show off their respective cultures in a different light to that which is constantly shed by the media." Muhammad Yousef Alhroob, one of the organizers, declared that "through our music and food, which are very similar in Palestine and in Israel, we wanted to teach the other students something about our two peoples."[27]

In 2006 ten young Israelis and Palestinians met in Bonn and Berlin, and discovered a number of unexpected similarities. An article on the website of the Willy Brandt Center in Jerusalem expands upon this meeting, organized by the young socialists of the German Social Democratic Party (SPD), who invited a group of youths from Israel and Palestine to a seminar in Germany. The idea was to have them meet on neutral ground and give them the chance to directly encounter the other and test their own prejudices. The article from the WBC website tells the story of the friendship between Reem Mubarrak and Immanuel Stein in Berlin-Kreuzberg. Stein is Israeli, Mubarrak is a Palestinian from Ramallah in West Jordan, and that weeklong experience challenged their prejudices. Twenty-one-year-old Mubarrak maintained: "We noticed that, for the most part, we liked the same food and the same music" (*Wir stellten fest, dass wir großenteils auch das gleiche Essen und die gleiche Musik mochten*).[28]

The appeal of music and food was described by Stanley Fish as a typical feature of what he calls a "boutique multiculturalist"—someone who thinks that cultural differences can be easily overcome. "A boutique multiculturalist may find something of value in rap music and patronize (pun intended) soul-food restaurants," Fish maintains, "but he will be uneasy about affirmative action and downright hostile to an afrocentrist curriculum."[29] For Fish, food and music are superficial markers of identity that do not account for actual, substantial similarities: boutique multiculturalists, on the contrary, are inclined to believe that eating the same food and listening to the same music shows that differences among cultures are fabricated and instrumental.

The Jordanian writer Rabih Alameddine has put the argument about the similarity between the two cultures in striking terms. He pushed the idea of the Israeli and Palestinians as *cultural* twins in an interview in the Italian newspaper *Corriere della Sera,* where he maintained that the Israeli-Palestinian schism has escalated to the current level precisely because the rivals are hardly distinguishable from one another:

> I look around and see only the same people. With minimal—sometimes negligible—variations of the same stories. Or, for that matter, of the same recipes. Tell me where the difference is! . . . They are all the same. Their food is the same, their music is the same. . . . Look at the Palestinians, who had to leave their houses and become refugees in Lebanon: they behave exactly like the Jews of the Diaspora. This is why they kill each other: *because they are identical.* Pepsi does not hate Seven Up, it hates Coca-Cola.[30]

What is remarkable about Alameddine is that his argument turns the boutique view upside down. Alameddine did not simply criticize this view by opposing a strong form of multiculturalism to a weak or boutique one. He argued precisely the opposite of boutique multiculturalists, who are keen to believe that the more similar people are (or think they are), the easier for them to make, or live in, peace.[31] So to Alameddine there is no point in encouraging people to acknowledge their similarities, for this would do nothing but strengthen their mutual hostility.

Food as a marker of cultural identity features in the film *You Don't Mess with the Zohan* (2008), where hummus is represented as an ecumenical meal that both Palestinians and Israelis eat in abundance (and Zohan, the eponymous Jewish superhero, uses as toothpaste).[32] In the film, former Israeli commando Zohan moves to America, where he dreams of becoming a hairdresser. America is the place that assimilates all creeds and races, to the point that the people living there no longer see those differences and dissimilarities that both Israelis and Palestinians have turned into a political raison d'être. In the film, a Palestinian immigrant says, "People hate us. They think we're terrorists." And an Israeli immigrant replies, "People hate us, too. They think we're you." The "people" are the people of America, the outsiders of the mimetic game of imitating one another "to the extreme."[33] And neither Zohan nor his nemesis, the Palestinian superhero "the Phantom," manage to escape this mimetic predicament. Zohan wants to be a hairdresser, whereas the Phantom has a dream of simply opening a shoe shop. Both want to tend to their own businesses and pursue their petit bourgeois dream of living normal lives. They want to move to the outside of the conflict where differences evaporate and where their absolute likeness would be finally exposed. But mimesis takes over unacknowledged, and both Zohan and the Phantom become superheroes again, reinstating the internal space in which their similarities dissolve and the differences reappear.

Here we are faced with two distinct universalities. On the one hand we have the dynamic of violent imitation "which makes adversaries more and more alike." This dynamic is universal inasmuch as it "*is at the root of all myths and cultures.*"[34] On the other hand we have the tendency "to see differences where in fact there are none," that is, to refuse to internalize the "external" insight that what is growing to the extreme is precisely a furious, reciprocal imitation heading to the eventual "undifferentiation" of the scene.[35] Reem Mubarrak and Immanuel Stein, displaced in Berlin-Kreuzberg, are a case of successful internalization of this knowledge. They stopped acting as insiders in the "reign of violence" when they realized that their feigned differences were illusory.

The rivals, stuck in the reign of violence, engage in a frantic work of symbolic production of the differences they need in order to construe themselves as *others*. But once displaced from the symbolic milieu they fabricated, and placed in that elsewhere of the reign of violence in which they may dispassionately look at each other, the rivals may see that their "matching images of violence" were the unintended effect of a protracted and unconscious process of reciprocal imitation.[36]

The following section is meant to challenge the assumption that the principal goal of NWs is "political mobilization on the basis of identity."[37] Mimetic theory deconstructs identity claims by arguing that markers of identity are "reminders of difference" in a situation of escalating mimesis;

these markers serve to suppress and rationalize the mimetic flattening of all differences between the rivals.

## Beyond the Politics of Identity

To be sure, the whole paradigm of NWs is less a centralized forum of discussion than an archipelago of views sharing a limited number of empirical claims. A special focus on identity, together with an emphasis on low intensity, intransience, deterritorialization, and the demise of the nation-state pattern in managing warfare, is the defining characteristic of the NWs. Identity, though, unlike these other more empirical properties, determines the rationale of NWs and provides the actors with new gripping concepts concerning normativity, legitimacy, and a viable meaning-making structure to address, and respond to, a number of fundamental queries, both existential and political.

"First-generation" NWs theories include "new wars," "postmodern wars," "wars of the third kind," and "people's wars."[38] More recently, scholars have developed other forms of NWs thinking: theorists of "fourth-generation warfare" have tried to slightly repair the theory by adapting it to the changing environs of new conflicts.[39] But the tenets of the theory, notably the dynamics of mobilization of actors operating without the grand legitimation schemes of the past, are still there. After the dismantling of old political allegiances and ideological positions a number of actors were left with no clue about how to mobilize consensus and build a novel and durable political outlook. By the same token, international actors failed to understand the impact of "cultural issues in international affairs."

The NWs paradigm has been challenged by scholars who stressed the continuity of conflict patterns throughout the twentieth and twenty-first centuries: critics of the paradigm have argued that there is no evidence that the NWs are "fundamentally different" from old wars.[40] Here I am using NWs theory as a useful means of demarcation to highlight a slight adjustment of the pattern, one that can be empirically observed and that explains the enduring appeal of the theory.

NWs theory shares with the mimetic approach to international conflict the emphasis on escalation of war across state-boundaries, and for this reason it could be argued that the theory is an ideal companion for the mimetic theorist who seeks to find a point of access into the larger discourses of IR theory.

One thing that should be stressed is that this access to the discourse of IR cannot be organized by specialization: such topics as cosmopolitan democracy, NWs theory, theories of humanitarian intervention, and a number of normative approaches to conflict and rivalry straddle the realms and distinctions of IR theory.[41] In this chapter I acknowledge the findings of NWs theory and seek to repair its logic by tracking mimetic dynamics in new conflicts, by spotting dyadic patterns where NWs theory sees only a multiplicity of disconnected actors.

Interestingly, NWs theory failed to provide a decidedly novel paradigm for conflict resolution. The idea that diverse identities are bound to clash is very much ingrained in the ways we think about violence, and we are inclined to approve the liberal solution, that by erasing the differences we will get to something approximating "perpetual peace."

Political scientists Pippa Norris and Ronald Inglehart have put the point strikingly:

> In the post–Cold War world, the widening gap between the core values held by the more religious and more secular societies will probably increase the salience and importance of cultural issues in international affairs. How well we manage to accommodate and tolerate these cultural differences, or how far we fail, remains one of the core challenges for the twenty-first century.[42]

It is the "democratic hope" of international humanitarian organizations that people caught in mimetic rivalry might be persuaded to step back and defy mimesis.[43] Difference, however, has reached a critical point in the academic discourse on the origins and rationales of NWs. Land, the search for precious metals (the age of European imperialism), and a workable Lebensraum (Nazi expansion in Europe) are no longer the triggers and rationales of war; rather, identity and identity issues are increasingly fulfilling this role. Kalevi Holsti has given a sweeping genealogy of the dwindling of the age-old rationales for war, stressing how state-building in many areas of the world has become "one of the most fundamental political-psychological values of an era obsessed with questions of community and identity."[44] According to Mary Kaldor,

> The politics of identity . . . has a tendency to spread. All identity-based groups, whether defined in terms of language, religion or some other form of differentiation, spill over borders; after all, it is precisely the heterogeneity of identity that offers the opportunity for various forms of exclusivism.[45]

The idea that identity has taken over territoriality as the principal rationale for war is one of the central tenets of a cluster of insights that we could place within the same NWs paradigm only at the cost of overly generalizing. No longer interested in expanding their borders, states and international organizations have become the hosts to disputes and clashes over ethnic or religious identity. Herfried Münkler has complicated this relatively neat picture by claiming that it is becoming increasingly difficult to pin down the actual actors involved in disputes: NWs spill across ethnonational borders and feed on the general process of "debordering" spurred by globalization.[46] "State borders" and "sovereignty" are coeval concepts whose fate is tightly linked, and borders "are perhaps the most fundamental international institutions in the modern-state system." A number of phenomena related with large diasporas of ethnic groups and more generally the rise of ethnicity as a marker of identity gave rise "to substantial incongruences between the sovereign territory of the state and the geographic scope of the polity."[47]

Kalevi Holsti argued, back in 1996, that "strategic studies continue to be seriously divorced from the practices of war as we have seen them in the West Bank, Bosnia, Somalia, and elsewhere."[48] But the whole NWs paradigm has now taken over larger segments of the discourse on war. Being still a fluid and not self-consistent paradigm, NWs theory may host insights that challenge some of its tenets, like nonpolarity, asymmetrization, and the primacy of identity. The attempt to repair the paradigm along the lines of mimetic theory may help prepare a new meaning-making framework more suitable to addressing a whole cohort of new conflicts.

I believe that the theme of mobilization on the basis of identity is particularly receptive to mimetic theory, which argues that claims concerning identity come *after,* not *before* the actual conflict. I am focusing in particular on this aspect of NWs theory, not a minor aspect but a distinguishing aspect.

And one thing that mimetic theory may help dissolve is the focus on identity as a prominent rationale for war.[49] To explain the new conflict in terms of radicalization of ethnic identity is wrong and it generates biased policy prescriptions.

The notion of "civilization" is often used to describe a set of exclusive markers of identity: civilizations are held together by a sense of purpose and Weltanschauung that tends to be local and exclusive. However, claims of civilizational status are less the stimulus of conflict between civilizations than the workable rationalization of a prior hostility of a different nature. Accordingly, not only is the *identity* cleavage between Israelis and Palestinians largely fabricated, but so too are the ethnonational, cultural, and religious differences of groups at war in Somalia, Rwanda, and Sudan.

To be sure, most of these groups "were comfortable with multiple identities," and the creation of racial distinctions was contingent on ad hoc and cogent political strategies.[50] In Sudan the central government has been promoting, since the early 1980s, "Arab identity at the expense of Sudanese national identity," creating a novel cleavage line between Arabs and non-Arabs.[51] In both Sudan and Rwanda civil wars were fought on issues of identity that, on closer scrutiny, emerge as rationalizations of ingrained mimetic attitudes. Here, just like the "miniature" case of the Israeli-Palestinian conflict, the African ethnic wars of the last decades were fought by groups that had existed for centuries in contexts of multiple intersecting identities. Large-scale mimetic lineups of "new" ethnic realities were the effects, possibly unintended, of new political circumstances. Here one can observe very similar patterns, where the rivalry is compounded by underlying dynamics of reciprocal imitation.

But save for the several African cases to which we might refer, it is quite obvious how scholars concerned with new types of warfare found a particularly congenial terrain in the Yugoslav wars of the 1990s. These wars revealed a consistent pattern, with the fragmentation of all political spectra into myriad units amenable to manipulation by new political leaders. Indeed, "during the regime transition of 1990 no significant political force put forth an all-Yugoslav vision and agenda."[52] Nonethnic contenders fared poorly in the democratic elections of 1990, whereas ethnonationalists mobilized most of the votes across national borders. Ironically, the elections compounded a dangerous alienation of ethnic communities from democratic politics and fragmented the Bosnian society along ethnic lines.

The war in Bosnia-Herzegovina

has become the paradigm case, from which different lessons are drawn, the example which is used to argue out different general positions, and, at the same time, a laboratory in which different ways of managing the NWs are experimented.[53]

Again, Kaldor points to ethnic identity as the deciding factor in the wars that brought havoc upon the ex-Yugoslavia in the 1990s. She treats Bosnia in particular as yet another miniature case of a new and highly widespread modality of conducting war. Kaldor acknowledges the relatively peaceful arrangement of Bosnian society before 1990 and the instrumentality of the reinvention of "particular forms of history and memory to construct new cultural forms that can be used for political mobilization."[54] Kaldor's psychohistory of the war shows the hidden stakes involved in the rupture of the Yugoslav state along ethnonational lines: ethnonationalists undermined the symbolic construal of Yugoslavia as a multicultural space in which different ethnic groups could hardly experience the gap between being friends with local Muslims and shooting a Muslim depersonalized enemy from the hills surrounding Sarajevo.

Mimetic theory suggests a different etiology of the conflict, a story of reciprocal modeling of the rivals escalating into a conflict with genocidal implications. The mimetic strain in the Yugoslav wars becomes apparent as soon as we see that identity was being used to rationalize ethnic violence, but, on closer inspection, it was not the actual *cause* of ethnic violence. Mimetic theory suggests that identity, just like nonpolarity, is a distorted visual effect that renders new conflicts elusive and hard to pin down. NWs are characterized by a radicalization of identity, but this radicalization is the *consequence* of the mimetic crisis, rather than what sets it off. In conflicts in which animosity is explained in terms of the territorialization of identities a mimetic dynamic is arguably at work, pushing the rivals against each other and forcing people who socialized in an environment with weak identity ties and possessing unclear identity marks (children of interethnic marriages and, in Bosnia, non-ethnically Bosnian Muslims), to take on a clearly perceptible identity and thereby engage in the ongoing polarization. Claims of exclusive possession of a given portion of land often take place in environments in which identity issues become politically sensitive only *after* individual and group rivalries set in. Nevertheless, identity is used by both rivals and third parties to rationalize the ensuing conflict, thereby contributing to the concealment of the mimetic activity that polarizes the scene. And indeed ethnonational identity was to be blamed as the cause of the myriad civil wars—fought at the micro-level in towns and villages with an ethnically mixed population—that punctuated the blurred map of what was left, in the early 1990s, of the ex-Yugoslavia.

In Bosnia, in the early 1990s, towns and villages with a very high concentration (up to 40 percent) of ethnically and confessionally mixed marriages bore witness to a shocking escalation of violence between ethnic-based factions, and people caught in the mimetic thrall of the mounting civil war were understandably losing their bearings. And the many who had married across ethnic lines realized that the world that had once been indifferent to their marriage had "changed so profoundly that what had been accepted and even treasured only a few years ago has suddenly been rendered vestigial and taboo."[55]

I doubt that this turn in the psychological attitude and outlook of people can be explained by means of a psychological story of political disillusionment and symbolic vacuum. The causal mechanism adopted to make sense of the harsh polarization between ethnic groups starts with a claim to ethnic belonging and ends with terror and genocide, but it omits the passage from a condition of overall ignorance of one's belonging to the first germs of hostility: "the mimetism of the lynchers."[56] And lynchings occurred several times during the Bosnian wars.

Scapegoating is a highly regressive phenomenon that lets up only occasionally. In fact, mimetic violence is not superseded by a new "sacred" arrangement of the group hierarchy; it continues escalating to the extreme, contained not so much by sacrificial obstacles or mimetic exhaustion but by an external containment—a ban on further conflict (and mimetism) launched by external players.

## Mimesis Vindicated

"There is no totality that does not run the risk of being affected by the doubling that used to be contained by sacrifice."[57] And mimetic violence is bound to grow to the extreme because "Eteocles and Polynices will never be reconciled. Only democratic hope can claim to put an end to the tragedy, but we now know that this is a modern platitude."[58]

Girard is adamant about the pervasiveness of mimetic violence; his book on Clausewitz is meant to move the analysis of mimesis to a new scale. It is an inquiry into the collapse of the age-old boundaries that kept mimetic conflicts from spilling across boundaries. It suggests that modern states have sacrificial origins that fail to do their job of containment correctly.

Mimetic dynamics are expanding and escalating, but they remain difficult to detect. Ontological biases and erroneous psychological presuppositions make it difficult to recognize the actual working of mimesis in global politics. Girard has pointed out that "it is not surprising that in the era of globalization . . . when wars are increasing, mimetism has gained ground since 1945 and is taking over the world."[59] Assumptions of nonpolarity add up to yet another attempt at overlooking the mimetic structure of human relationships—the perception, acknowledged by Benoît Chantre, "of the duel as the hidden structure of all social phenomena."[60] If the duel is omnipresent and structural, nonpolarity is yet another disguise for mimetic dynamics to conceal themselves.

If we look at mimetic rivalry from the perspective of canonical theories of international relations it seems unclear how the actors could be misled in their choices and motives to the point of fabricating entirely fictitious causal stories about their behavior. It is not intuitive to think of political behavior in mimetic terms, as if social structures could decide about their course without human intervention, as if some kind of mimetic causality subsumed human agency and acquired patterns of its own. And it is difficult to predict whether the fate of global politics will be shaped by the relentless production of mimetic twins, namely, by a process of undifferentiation that "grows behind the backs of those involved."[61]

Another point that theorists may find puzzling is the fact that the growth of this process of undifferentiation is no longer contained by sacrificial barriers; nation-states are on the wane under the impact of globalization, and identities have become mobile and ubiquitous. More important, *local* identities feed on a broader scheme of identification that provides a practical distinction between us and them and draws a major line of enmity whose impact is felt across local and global venues. East and West are in fact the two main sides of a worldwide mimetic confrontation; their alleged differences are inspiring the ideologues of local conflicts desperate to find markers of difference in order to conceal and rationalize their mimetic rivalry.

The "worlds at war" that constitute the current mimetic structure of global politics are facing one another with neither sacrificial nor legal devices to inhibit the growth to the extreme of their reciprocal enmity.[62] I stressed the mimetic outlook of the Israeli-Palestinian schism and tried to show how this arch-conflict of our time is projecting its mimetic core onto global politics.[63] To be sure, the struggle between Israelis and Palestinians is the hotbed, the arch-conflict, to which the two worlds engaged in this global mimetic contest look in order to frame their inimical imagining of the other. It is a powerful source of metaphors that reverberate globally and sustain the current reciprocal struggle on an unprecedented scale.

Local and global exist simultaneously, each informing and influencing the other, and both caught in the same process of growing undifferentiation. The myriad reciprocal actions that occur in this global scenario can be broken down in single reciprocal events, tiny mimetic units—or "mimetic foci"—which are highly likely to escalate: reciprocal action is amplified by globalization inasmuch as globalization can function as "the planetary reciprocity in which the slightest event can have repercussions on the other side of the globe.[64]

Several mimetic units—the NWs that are currently fought worldwide—can be seen as miniature copies of "a struggle to the death between Islam and the West," as synchronic moments in a process of escalation that could "take place between Arab countries and the Western world."[65] But if we push the implications of mimetic theory as far as they go and stick to a perfectly dyadic vision, we end up losing a good part of the normative language used by theorists of the international relations, especially when they make a point about the *ethics* of the international relations. "The symmetry of the overall picture" sets constraints on our tendency to praise and condemn: discourse of "failed" states, of "terrorism," and, more significantly, of "victimhood," loses its normative edge so long as each member of the dyad can be seen as both good and evil, both perpetrator and victim, depending on perspective.[66] With regard to the Israeli/Palestinian schism, neither—or both—could make an exclusive claim to the status of victim.[67] Mimesis dissolves the discourse of victimhood, which makes sense only within the closed system of the respective languages.[68]

We are now left with the question whether the mimetic framing of the issue of NWs is epistemically warranted. Could it be that when we peek below the theoretical edifice in search of epistemic foundations, the mimetic argument is seen to rest on ground no firmer than Girard's intellectual authority alone? This easy objection to mimetic theory triggers a simple counterobjection, namely, that there is no "external" epistemic warrant that decides that the individuationist model is right. It all seems to come down to authority and rhetoric. The model sets constraints on our ability to envision new approaches, to upset intellectual routines, and to think in radically different terms. The challenge is to see how far our hypotheses can be pushed beyond the reach of a model—the mimetic model—that remains epistemologically amorphous and rhetorically unconvincing. Sensitive topics in IR theory may benefit from a different insight, and speculations inspired by a mimetic understanding of political phenomena could be morphed into a coherent whole, into a more comprehensive level of analysis. The distinction between Girardian insights and actual theoretical premises is still fuzzy, and the premises—and their implications—need to be researched thoroughly. The mimetic model needs to be pushed beyond its original (or pseudo-original) Girardian matrix and its possibilities need to be explored in a more thorough way.

To be sure, the individuationist model and the mimetic model are each grounded on a distinctive ontology, each defined by what items are considered to have ontological preeminence. One approach considers the individual as the ultimate reality. The other approach considers groups the decisive realities in political processes. The mimetic perspective highlights neither individuals nor groups, but "doubles," or "mimetic twins." The mimetic approach has one strong epistemic advantage, though, as it connects contemporary events and arrangements with social and cultural origins, and shows that "violent imitation, *which makes adversaries more and more alike,* is at the root of all myths and cultures.[69] Thus, if we push our genetic stories backward not just years or decades, but to the very origins of society and culture, we could see what we have thus far repressed, make up for the spiritual hubris that broke down these mimetic units into individual loci of agency, and restore the fundamental mimetic structure of political exchange.

CHAPTER 3

# Cleavage Lines
# in Global Politics

<br>

This chapter revisits the "heuristic value of the left-right dichotomy" for understanding global politics and brings mimetic theory to bear on left and right as "mimetic opposites." The chapter explores the impact of the mimetic antagonism illustrated in chapter 2 on the political discourse and processes of Western democracies. It argues that the Israeli-Palestinian schism reverberates at the global level and affects both the democratic processes of Western nations and the political orientation of what Alain Noël and Jean-Philippe Thérien call the "world public sphere." So this chapter explores the spilling-over of *real* conflicts into the political discourse and processes of Western democracies. It shows that the escalation to the extreme of the conflict in the Middle East triggers a similar escalation between opposite sides within the political spectra of both the United States and the European Union. Ultimately mimetic dynamics operate unacknowledged, and the harsh left/right polarization in both the United States and the EU is an expression of this mimetic radicalization, of a rivalry that is in the process of losing its checks and boundaries.

This chapter explores the spillover effects, *outside* of the Middle East—and notably in the United States and the EU—of the arch-conflict of our time, and shows how tensions and dynamics of rivalry in the West feed on that arch-conflict. The mimesis of the Middle Eastern rivals has its Western epiphany within the political spectrum of each and every democratic nation of the West, where the left-right axis turns out to be exceptionally sensitive to that conflict.

The tension between left and right is deeply mimetic in nature. The mimesis of political polarization is all the more evident in times of harsh polarization, where parliaments, and notably two-party systems, fail to do their job correctly, namely, neutralize the political thrusts of society and displace it on a semisymbolic level where political decisions will be made. Nevertheless, as it has been pointed out, "the two party system of modern parliaments uses the psychological structure of opposing armies. . . . the two factions remain; they fight on, but in a form of warfare that has renounced killing."[1] The dynamic of parliamentary democracy is therefore the same dynamic of Clausewitzean warfare, a duel-like dialectic between two sides that cannot help imitating each other, and whose secret aim is to defeat and ultimately annihilate each other. This rather grand and suggestive statement becomes vaguely plausible as soon as we make room for the subtext that Girard has pushed to the foreground of his political analysis of globalization, namely, anthropology, the idea that human nature is structured by the universality of a few anthropological constants that bind behavior to relatively limited social patterns.

The structuring of modern politics through mimetic dyads is the effect of a process of adaptation of our mimetic psychologies to complex social systems. The advent of large-scale polities, of democracy and universal suffrage, has created a new context for mimetism to operate. Left and right are critical indexes for orientation within the *democratic* political space. The left/right distinction is designed to *suspend* the trend to the extreme of social conflicts, namely, the eventual escalation of the polar contest between "mimetic twins," and it aims to keep political processes within the fragile boundaries of democratic politics. Their ever possible "going to extremes" can be gleaned when more cleavage lines compound themselves and give rise to potentially explosive "cumulative cleavage positions."[2] The chapter illustrates the potential collision of three different cleavage lines: left/right, East/West, earth/heaven, and introduces a theme that will be explored in chapter 4, namely the theme of *political theology*.

This chapter shows what happens when mimetic opposites are pressured apart by a powerful polarizer. These opposites, or extremes, often resort to a theological jargon in order to legitimize their exclusiveness and mutual incompatibility. Instead of framing the conflict within the ritual dialectic of democratic exchange, left and right become the indexes of a radical incompatibility between the rivals.

## Left and Right: A Genealogy

Despite pronouncements of its imminent end, the left/right dyad is undergoing a notable revival.[3] Its resilience seems to lie in the fact that left and right are "empty vessels" that can be filled with any sort of content.[4] The dyad is relatively old, a child of the French Revolution, when, in the political void left after the collapse of the ancien régime, it worked as a viable device to frame the post-Revolution political space. The "people" (an old term filled with new meaning) was in need of orientation and a polarizer was deployed to orient new political actors—the *citizens*—on issues that were deemed critical to the moral design of the polity that had emerged from the debris of the old order. Back then, the notion of equality was still a relatively abstract notion, foreign to the political lexicon of the ancien régime, but it helped polarize the public into two major areas of opinion: supporters of more equitable social arrangements on the left, and advocates of the old, hierarchical order on the right.

Over the last two hundred years, a variety of polarizers have played active and distinctive roles in framing the political space.[5] However, in a world increasingly exposed to the pushes and challenges of globalization, people's political bearings depend more and more on perceptions of *international* issues, and international politics is providing both the agenda and the stakes for further left/right polarizations at a *global* level.[6] Pro- and antiglobalization movements, Middle Eastern politics, international terrorism, and environment-related issues pose policy challenges that generate polar reactions in the global public sphere. And such reactions can be sorted under the all-purpose headings of left and right: people locate themselves on a left-right continuum depending on their views on a number of global issues.[7]

This chapter addresses problems that are urging political scientists to revisit the "heuristic value of the left-right dichotomy" to understand *global* politics. Alain Noël and Jean-Philippe Thérien have wondered whether the left-right distinction is "powerful enough to extend beyond the politics of equality and distribution it usually captures, and help us understand other global issues."[8] Marco Revelli, for one, is more skeptical about applying the left/right dyad to global politics: "the traditional criteria of spatial orientation that applied to the smooth and seamless plane of 'modernity' haven't stopped working, although they have lost their 'ordering' character. Instead of clarifying political discourse, they generate more distortions and optical illusions, more diversions and disorientations."[9]

In the following I shall argue that the notion of equality has lost momentum in polarizing political spectra, and that over and beyond "the politics of equality and distribution" a new politics of identity is placing strain on the left/right continuum.

In the Western world, notably in Europe and in the United States, the left/right dyad relies more and more on a discourse of orientation in which some new words have taken over the discourse of class, equality, and social justice. Talk of identity, though, bears an inherently polar structure, as its attendant us versus them outlook is mainly organized along the range from West—its cultural mores and its politics of the partition between "earth" and "heaven"—to a supposedly harmonized East, with its distinctive amalgamation of politics and religion. In political debates structured along the left/right continuum, the discourse of West and East has acquired the power to set opinions apart precisely along that continuum. And this streamlining of the left-right continuum along the East/West axis is the result of the emergence of a new polarizer. No longer an ideal, although ideals and values are commonly attached to it, this polarizer is the state of Israel.

One thing that should not escape our notice is that the "empty vessels" of left and right are filled with slightly different meanings in Europe and in the United States. It is especially in Europe that the left/right distinction has proved to be remarkably sensitive to the East/West divide, although not in the sense that the left is defining its leftist political outlook in terms of direct support of "pro-Eastern" agendas and values, and that, by the same token, the right is leaning westward. To be sure, neither right nor left in either Europe or the United States is perfectly unified in its support of one side or the other, and the deep and enduring divisions between right and left on both sides of the Atlantic are shaped—more or less critically and enduringly—by numerous issues, both domestic and international.

International issues, to be sure, are gaining unprecedented momentum in shaping the left/right distinction, and compete with domestic issues in orienting public opinion and public policy in both Europe and the United States. The rise of international issues in electoral agendas and in people's everyday understanding of politics, combined with the emergence of identity as the new grammar of political orientation, makes the East-West divide into a powerful psychological cleavage that compounds the pressure that pushes left and right apart.

It is not only that the political systems of both the United States and the EU have become increasingly sensitive to nondomestic issues. In a global environment in which all actors have become more and more porous, a number of international actors (including foreign governments) can condition and even penetrate the body politic of a nation.[10] Spillover effects from foreign policy areas to domestic areas are part of the normal political process in Western democracies, and the citizens of Western democracies are often influenced by global issues that can determine their political orientation. The Israel-Palestine conflict "takes place over one of the great ideological and civilisational fault-lines of the modern world. It matters to everyone who takes global affairs seriously."[11]

Overall one can say that the "world public sphere," with some still significant differences between geographical areas, is subject to a significant polarizing tension, and the general perception of the role of political agencies representing Western values and policies seems geared along a left-right continuum.[12] The discourse about Israel builds on this preexisting tension, and seems to have the power to dramatize (or even overdramatize) an already sensitive cleavage.[13] Israel is omnipresent in the global political discourse, and the struggles for identification of both left and right unfold through the tracking of each move of either Israelis or Palestinians, as part of a more general "scorekeeping" attitude specifically focused on political developments in the Middle East. Andrei Markovits has argued that

> a new European (and American) commonality for all lefts—a new litmus test of progressive politics—seems to have developed: anti-Americanism and anti-Zionism.... I cannot think of two more potent wedge issues that define inclusion and exclusion on the left today. In a hierarchy of key items defining what it means to be left in contemporary Europe and the United

States . . . opposition to Israel and America figure at the very top. . . . There
has not been a common issue since the Spanish Civil War that has united
the left so clearly as has anti-Zionism and its twin, anti-Americanism.[14]

In the following I will present a more nuanced and much expanded
version of this argument and will discuss a number of clues that appear to
vindicate the claims presented above. I shall first focus attention on the transformations the left has undergone both in Europe and in the United States
after World War II. I shall then focus on clues suggesting that in Europe—
both at the EU level and at the member-state level—the political spectrum is
sensitive to the polarizing thrust described above. In the third section I shall
expand on the "Atlantic cleavage" that is opening up between the American left and the European left. In the fourth section I will discuss the earth/
heaven cleavage and will show how it intersects with the other cleavage lines.
In the fifth section I will focus attention on the polarizing tensions radiating
from the hub of the East/West cleavage (i.e., Israel), and will show how these
*local* tensions reach out to *global* politics.

## The End of the Class Cleavage
### and the Politics of Identity

When it comes to the left-right spectrum, polarizers have changed considerably over the last forty years. For a little less than two centuries the main left/
right cleavage was the "class cleavage," and all political tensions came to bear
on the notion of equality.[15] *Class* remained the spur of political mobilization
until the late 1970s, when a mechanism of polarization focusing on *identity*
issues emerged. Current dynamics of polarization in American politics would
be hard to understand outside of this major shift from class to identity.[16]
Constituencies traditionally located on the left became sensitive to issues
whose rise in American political discourse was brought about by the civil
rights movements.[17] Equality (of income and social treatment) was no longer
the principal polarizer, and social change brought about a dramatic restructuring of the cleavage line. In the 1950s and 1960s people's sense of position
within the symbolic-political space was challenged by new stimuli. Race and
gender turned out to be new powerful pull-factors that gave intelligibility

and meaning to politics. It was *identity* now, more than wealth and welfare, that determined the people's political orientation.

This was by no means the end of the class cleavage. Anthony Giddens has described "the polarizing effects of what, after all, remains a class society."[18] The tensions produced by a class cleavage still exist, although they are reframed in terms other than class. Issues that were hallmark to the (old) left, such as welfare, are now shared more or less ecumenically by both left and right. Involvement with issues of welfare and basic social services by right-wing government coalitions is especially noticeable in Germany, Italy, and France.

However, the rise of identity as a new grammar of political orientation, as suggested at the outset, implied that the East/West dichotomy could come to play an unprecedented role in articulating antagonistic political orientations.

The "structuring of the cleavage line" along a new polar continuum followed a slow course.[19] As the old cleavage receded, perceptions of left and right became less focused, and the allegiance to either left or right more volatile. Rapprochement is in these cases the standard reaction, until the inception of a new polarizer rewidens the gap.[20]

As soon as the class cleavage gave signs of remission, a new phenomenon surfaced in the political scene: multiculturalism took over the political and polemical language of the left, and the left, since the late 1950s, especially in America, started to define its agenda and goals in terms of advocacy of *minor* identities. The empty vessels of left and right were filled with new content, and identity-related issues turned out to be a natural ground for a new sharp left/right polarization. The new politics of identity, namely, the politics of religion, gender, and ethnicity, concerned individual and group representation and recognition in public life, and the struggle over curricula in Western educational institutions proved how fertile this ground was.

Speaking of curricula, if we shift the attention from left to right we notice what looks like an attempt to relaunch the values originating, in Hobbes's words, in "these Western parts." Advocates of a set of eponymous and perennial Western values, safely and squarely located on the right, seek to outshine the values and reasons of the multiculturalist left. And the left, by contrast, is articulating a new discourse of discontent in which the values, great books, lifestyles, and moral outlooks that we conventionally consider Western are seen as sustaining the imperialistic and neocolonial claims of the West.

In the West, the East/West cleavage has been constantly renegotiated since the Greek historian Herodotus drew a tentative version of it some 2,500 years ago.[21] And it is precisely the geographical area where the East/West cleavage runs that produces the tensions that reverberate in the global public sphere. Tensions in Middle Eastern politics resonate globally, and the East/West fault line is being displaced from its original setting between Asia and Europe, and it now runs within *each* Western democracy. Niall Ferguson has argued that "a hundred years ago, the frontier between West and East was located somewhere in the neighbourhood of Bosnia-Herzegovina. Now it seems to run through every European city."[22] And while the right supports the reasons of "Western modernity," the left appears to be more sensitive to reasons radiating from the narratives of oppression and retribution invoked in the East.

Noël and Thérien argue that it was the Cold War, and the attendant division between capitalism and communism, that

> gave rise to an East-West division that incorporated most other issues of international politics, and polarized positions on the right and on the left. Even decolonization and the birth of new states tended to be interpreted as battles in the war between communism and capitalism. In due course, however, the rise of poor nations and the question of development imposed their own logic, to define a distinctive North-South cleavage.[23]

According to these authors the end of the Cold War marked the vanishing of the East-West divide as an effective political cleavage: "In world politics, the 1980s and 1990s also saw the triumph of conservative forces. Communism was defeated and the East-West division abolished. Only the North-South cleavage remained."[24]

To be sure, the structuring of a powerful inequality cleavage along the North/South axis is crucial for the restructuring of the left/right spectrum in the global age. Critics of those neoliberal policies that go under the rubric of "corporate globalization" think that world politics should be focused on redressing the North/South equality gap. I think that the emergence of articulate and coherent talk of identity has largely replaced the classical talk of inequality and class. Nations that are "victims" of the inequality gap apply for economic support from the affluent North, but the plea that they make in venues such as the World Social Forum is largely framed in a discourse of (national, Muslim, and postcolonial) identity. Actors that speak *on behalf* of these nations, such as social movements and, more generally, critics of "corporate globalization," are crediting the North/South schism as a more viable framework.

I believe that the North/South cleavage is largely subsumed in the East/West cleavage, so long as the "other" pole—the one challenged and contested by such nations as Algeria and Sudan—is not the "North" but the "West." Brazil could be seen as a typical outlier in this picture, but this chapter is concerned with factors mobilizing opinions along the left/right spectrum in Europe and the United States. Brazil features in European newspapers for a short span of days per year (normally in January, on occasion of the WSF); Israel and the Middle East (let alone, at the time of writing, Libya), are incomparably stronger factors in mobilizing opinions and in structuring the left/right cleavage line. Immigration, security, and terrorism are sensitive issues that activate an "identity talk" oriented along the East/West axis.

If we push this line of reasoning as far as it goes, people who identify themselves with the values and political outlook conventionally attached to the left are sensitive to *reasons* adopted to advocate issues that figure in the agenda of pundits and policymakers particularly aware of the plight of a number of "Eastern" nations and peoples. The shaping of one's polar identity, admittedly, is on *reasons,* on the viability and moral dependability of the reasons given to justify, or vilify, a course of action leading to the making of policies.

The European lefts, especially in countries with colonial histories of lesser significance, were late in discovering identity. Italy's political elections of May 2008 are indicative of this transition, which in countries with a sweeping colonial past was not nearly as abrupt. Here, the shift from class to identity not only brought about a dramatic restructuring of the traditional outlook of the left but it had more immediate political effects on the left's traditional constituency, causing a significant migration of a large portion of voters from left to right.[25] Voters in the Italian political elections of 2008 mass-migrated from the far left to the right, attracted by the much more effective (and identity-centered) political talk of parties like the rabidly "anti-Eastern" Northern League. Umberto Eco observed that many Italians have shifted their vote from left to right (namely, from the former Italian Communist Party to the right of Silvio Berlusconi and Umberto Bossi [respectively, the former head of the Italian government and the former chief secretary of the Northern League Party]), thus "redirecting their disdain from capitalists to immigrants."[26]

The Italian case suggests that this phenomenon of adaptation of one polar cleavage to another has affected Europe and America in different ways. Identity politics in America has failed to exploit the East/West cleavage as dramatically, and both left and right keep a distinctive pro-Western (and to a broad extent pro-Israel) attitude.

## Mobility along the Left-Right Continuum: The Case of Europe

The European political landscape is notably mixed, and European politics is not yet sufficiently integrated to allow for consistent generalizations.[27] European politics, though, has been deeply affected by a number of stimuli from the outside (at least since 9/11), and the reactions varied uniformly from country to country along a left-right continuum that straddles ideological partitions at the national level. The events of 9/11 have changed, not so much globalization per se, but the *perception* of global dynamics, making people highly sensitive to the "spillover effects" that I mentioned before. The "forging of global attitudes inside and alongside the national identities" described by Manfred Steger explains why the Israeli-Palestinian schism activates a sensitive discourse of identity in "these Western parts." It is, to be sure, "the eruption of the global imaginary within the national."[28]

One crucial parameter in current European political discourse is the recognition of the Holocaust. As Tony Judt has pointed out, there is little doubt that "Holocaust recognition is our contemporary European entry ticket," and the question whether the case for Israel should be grounded on "Holocaust recognition" is a significant factor of polarization.[29] It is as if the polity emerging from the debris of an old—but not yet obsolete—political order had become aware of its postsacrificial status, and the ban on its sacrificial past were the fundamental constitutional principle upon which the EU is built.

The Action Plan adopted by the Association Council between the EU and Israel refers to "anti-Semitism" as the principal obstacle to integration for prospective EU member states.[30] In other words, the EU construal of Israel's *moral* and political status is pretty much grounded on the open recognition of—in Mary Douglas's words—the "history of persecution and resistance" of the Jewish people.[31] On the one hand, the failure to recognize the moral and historical significance of the Holocaust is assumed to operate—deceptively and in a possibly unacknowledged way—in morally acceptable critiques of Israel's Zionist claims. Bernard-Henri Lévy has stressed the anti-Semitic implications of the anti-Zionism supported by much of the European left. In Peter Berkowitz's reading of Lévy's book *Left in Dark Times,* "the European left vilifies Jews for monopolizing the limited stores of human compassion by constantly invoking the Holocaust; for exaggerating the suffering and death Jews suffered at the hands of the Nazis; and for using Jewish compassion-mongering to justify Israel."[32] Similarly, Efraim Karsh has argued that "anti-Jewish prejudice and animosity, or anti-Semitism as it is commonly known, has served . . . to exacerbate distrust and hatred of Israel."[33] On the other hand, it is the plight of the Palestinian people to frame the discourse of those for whom it is critical, in the first place, to disambiguate legitimate critiques of Israel from the charge of a principled aversion for the Jews.

In the following I will survey—almost anecdotally and very much in outline—the attitudes and outlooks of three EU member states (Britain, Germany, and Italy), and I will conclude with a note on some aspects of the general orientation of the EU towards Israel.

◆ ◆ ◆

In the UK impulses of harsh polarization followed by moments of rapprochement have deeply affected the orientation of local constituencies. W. D. Rubinstein feared—back in 1982—that a growing consensus for Labor may entail the decline of pro-Israel political sympathies and an increasing support for the PLO.[34] Rubinstein, though, could not anticipate two things, that the years of Tory rule were pitched to a *longue durée* (1979 through 1997), and that during the Thatcher era the "class cleavage" was bound to lose much of its political momentum. Tony Blair was the man who rebalanced the party towards the center, supporting policies that broke with Labor's socialist heritage. New Labor, which won the elections in 1997, was ready to frame its agenda by reclaiming a quasi-nonpartisan political outlook, and by pushing to the almost fringe left the kind of socialist orientation feared by Rubinstein.[35]

If we take British politics as a revealing case study we observe that the general attitude of the left towards Israel "was the effect of an encroaching New Left agenda during the 1960s and 1970s."[36] Interestingly, Rubinstein's fearful anticipations are not completely superseded by history, and the new political climate that followed Tony Blair's open support of G. W. Bush's war in Iraq,[37] and a steady buildup of pro-Palestinian or even pro-Arab public opinion, have boosted the leftist discourse in Britain.[38] Media surveys by Arab Media Watch (AMW) reported that the British media are slowly redressing an alleged pro-Israeli bias, especially in the use of language.[39] And language, to be sure, remains the sensitive medium of a widening cleavage between a pro-Israel and admittedly conservative orientation and a pro-Arab and politically progressive attitude.

AMW surveyed the words used in the British press to describe, respectively, Israel's attack in the Gaza Strip in early March 2008, and the killing, days later, of eight students in a Jewish seminary in Jerusalem. While in the case of the Israeli attack the language is somewhat neutral, and the most recurring words are "offensive," "incursion," and "operation," the description of the Palestinian action is loaded with terms such as "massacre," "bloodbath," and "atrocity."[40]

◆   ◆   ◆

German politics provides a revealing perspective, for obvious reasons. However, it is difficult to say whether Israel is polarizing the German political spectrum, and a survey conducted by the weekly magazine *Der Spiegel* has shown that 91 percent of the interviewees want to remain neutral towards the Israeli-Palestinian conflict, although only 3 percent declared themselves to stand openly on the side of Israel. It looks like a sense of caution is keeping Israel from becoming a major polarizing factor in German politics. However, a noticeable strand in German media and politics indicates that opinions and policies are sensitive to the same polarizing factors at work in British politics.

On the left, the party that better understood the risky implication of breaking with caution and taking an openly critical stance on Israel is the Green Party, once the "special spokesperson for the Palestinian perspective."[41] Distinguished members of the party, like former minister for foreign affairs Joschka Fischer, have tried to keep the debate within the bounds of political correctness dictated by the ever possible—and politically danger-ous—short-circuit between anti-Zionism and anti-Semitism.[42]

The German left fits well into the pattern presented by Rubinstein in 1982, for it tends to conflate Israel and the West as a consequence of its "anti-Occidentalist" bias. In 2006 the Linkspartei had invited a delegate of Hamas to Berlin (a political statement per se), whereas Die Linke, since its inception in June 2007, has consistently described the Israeli occupation of the territories in terms of "ethnic cleansing." But it was in November 2008—on the occasion of a memorial event for the seventieth anniversary of Kristallnacht—that the cleavage line between an avowedly pro-Western and pro-Israel government coalition led by Angela Merkel and the new party on the far left of the spectrum, Die Linke, increased in salience.[43] However, the overall attitude of the party towards Israel remains ambiguous: Die Linke is avowedly pro-Israel in terms of its right to exist, although a number of official statements suggest that the party is not at all clear about what kind of polity Israel should be: Gregor Gysi has written (in the party's official website) that "Israel should not further try to be a cultural Europe in the Middle East [*kulturell Europa im Nahen Osten*], but should rather become a cultural power *of* the Middle East."[44] So Israel *should* exist, but it should give up its Western credentials. Or it should stop making political use of them.

◆　◆　◆

Another revealing case is Italy. I have no space here to elaborate on the imposing use of the word "Israel" for identification purposes in the current left versus right political contest in Italy. However, the polarizing effect of the discourse on Israel is a case in which a *global* issue is having a much stronger impact on the orientation and allegiance of the leftist constituency than the usual and apparently worn-out discourse of equality and labor.

The force of Israel as a polarizer in Italian politics escalated to vertiginous heights during the Israeli attack on Gaza of January 2009. Massimo D'Alema, one of the political leaders who led the transition from the former Italian Communist Party (PCI) to the Democratic Party (PD), and former minister for foreign affairs, was, respectively, praised by the league of the Arab ambassadors for his standing on Gaza, and reprimanded by political analyst Angelo Panebianco. According to Panebianco, D'Alema's take on Gaza contained no reference to either "jihad" or "Iran."[45]

If the discourse of the left was still structured around the class cleavage, the right-wing political coalition led by Silvio Berlusconi successfully exploited the "orientation gap" created by the fading of the leftist traditional ontology (workers, unions, classes, etc.). Both the former secretary of the right-wing party Alleanza Nazionale, Gianfranco Fini, and, more recently, the former neofascist mayor of Rome, Gianni Alemanno, arranged their visits to, respectively, Jerusalem (Fini), and Auschwitz (Alemanno), to take political advantage of the new (*identity*-centered) cleavage line.

◆ ◆ ◆

If we switch to the general orientation of the EU, we see that the public spheres of each single member state remain sensitive to issues of *national* interest, and when exposed to the same issues and challenges, they react in ways that are far from uniform. Public opinion in EU member states has occasionally reacted in a relatively uniform fashion, but the reactions are normally articulated in languages that remain fundamentally autochthonous.[46]

However, new major fault lines opened up, especially in Europe, and straddled traditional national divisions. American foreign politics elicits debates and divisions at a level deeper than the member states of the EU. Jürgen Habermas has pointed out that "the divisive force of divergent national histories and historical experiences that traverse European territory like geological fault lines remains potent. The earthquake unleashed by the illegal Iraq policy of the Bush administration has also torn our countries apart along these historical fault lines."[47]

Post-9/11 international politics has produced occasions for a left/right polarization across national borders, and the intervention of an American-led military coalition in Iraq has driven a rift between the left and the right of each European nation, prompting each nation to place itself on either side of the polar continuum, depending on whether it joined the coalition or not.

Let us look at the specific case of Israel. Relationships between the EU and Israel are specified in a number of protocols, notably the aforementioned Action Plan, a document that endorses the standard justificatory discourse deployed by Israel in its relations with the (Arab) world.[48] It is a contentious document, which presents a "comprehensive settlement of the Israeli/Palestinian conflict and a permanent two-state solution" as the arrangement favored by the EU.[49] Its emphasis on anti-Semitism and, more implicitly, on the agency of a pan-Arab *metus hostilis* threatening the unity of the Jewish state, is pitched to the right, and the fact that the construal of an issue currently so high on the agenda of the EU is leaning to the right is bound to affect the making of such critical items—in the EU political ontology—as a EU public sphere and a EU constitution.[50] And the fact that "the draft constitution appears to be strongly tilted to the right" suggests that the polarizers operating at the level of EU politics are not the same as those that operate at the domestic level.[51]

The activities of the European Parliament are monitored by www.votewatch.eu, a nonpartisan website that scrutinizes the attendance of members, their voting, and general activity data broken down by nationality, national political party, and European party grouping. On June 17, 2010, EP voted a resolution on the Israeli military operation against the humanitarian flotilla and the Gaza blockade. The resolution condemned the attack against the flotilla as a breach of international law, but it also stressed that the attitude of the EU towards a single policy item was to be seen within a comprehensive EU policy framework towards the Middle East. The resolution mentioned the damaged relations between Turkey and Israel, the opening of the Rafah crossing by the Egyptian authorities, and the release of the Israeli sergeant Gilad Shalit. Nevertheless, two parliamentary groups located on the right of the EP (namely, Europe of Freedom and Democracy and the European Conservatives and Reformists) voted against the resolution, with all other forces (including the European People's Party) voting in favor. Other votes concerning the attitude of the EU towards the Middle East exhibit a similar pattern.

It is difficult to determine the extent to which global issues and world politics will affect the EU Convention via the formation of an EU public sphere. The "democratic deficit" of Europe—over and beyond the mere "falling off in voter interest" in the European elections—owes less to political ennui than to the lack of powerful elements of orientation at the EU level.[52] And it is not via a certain kind of "affirmative action" aimed at making EU citizens aware that a new transnational polity has emerged that the deficit will be overcome. In fact, the perception of transnational issues and challenges is still biased by the ways those issues and challenges are construed through idioms with little currency out of the borders of each member state.

If we look back to the shift from class to identity, some of the parties that in Europe stand squarely on the left seem unable to recognize the shift, and have thereby failed to reckon with the polarizing thrust of new, identity-oriented, factors.

## The Atlantic Cleavage and the Role of Ideology

The collision of two different structures of polarization—one spatial, and the other political—may have momentous consequences, and may lead eventually to the formation of "cumulative cleavage positions." The political agendas of European democracies would be shaped by a new criterion, in the sense that an East/West cleavage finally subsumed into the left/right dyad might determine priorities in the agenda of the EU, and might as well structure the policymaking processes. That is not to say that the political orientation towards Israel may have a direct spillover effect on other policy areas (in the sense that adopting a pro- or anti-Israel stance will immediately affect other unrelated policy areas), but rather that the general policy orientation may be affected by a strong polarizer.

A possible outcome of this collision of the spatial cleavage East/West with the political cleavage left/right could be the increasing separation between the European left and the American left, a sort of Atlantic rift between the two lefts. Here the *force* that widens the gap is, as stated above, the different *perception* of the same issues. This perception, to be sure, is becoming more and more marked and focused thanks to the impact of international issues on the public opinion of each nation. The perception of demarcated political fronts, though, is mediated by existing values and political mores, and here the difference between Europe and America is famously marked. But the *psychological* force that drives people to build polar fronts is, in Europe perhaps more than in America, *ideology*.[53] It is tempting to argue that the collision described above would be effected by the driving force of ideology, for ideology is, in Europe, the classical medium of political perception. In Italy, for example, appeals to communism and fascism are commonly used to define the political identity of one's opponent, whereas each side of the divide (with the exception of the extreme fringes) duly disavows any allegiance to these "classically European ideologies." But the rhetoric *works,* in the sense that people are keen to locate their adversary on a continuum whose extremes are fascism and communism.

In the European public discourse the construal of one's opponent as quasi-fascist, or quasi-communist, is part of a shared psychological effort to find one's bearings in a political landscape in which people seem to have lost their sense of position. A space structured along clearly traceable poles, in which one can discern the contours of both oppressed and oppressors, in which the grammar of right and wrong is clearly spelled out and placed on a symbolic continuum, offers obvious epistemic advantages, and provides valuable means of political orientation. It all depends, so it seems, on the ability of the polarizer to create a clear-cut distinction and narrow the blurred area of psychological rapprochement. The polar opposites advertise themselves as shorthand indexes that people may refer to in order to frame their political judgments. In this sense the left/right continuum is a viable, and even necessary, *complement to ideology,* inasmuch as people are given a chance to modulate their penchant for different ideological options by locating them on a left-right continuum.

It would be a mistake, though, to consider the American public discourse entirely immune from the kind of ideological polar bias affecting European political talk. And ideological is, admittedly, the *specular* construal of the nexus anti-Semitism/anti-Zionism: on the one hand, people like Alan Dershowitz have maintained that anti-Zionist propaganda feeds on Holocaust minimization, whereas Dershowitz's nemesis, Norman Finkelstein, has targeted those who "exploit the historical suffering of Jews in order to immunize Israel against criticism."[54]

In America it is especially at the level of language—as we saw in the case of Die Linke in Germany, or in the media surveys of AMW in Britain—that one can detect a biased understanding of topics that have the power to polarize the left/right cleavage. On the right, Peter Berkowitz has pointed out that the American left "has been all too ready to join forces with the vilifiers of Israel," while on the left Geoff Nunberg has argued that the "hackles" of conservative media watchdogs rise especially "when they hear a report on Israel that mentions 'cycle of violence,' 'peace process,' or 'occupied territories.'"[55] As in the case of a recent statement by the Czech foreign minister, Karel Schwarzenberg, the use of language here has immediate political implications. In politics, to be sure, the candor of some "neutral" descriptions of facts serves to conceal the commitment to *political* views that are bound to perpetuate, or even compound, existing cleavage lines.

I will elaborate in more detail on these issues—as well as on the widening left/right cleavage in American political discourse—in the following section, where I shall expand on the earth/heaven cleavage and on the effects of its closure on the other cleavage lines.

## The Earth/Heaven Cleavage

A feature of American politics is that, as we move along the political spectrum from left to right, we notice the closing of yet another political cleavage, the heaven/earth cleavage. And the closer we draw to the right end of the spectrum, the more likely we are to encounter a policy outlook grounded on appeals to heaven and to the quasi-messianic nature of America's standing and goals.[56] The tension in American public discourse between the divine politics supported by the right and the "enlightenment values" put forth by the left has been illustrated by Anthony Pagden:

> despite the resurgence in some Western states of Christian fundamentalists (on the political right) and multiculturalists (on the political left)—both of whom, in their very different ways, seek to privilege religious belief and the ingrained and unexamined customs which John Stuart Mill once described as "the standing hindrance to human advancement"—broadly enlightenment values still predominate throughout all the Western democracies, and still dictate the actions of their governments.[57]

It is difficult to predict for how long these "enlightenment values" will endure, but one fact about globalization, and the attendant polarization of the globe along an East-West continuum, is that both the "fundamental theological difference" between West and East—or, for that matter, Christianity and Islam—and the separation between law and religion are called into question. Earth and heaven threaten to collide and to give way to a novel political configuration with little bearing on the tradition of political thought (let alone political *practice*) that contributed to the making of the American polity. And the closer the two extremes come to one another, the stronger the drift will be towards the kind of sacrificial politics from which the American polity departed. New acts of "political spirituality"[58] were aimed at purifying

America by strengthening its original nexus with the divine. The sacrificial rhetoric of the internal enemy is a powerful means of identification and purification, but it is an easy means that was banned by the collective decision of the early American republic to embrace a postsacrificial kind of politics, and was eventually reinstated in order to restore the boundaries of the American nation and to reshape and refocus its messianic goals.

The earth/heaven cleavage is clearly embedded in the tradition of political thinking that inspired the framing of the American Constitution. The cleavage, though, lost much of its depth and clarity during the G. W. Bush administration: presidential addresses and informal remarks suggested that the president was targeting precisely the "fundamental difference," by seeking to reduce the gap between earth and heaven in American politics.

In the early years of the G. W. Bush administration, the attorney general and Pentecostal Christian John Ashcroft made an even more direct attack on the founding principles of the American democracy by telling an audience at the Bob Jones University that "the separation of Church and State was 'a wall of religious oppression.'"[59] As argued by Howard Fineman in an article in *Newsweek* magazine, Bush's presidency turned out to be "the most resolutely 'faith-based' in modern times, an enterprise founded, supported and guided by trust in the temporal and spiritual power of God."[60]

It was the closing of the earth/heaven cleavage that widened the Atlantic gap between Europe and the United States. G. W. Bush's first executive order as president was "to establish the Office of Faith-Based and Community Initiatives at the White House." With Bush—and in Bush's own words—the federal government would

> put money up to allow faith-based programs to compete, side-by-side, with secular programs, all aimed at making sure America is the greatest country possible for every single citizen. And it's going to happen in this country. I've had the honor of traveling the world for our country, I went to Europe. And we're different, in a positive way; we're unique in an incredibly positive way. It's important for our nation to never lose sight of that.[61]

And America is certainly *not* losing sight of that. Pippa Norris and Ronald Inglehart have drawn a general pattern of dwindling religious convictions based on "lapsed churchgoing habits" in the Western Hemisphere; and the pattern they drew would be just too perfect were it not for the behavior of the American "outlier."[62] The two authors have called this gap in the pattern "the puzzle of secularization in the United States and Western Europe."[63] To Norris and Inglehart, what makes the *expanding gap between the sacred and the secular societies around the globe*" problematic is the borderline position of the United States, and the fact that America seems to resist the secularization drift that swept over "these Western parts," and seems thereby co-responsible for the rise of the role of religion.[64]

This view may look overly simplistic, as it fails to acknowledge the diversity in options inherent to what the authors call, quite monolithically, "religion." I have no space here to expand on this critique, but I believe that the real divide that is opening up is not so much one between nations where people declare their allegiance to an institutionalized credo on one hand, and more secularized nations on the other. The divide is rather between nations that pursue a *divine* politics—and believe that the will of God is intelligible—and nations that, in James Madison's words, are committed to the *political* belief that "a practical distinction between Religion and Civil Government is essential to the purity of both, and as guaranteed by the Constitution of the United States."[65]

The Obama administration has tentatively opposed the trend towards a further widening of the cleavage, and a number of sensitive policy areas are less permeable to the agency and initiative of God. In American politics, however, left and right have clustered around both a set of issues and a method of address, and the gap between earth and heaven has become a critical factor in current political polarizations. In a much-cited entry in the *Huffington Post,* Naomi Wolf has shown that a number of conservative venues (all nodding to the Tea Party) are reframing their plea for constitutional values in religious terms, thus departing from the age-old genuinely secular, and exclusively constitutional, concerns of American proto-conservatism. A democratic administration can shelter politics from God impinging on the process, but the next Republican administration is likely to be more focused on religion than ever, and more keen on closing the earth/heaven gap.[66]

If we consider these issues in a global perspective, the endorsement of a "terrestrial" political philosophy, polemically opposed to a view that seeks political direction from heaven, could be fertile ground for a further left/right mutual repulsion and the construction of a new space for orientation in a left/right continuum. Stem-cell research and the status of the human embryo, for example, might in the near future spur a new powerful left/right polarization in America. Peter Singer has put the point strikingly:

> one source of new ideas that could revitalize the left is an approach to human, social, political and economic behavior based firmly on a modern understanding of human nature. It is time for the left to take seriously the fact that we are evolved animals, and that we bear the evidence of our inheritance, not only in our anatomy and our DNA, but in our behavior too. In other words it is time to develop a Darwinian left.[67]

In a country in which the heaven/earth cleavage threatens to close up, the discourse on "human nature" is obviously sensitive. It is difficult to predict whether a "modern understanding of human nature" will gain credit as a viable candidate for purposes of political orientation on the left. However, the current shift in "the relationship between science and the public"[68] may suggest that the stakes of political exchange in America are changing, but it is still hard to imagine that "human nature" could become any time soon the stake of a polar redistribution of public opinion in which science and religion will become the pulls of political orientation.

The Bush administration's disrespect for science became commonplace;[69] and commonplace, in current efforts to sketch a viable intellectual agenda for the American left, is the attempt to restore the earth/heaven gap by stressing the secular and democratic foundations of the American polity.[70]

It is difficult to predict how the earth/heaven cleavage will react with the widening of the other cleavages, but again, a secular left traditionally in favor of a nonconfessional and nonreligious arrangement of political conflicts is likely to bring its secularist outlook to bear on the Zionist-Arab political schism. It will continue to favor the creation of a single polity hosting both Israelis and Palestinians, and will oppose Israel's classical rationale for its existence, grounded on a relatively thick religious rhetoric.[71] By the same token, some people have taken notice of a sort of "theological convergence" of Israel's Zionist discourse of legitimacy and the religious right in America. When Israeli prime minister Benjamin Netanyahu visited Washington in January 1998 "his initial meeting was not with President Clinton but with Jerry Falwell and more than 1,000 fundamentalist Christians."[72] The meeting was designed to strengthen a link established by Netanyahu's mentor, Menachem Begin, during the Carter and Reagan administrations between the Likud government and the U.S. religious right. Its objective was precisely to ease the pressure on Israel to comply with the Oslo Accords.[73]

The roots of evangelical support for Israel lie in the long tradition of Christian thinking about the millennium. And it is in fact the very language used by Zionism that places the current struggle among different views for political recognition in a space distant from earth, a sort of ultraterrestrial heaven in which a number of competing gods have an ultimate say on political matters. In this sense, it seems correct to present the theological-political convergence of the American right with the Israeli right as "a match made in heaven."[74]

## Conclusions

The French Revolution gave the West a durable set of institutions and ideological tenets. It forced political struggles to unfold on a horizontal plane and named *laïcité* its most enduring legacy, an influential creation that thrived in the cleavage space between left and right. It fixed in the Western imaginary the kind of Orientalist discourse through which the East/West distinction has been articulated ever since. It drew a firm fault line between "earth" and "heaven" and destroyed what was left of Christian confidence in the ability of the Church to build a temporal polity modeled on heavenly hierarchies.[75] For about two centuries the West has aimed to stabilize structures acquired through the French Revolution, and in times of crisis the existing cleavages functioned to articulate allegiances and draw the borderline limits of political enclosures. *Enemies* were located beyond these lines, in spaces either symbolic or geographical, but ultimately distant and unapproachable by previous sacrificial strategies.

The time between the fall of the Berlin Wall and 9/11, the "self-deluding harmless few moments" *before*—in Philip Roth's prophetic words—the "awakening . . . to the horror of self-reflection," created the illusion that *human* history had come to an end, and that the dyads and cleavages that the posthistorical humankind had inherited from its historical past could serve mere orientation purposes.[76] It was indeed 9/11 that destabilized the pattern: it brought about the ideological alignment of right and West (and, accordingly, of left and East), and spurred the attendant tapering of the earth/heaven cleavage.

Old dyads and cleavages have now gone global, and the clues considered in this chapter suggest that they are aligning themselves in new directions. If politics goes global, if left and right "reach out" from local to global politics and become tied up with identity issues, the risk then lies in the possible formation of a "cumulative cleavage," an explosive compound of the three cleavage lines detailed in this chapter.[77]

Left and right have reached out to global politics and have spurned rapprochement by seeking the repulsive force of a polarizer. The "Israel effect" on the left/right cleavage in Europe and in the United States is gaining momentum, to the point that old ideological tensions may now escalate to a new level of animosity. The risk is that once the left/right cleavage is shaped along *real* conflicts and not ideological divisions, the dyad is likely to lose its original function, which was to *sublimate* radical alternatives into options, and mutual loathing into debate. The risk, then, is that the blurring of the earth/heaven cleavage may compound the spillover effect from "local" (i.e., Middle Eastern) to "global," and recast the ensuing cleavage in theological terms.[78]

W. D. Rubinstein pointed out in 1982 that a poor peace process in the Middle East would lead to the alignment of avowedly anti-Zionist political platforms and the left.[79] To be sure, the gaps and failures of the peace process brought about a sharper left/right polarization at a global level. A functional and ultimately successful peace process in the Middle East will not rid us of the left/right dyad, for the void possibly created by a lasting settlement of the Israeli-Palestinian conflict—and the consequent demise of a strong polarizer—would be filled with the emergence of other polarizers, capable of displacing opinion and consensus along the same continuum. But what we should hope for is to continue to inhabit a political space in which harsh divisions are sublimated into forms of constructive disagreement, with options instead of alternatives, and debate instead of open clashes.

# CHAPTER 4

# A Mimetic Perspective on Conflict Resolution

W hen democratic politics fails to do its job correctly (that is, to embed social conflicts in normal democratic procedures), mimetic confrontations may exceed the bounds of a normal democratic contest and escalate into explosive crises. International actors obey the same logic: when they operate in contexts in which democratic norms of conflict resolution are absent, they may resort to war to settle their disputes.

Current theories of international justice and conflict resolution rest on the assumption (supported by the late John Rawls) that peoples of genuinely democratic and liberal societies "have nothing to go to war about." This chapter seeks to show that the Rawlsian notion of "peace by satisfaction" is problematic: people's needs and desires, being mimetic in nature, are hardly extinguishable. I contend that classical approaches to conflict resolution fail to address this mimetic dynamic and wrongly assume that there is an objective measure of desire to be filled to satisfy the contenders.

An alternative theory of conflict resolution may benefit from descriptions of the origin of human discord that deviate from the classical approach. In proposing an alternative account I shall consider cases in which conflict *does not* arise over the appropriation of goods. Rather, it is discord itself that generates the stakes, in the sense that they come to function as rationalizers of *prior* inimical attitudes.

As discussed in chapter 1, the alternative theory—alternative to the standard *normative* view alleging that conflicts arise on scarce resources and de-escalate once we reallocate them *fairly*—would be grounded on disciplines such as social psychology and behavioral biology and psychology, disciplines that seek to replace the normatively loaded notion of *agency* with the more neutral concept of *behavior*. However, while these very same disciplines offer a challenging description of the wellsprings of human behavior, they have failed to articulate a naturalistic solution to a problem, reconciliation, whose grammar remains ultimately normative, that is, articulable by means of concepts such as justice, equity, and retribution.[1]

Some authors have stressed the "natural propensities that underlie our capacity for peacemaking."[2] However, accounts of reconciliation based on biological dispositions fail to register the normative force brought about by peacemaking arrangements, namely, the role of choice and deliberation in stipulating conditions of live and let live with former rivals. *Dispositional* peacemaking—or "natural conflict resolution"—as observed among primates, is also overly sensitive to adverse environmental stimuli.[3] It can certainly be observed in patterns of reconciliation among primates, but cannot be used as a normative tool to design reconciliatory strategies for humans.[4] In this chapter I shall seek to delineate a viable alternative to strategies focused on biological dispositions without ignoring the biological makeup of our psychologies, namely, the anthropological constants detected by mimetic theory.

One of the key concepts in contemporary theory—and a key concept in Rawls's account of the "Law of the People"—is, again, "satisfaction," a term describing a psychological condition of contentment and fulfilment whose subject is an actor (a person, group, or state) taken in isolation from other actors. To Rawls the peoples of genuinely democratic and liberal societies are "satisfied peoples," in the sense that "their basic needs are met, and their fundamental interests are fully compatible with those of other democratic peoples. . . . All being satisfied in this way, liberal peoples have nothing to go to war about."[5]

A theory of justice is meant to provide satisfaction in conditions of scarcity, and to appease rival interests through a mutually satisfying management of extant resources. But satisfaction is a *normative* notion, not a *biological* one, inasmuch as people are satisfied (and therefore prepared to make peace with their former rivals) not after gaining a *given* amount of goods but rather after receiving what they perceive to be a *fair* amount of the available goods.

The solution to the dilemma is therefore normative and not natural, in that it involves the reflective ability of the people involved in a dispute to address the (mimetic) sources of their animosity and thereby (reflectively) undo the biased presuppositions that sustain hostility and conflict.[6] The chapter refers in the end to the notion of "reflective justice," a form of collective, reflective recognition of the mimetic biases that distort our understanding of our interests, needs, and perceptions.

## Normative versus Empirical Strategies of Conflict-Resolution

According to one canonical story, discord and animosity among humans arise when more people strive to attain some nondivisible goods. Peter Wallensteen has proposed "a complete definition of a conflict as *a social situation in which a minimum of two actors (parties) strive to acquire at the same moment in time an available set of scarce resources.*"[7]

Conflicts also arise when people dictate rules concerning the distribution of available resources that benefit only a limited number of individuals.[8] Discord escalating into open conflict may arise out of diversity in people's beliefs and practices, or when people have biased or distorted opinions or perceptions that lead them to "assess a conflict and evaluate a case or the worth of an item differently because of differing perceptions."[9]

A rather obvious solution to conflict consists in authorizing a third party to bring the two sides together and frame the point of contention in a different light. As terminus of a long-standing tradition, Hegel argued that the *settlement* of all "civil suits" requires "a third judgement which is disinterested *in the thing.*"[10]

Invoking *justice,* namely, a just and "disinterested" way to handle a dispute, is arguably a natural option for those committed to its successful resolution, and one may argue that theories of justice find in conflict resolution their elective field of application:

justice issues often play a central role as sources of civil wars, and are therefore important to address if peace is to be restored and endured. These
issues may concern the division of political power, territory, and other
resources; procedures for democratization including the holding of elections; and the establishment of human rights commissions, amnesty and
compensatory justice for war crimes. Earlier research has demonstrated
that justice principles and related concepts influence the dynamics of
international negotiation and the content of agreements.[11]

The aim of the following pages is to expose the biases of the canonical story by showing how theories of justice are subject to a number of
assumptions about the ontological status of *the thing* (e.g., "political power,
territory, and other resources"). I will discuss the standard view according
to which conflict prevention and peace-building (as distinct from peace
enforcement, whose case is not discussed in this chapter) involve "building a viable democracy and its institutions, creating confidence between a
government and population, structuring the protection and promotion of
human rights, the elimination of all forms of gender discrimination, and
respect for minorities."[12]

I shall argue that by sticking to a classical ontology (or "serious ontology," as in John Heil's book of 2003), to the view alleging that discord always
arises over the possession of things that are there, current theories of conflict
resolution fail to capture a vast penumbra of phenomena in which the classical nexus between justice and peace does not seem to work.[13]

When pushed by reciprocal animosity people seem to descend into what
Quine called an "overpopulated universe" pullulating with items to which
only a nonserious ontology would grant existence.[14] This chapter focuses on
situations where the pull of the object is not critical to the outcome, where
the "ontological commitments" that people make to the world do not explain
the course of their actions.

The very word "ontology" may sound a bit puzzling in this context,
especially when it comes to such practical issues as conflict resolution, and
one might get the impression that the argument is becoming too abstract.
It is not.[15] The couching of issues of conflict resolution in ontological terms
may help tease out the mechanism by which "civil suits" are settled. If conflict
arises over the appropriation of some stakes that ultimately constitute reasons

for action, a fair settlement of the stakes, however partial, may "satisfy" the contenders.[16]

The players with a stake in the suit appear to be committed to obtaining goods to which they ascribe a "good making quality."[17] They can describe the facts that prompted their actions in terms that make explicit the scope of their commitments. Ontology and the theories guiding a fair resolution of conflicts bear intimate mutual relations and in fact major concerns for international justice guide the policies of "truth commissions and *fact-finding* bodies."[18]

In the following I shall consider how a workable theory of conflict resolution may benefit from descriptions of the origin of human discord that deviate from the classical approach.[19] I shall focus attention on instances of human discord that seem typically insensitive to the arrangements dictated by a third party "disinterested in the thing."

The conventional approach on the origins of human discord fails to account for a blind spot, a gray zone that remains unaddressed by the theories that adopt this approach, an area in which conflict *does not* arise over the appropriation of existing goods. Rather, it is discord itself that prompts the stakes, in the sense that they come to function as rationalizers of *prior* inimical attitudes. The mutual signaling (blaming, scolding, etc.) that eventuates in open manifestations of hostility expresses the depth of the agents' appreciation for the thing at stake. It expresses, in other words, the "ontological commitments" to things or facts whose existence seems, on closer scrutiny, instrumental to discord itself. Here, while an entirely new level of reality is brought to light, in which anonymous items are turned into bones of contention, animosity and discord are thereby fueled. In the following I shall make a case for the *nonexistence* of such items. I shall argue that they do not have an existence separate from the commitments that people make as soon as they start looking at their rivals—for reasons that have little to do with ontological scarcity—as *enemies*.

## Conflict Resolution and Theories of Justice: An Overview

Discord manifests itself when individual purposes conflict; when, for instance, the supply of goods is insufficient to satisfy the wishes and expectations of the parties. A case in point is Hobbes's *De Cive* i.6, where it is claimed that "the most frequent reasons why men desire to hurt each other, ariseth hence, that many men at the same time have an Appetite to the same thing [*quod multi simul eandem rem appetant*]; which yet very often they can neither enjoy in common, nor yet divide it."[20] A similar formulation of the same approach is in John Milton's *Paradise Lost* ii.30–32, where Satan states that "where there is then no good / For which to strive, no strife can grow up there / From faction."

The causal nexus between injustice and violence has permeated theories of justice since the early philosophical speculations on justice and its relationship with human sociability. It seems likely that this way of thinking originated in Plato, who maintained that "it's over the gaining of wealth that all wars take place."[21]

Elias Canetti aptly described justice as "the law of dividing" and showed how in archaic societies the fair distribution of available goods was commonly perceived as a powerful means to forestall discord within the group.[22] As sources of grievance have often been "associated with structural injustice," in the shape of power imbalances and inequitable social and economic relations, Western political philosophy has held theories of justice to be the most powerful means to build a well-ordered society.[23] As a consequence, it is consistently assumed by students of conflict resolution that any viable mechanism of peacemaking bears on "the creation of independent procedures in which the parties can have confidence."[24]

An influential strain in Western political thought contends that major political evils, such as unjust wars and oppression, could be eliminated by following just (namely, publicly justified) social policies. John Rawls, for one, has mentioned two basic "limits to reconciliation," such as religious fundamentalism and the sense of spiritual emptiness that befall us when our institutions neglect our ideals. A liberal education should support our search for such ideals but should also avoid *politicizing* them, namely, perverting and diminishing them "for ideological ends."[25] Driven by ideological concerns, political institutions reinforce some widespread delusions about the construction of social justice or the identification of the actual causes of social poverty and unrest.

Although the idea that only justice provides a workable foothold for social policies aimed at securing order and stability is old, dating back to the writings of Plato and Aristotle (and Cicero, who claimed in *Pro Sestio* that "if we would have violence abolished, law must prevail, that is, the administration of justice"),[26] it has been reworked a number of times in the course of the intellectual history of the West.[27] A clear statement of the idea that conflict prevention resides in the ability to allocate goods fairly was put forward by the philosopher Diogenes Laertius, who stated that "natural justice is a symbol or expression of expediency, to prevent one man from harming or being harmed by another."[28]

John Stuart Mill maintains that "in many cases, an individual, in pursuing a legitimate object, necessarily and therefore legitimately causes pain or loss to others, or intercepts a good which they had a reasonable hope of obtaining.[29] Mill further identifies "bad social institutions" as ultimately responsible for vicious social arrangements, and for generating de novo the divisions and conflicts that they were supposedly designed to prevent. If the purpose of institutions is to keep people from pursuing goods that, in Hobbes's words, "they can neither enjoy in common, nor yet divide," *sound* social institutions are those best suitable to prevent civil strife.

This standard view on conflict resolution is supported by major international agencies, commissions of conflict prevention, and "contact groups." In their routine pronouncements these agencies insistently refer to such obstacles to the achievement of peace as resurgent economic nationalism and protectionism. Governments and international agencies seem far more capable today than ever before of facilitating cooperation among different groups through communication and regulation, but a slight lapse from a just set of arrangements in international disputes may pave the way to a "road . . . to conflict and violence and war."[30]

Among contemporary scholars of international politics, "democratic peace" theory similarly presumes that democracies promote peaceful resolution of differences because they offer fairer distribution of valued resources. Democracies supporting liberal principles are, according to the brief genealogy outlined above, better prepared to check internal conflict. According to the canonical liberal assumption, material gains, if supported by just institutions, increase the likelihood that people will be satisfied, and thereby reduce their mutual hostility. Not all scholars agree, however, that this principle can be extended universally. Some have challenged the "liberal assumption" that foreign investment in developing nations is "always an engine of development or that development necessarily means better human rights standards," that is to say, less repression and *less civil war.*[31]

The idea that hostility and conflict can be eradicated by means of properly designed social institutions has been challenged by Stanley Fish, who counters that this "is the lesson liberalism is *pledged* never to learn because underlying liberal thought is the assumption that, given world enough and time (and so long as embarrassing 'outlaws' have been discounted in advance), difference and conflict can always be resolved by rational deliberation."[32]

To follow this argument between advocates of liberal institutions and the skeptics, over the logical nexus between "rational deliberation" and conflict resolution, I propose to begin with a minimal definition of liberalism. If we assume that liberalism is a philosophical orientation whose resurgence in American public discourse in the early 1970s was accompanied by a broader reemergence of normative political theory, the kind of liberalism that Stanley Fish seems to have in mind is the liberalism that was discussed mainly in academic forums after the publication of Rawls's *A Theory of Justice.* It is one basic precept of at least this specific kind of liberalism that discord can in principle be settled by means of a fair arrangement of stakes that constitute reasons for action. The arrangement is valued and ultimately supported by the parties involved, who signal their commitments to reformulate their earlier claims over the goods at stake.[33]

The talk of justice and economic appeasement issued by the "third party" is a *reason-laden* discourse in which the former contenders express satisfaction and recognition of the rules by which the stakes are assigned. Yet this discourse can generate difficulties and areas of misunderstanding among people if they think that they are being treated badly or unfairly by their institutions. In a situation in which people have "conflicting views about aspects of the world," the expected "mutual reckoning" is hardly likely to lay the groundwork for a more comprehensive level of discourse by which a disinterested third party "can assess the goods that are distributed in society."[34]

Mutual reckoning is possible only if the people involved in a dispute share the same ontological framework and reflectively review their psychological biases and evaluative mistakes. Such mistakes can be easily amended by interventions of recognizably *sound* social institutions, which play the role of a third party disinterested "in the thing." People who rationally agree on a given arrangement can ideally converge on a set of assumptions on the stake's *intrinsic* value. In a sort of ideal situation they have a clear under-standing of what is there, and the decisions they make are made according to feedback, information, and reflection. A difficulty arises when people's reasons for action are guided by commitments to facts or items that are apparently "not there."

## Mimetic Desire

According to the classical view, when self-interested pursuit of some things is driven by correct information and feedback, just institutions can provide a reliable vantage point by which the parties can reach a fair and unbiased assessment of the value of the stakes. However, the idea that neutralization of conflict is best achieved through the equitable distribution of goods obscures the nature of violence that arises *in the absence of* goods. Objections to the classical approach seek to explain how it is that one acts in a certain way even though there is no "fact of the world" that may explain the action.

Alternative explanations are often drawn from disciplines that have adopted the notion of "behavior" to make sense of a number of social phe-nomena. Indeed, if a characteristic mark of good science is a commitment "to challenge its assumptions based on findings in other scientific fields," conflict resolution as a field of study should be cross-pollinated with other disciplines.[35] Approaches that eliminate the moment of agency from the explanation of human behavior, I noted, rely instead on the biological drives and in-built dispositions of both humans and other great apes, and offer comparative accounts of patterned strategies of reconciliation and conflict prevention. But these accounts miss the normative moment, that is, the moment of thoughtful deliberation about the best or more profitable course of action in the attendant circumstance.

An approach firmly grounded in human biology but widely appreciative of the normative possibilities of human cognition could possibly be derived from the general theory of human behavior put forward by René Girard. His lifelong speculation on scapegoating dynamics and patterns of mimetic vio-lence in myth and literature has yielded important insights into the nature of human agency and rationality. His work has contributed to the relativization of two fundamental and tightly connected assumptions about rationality:

that people, if rational, are in principle both *reflective* and actively responsive to reasons.[36]

In the pages that follow I shall try to bring to bear some critical notions from Girard's theory on a radically alternative approach to conflict resolution. It is difficult to say whether my proposal remains consistent with the anthropological premises formulated by Girard. The only text in which he hints at a possible theory of conflict resolution, *On Things Hidden since the Foundation of the World,* makes the peculiar claim that the final overcoming of all conflict is an "easy" pursuit and the path we should take is one leading to the eventual accomplishment of the "Kingdom of God."

To Girard the "failure of the Kingdom" is not the failure of Jesus Christ's mission in the world, but rather "the inevitable abandonment of the direct and easy way, which would be for all to accept the principles of conduct that he has stated."[37] In this chapter I propose taking a step back, to gather together the psychological premises, and explore tentatively how they could be tied to *actual* demands for peace and reconciliation made by *real* people and not potential candidates for final citizenship in the forthcoming Kingdom.

According to Girard the notion of desire handed on to us by a tradition that goes back to Plato fails to reckon with the inherent *symmetry* of human relationships. Girard, by stressing the essentially *relational* and *alterocentric* origin of human discord, seeks to find a way around the Western (Platonic-Aristotelian) model of "unsupported" or "celibate desire," namely, a desire centered on the subject and focused on things that, in principle, can be detected "out there." He seeks to deconstruct this Platonic model of desire by revealing "the way most men *are*," which is not the *egocentric* way we usually think it to be in our mistaken belief that every conflict that arises within a human community is between self-centered subjects desirous of appropriating goods.[38] In Girard's words, "the mimetic process detaches desire from any predetermined object."[39]

Some authors, representative of what Girard calls the "tragic tradition," have shifted the generative nucleus of desire from the subject to the *relationship* between subjects. They have replaced the egocentric concept of desire dominant in the West with the alterocentric concept, in this way undermining the classical model, which explained human agency by means of people's rational responsiveness to items or facts of the world that they treat as reasons. Where the classical approach envisaged a solitary agent and a limited set of goods, the alternative approach acknowledges only the existence of *rivals*. The scene in which rivalry and violence arise is in fact a scene *without objects*. Revelatory writers such as Shakespeare have shown the purely ideological nature of the desire centered on the subject.[40] These writers unveiled the existence of a kind of desire that, unlike the desire codified in the Platonic tradition, does not pursue an external good but seizes upon the desire of the mimetic rival. The rival imitates this desire and, in turn, its desire is imitated by the subject. Through this notion of "emulous desire" Girard strips the "object" of the ontological privilege that made it the simple and absolute desideratum of the Western philosophical tradition and brings to the forefront the figure of the rival.[41] His primary objective is

> to define the rival's position within the system to which he belongs, in relation to both subject and object. The rival desires the same object as the subject, and to assert the primacy of the rival can lead only to one conclusion: rivalry doesn't arise because of the fortuitous convergence of two desires on a single object; rather, *the subject desires the object because the rival desires it.*[42]

The crisis that results from this surplus of reciprocal rivalry triggers actions aimed at destroying the mimetic adversary. Girard maintains that what is most remarkable about the Western philosophical tradition is its failure to acknowledge the working of this mimetic dynamic. We fail to capture the mimetic outlook of human discord because we are inextricably wedded to the classical belief that "we cannot have a desire except for a reason."[43]

According to Girard the classical model enjoys strong warrants and protections, and so it is unlikely that it will be readily displaced by other noncanonical approaches. Such replacement "seems unthinkable only because the existing situation, once solidified, shapes reality in such a persuasive way that it seems to possess the attributes of a natural phenomenon."[44] The antimimetic humanism that reflects the way we organize our lives has pushed mimetic phenomena to the margins of our mental universe. Mimetic rivalry "is the scandal of human relations that most of us elude because it offends our optimistic view of those relations."[45] It challenges our ingrained belief in our autonomy and capacity for agency and presents a bleak picture of human behavior in which envy and resentment are the driving emotions.

Girard maintains that we are accustomed to thinking of mimetic dynamics (the alterocentric structure of desire) as being "inert" and thus we find natural and obvious anything that nicely fits the reassuring ontology supported by the classical case. The universe described by the "tragic" writers (Shakespeare, Stendhal, Dostoevsky, Kafka, etc.) makes us aware of a dimension of human relationships that the classical approach has consistently overlooked. If we shift our attention to the secret dimension of unsolicited rivalry and mimesis where a most destructive kind of violence arises, we find out that it is not true that "all wars" are fought over the appropriation of goods. In this mimetic dimension of human experience, in which the rivals seem to be rid of their supposedly "authentic" desires, there are in fact no objects, only "rivals."

According to the classical model two (or more) people would normally quarrel over an object to which they both lay claim. Here the emphasis is on the inherent paucity of the desideratum, not on the psychological outlook of the rivals. If we abandon the classical approach and give credit to a different perspective on the origins of discord, we see that the rivals refer to an ontological inventory that is instrumental to nothing but their rivalry. The object, in other words, cannot suffice to explain the intensity of the conflict: "*one can remove the object and the rivalry will continue.*"[46]

Rivals are *still* prompted by desires and driven by reasons, but there are no longer facts out there to sustain their commitment to act in a way consistent with their *avowed* reasons. The object has dropped out of sight, facts that are claimed to constitute reasons for action have become shady and vague and ultimately difficult to detect, and we are faced with the glaring absurdity of a situation in which "*violence operates without a reason.*"[47]

By arguing that discord is *prior* to people's commitments to what there is, Girard turns one of the key assumptions of the classical model upside down. By making human discord contingent on the commitments we make to the world out there, Girard reverses the "direction of fit" of reasons and actions and assigns a merely derivative status to the former.

The discourse of the rivals is full of claims of desirability and entitlement to possess by which they seek to build a rationale for their actions, but Girard's achievement is to suggest that there is no-thing out there to sustain their claims. Removing the object is in fact no guarantee that mutual discord will be resolved. Rather, a particular brand of liberal naïveté leads to the belief that discord feeds on reasons that can be appeased and ultimately offset by means of a fair distribution of the stakes. One may contend that there are conflicts that challenge the classical approach without being mimetic, such as those whose resolution does not in principle depend on redistribution. In such instances—a case in point being identity-related conflicts—solutions hinge upon rituals of reconciliation. But such instances are in fact explicable in the terms of the classical approach, for they often remain focused on land, on the possession or political control of areas that have produced age-old ethnic cleavages. Identity-driven conflicts are indeed often redressed—and the parties thereby reconciled—by means of material incentives, including redistributive remedies such as the redrawing of boundaries. In other words, this chapter is not arguing that redistributive means are powerless in any case, and that *all* conflicts are mimetic in nature. Under closer scrutiny, conflicts arising over an original act of injustice (the expulsion of an ethnic group from a patch of land) develop a mimetic momentum after the original deed and resist a settlement arranged by a third party.

At this stage I need to say something about the comprehensiveness and finality of my argument about the mimetic structure of human discord. The overall picture I have outlined is certainly schematic, fragmentary, and vague. I have relied on some anecdotal evidence and have tried to connect the few dots by means of a theory that does not rely on a comprehensive canon of theoretical (let alone empirical) investigation. Nevertheless, I think such an incomplete picture can be perfected by means of more extensive research, aimed at detecting mimetic strains in conflictual situations that are obviously asymmetrical.

There is one case where the mimetic dynamic is far from apparent, the case in which, however, reconciliation typically defies redistribution. It is the case of conflict between a victimized group and a dominant one identified as a "perpetrator." Here a number of discriminatory policies fuel resentment and animosity and are often sustained by identity claims. But what is remarkable in this case is the kind of "cold" animosity involved, that rarely eventuates in open conflict. South Africa is a case of (relatively) successful reconciliation, whereas Zimbabwe and Rwanda are cases in which the latent animosity between ethnic groups eventuated, respectively, in a brutally repressive dictatorship and in open warfare.[48] Here, if we look at the polemical languages of the parties, *land* always figures as a major stake in the disputes.

## Mimetic Ontologies

When we think about our attitude to discord, we somehow wonder if it is always undesirable, or how should it be contained, or channeled. Should it be tackled via market forces, education, regulation, or the criminal law? These questions, I believe, should be addressed not by indulging in large generalizations, but by preparing the ground for more sensitive and detailed research of the manifestations and effects of discord.[49] The merit of Girard's model resides in its radical questioning of the assumptions lying at the core of the classical approach. If we assume that human discord does *not* arise out of people's self-interested concerns for material as well as immaterial gains, we open up a dimension of human agency in which the sources of discord are no longer traceable to the motives of the people involved, and discord itself becomes impervious to the justice-centered perspective fostered by the classical approach.

In contrast to the classical view in which rivalry between individuals and groups could be easily overcome through a mutual recognition unfolding within the framework of just institutions, in the scenario opened by Girard, in the place of the *thing* responsible for the discord we find an empty space—a carefully dissembled absence. The commitments made by mimetic rivals, on closer scrutiny, suggest that there is *nothing* out there, and therefore the friction between the rivals initiates in an ontological vacuum. Once we abandon the approach that considers people's actions as manifestations of their first-person responsiveness to facts of the world, we see that the causes of discord are not to be looked for in the defective functioning of institutions allegedly "disinterested *in the thing.*"

The illuminating power of a mimetic approach becomes evident through its application to certain recent events. After 9/11, two discourses dominated in the media to explain the terrorist attacks and, possibly, vindicate what turned out to be a short-noticed American retaliation: the classical framework and one that I would call the "discourse of insanity," an explanation of the terrorist attack as based on mere irrational beliefs. Soon a third view emerged in the media debates. In *The Guardian* of September 29, 2001, Arundhati Roy pointed out that once a war begins, it is bound to "develop a momentum, a logic and a justification of its own." The sense of loss and despair unleashed by the war grew despite the "facts." Roy captured the logic operating in this psychological climate and pointed to the *lack of facts* that were to function as viable reasons for actions. She argued that once the logic of war took over, "we'll lose sight of why it's being fought in the first place."[50]

In the ontological vacuum in which mimetic rivalry operates, the conflict is bound to develop a momentum and logic of its own. But even though there is *nothing* out there, no valuable object that the rivals strive to appropriate before perceiving one another as rivals, they make commitments to what is there by consistently referring to *things* whose actuality depends on the representational efficacy of their claims. The existence of the thing is therefore a variable that depends on commitments made by the rivals, on their ability to identify and illustrate the good-making qualities that prompt them to act in a certain way.

David Weissman has made the ontological claim that "every thing is constituted of its properties."[51] Such a claim presupposes that the ascription of properties, as in the reason-laden discourse engaged by the rivals, is the minimal condition for the thing to qualify as an item in a serious, not chimerical, ontology. Indeed, we can hardly ascribe an ontological dignity to things that lack *any* property, given that it is only in light of its properties that we can assert that an object is. The case of mimetic desire is one in which people find themselves thrown in a vacuum of properties and nonetheless make commitments to some supposedly existent things. What people do is to blame their target of resentment and indignation, which may further be subject to "avoidance, reproach, scolding, denunciation, remonstration, and (at the limit) punishment."[52] Through avoiding, scolding, denouncing, and so on, people work out some evaluative standards whereby they express their commitments to some things. It is by signaling mutual scold and reproach that people articulate the properties of the *thing* at stake: it is *on occasion* of these special transactions that the thing comes into being and gains the status of a stake in the dispute. It is, in other words, by mutually addressing one another that they effect the construal of the thing as a compound of good-making properties.

Commitments to ontological sets are often assessed on the basis of a biased evaluation of the nature of desire, inasmuch as desire is always considered as authentic and genuinely egocentric, and not as the mark of unconscious mimetic drives. Egocentric desire or, better, the *illusion* of egocentric desire is a viable rationalization of an impulse whose mimetic springs are left unacknowledged. Failure to acknowledge the fundamentally mimetic dynamic of desire is what makes the classical approach ultimately useless for reconciliatory purposes. This approach appeals to reason in order to devise just social arrangements, on the assumption that justice neutralizes by default *all* conflicts: "humans apply universal, general, reasoning rules to all problems in making choices in their current environment, including interpreting and acting on signals in reaching a negotiated settlement of conflicts."[53] Both individuals and groups send credible signals to other individuals and groups of an aversion to using force, and in this way they expect to create a non-threatening mutual reckoning from which to build durable peaceful arrangements. But the choices people make are grounded on their perceptions of their "current environment," in the sense that they survey the environment and formulate reasons on the basis of perceived stimuli. The story of scarcity implied by the classical approach is grounded on the assumption that people operate in a shared ontological milieu in which information and feedback govern the kind of "interpreting and acting on signals" through which the parties stipulate a possible agreement on what there is. This hermeneutical process entails the exchange of crucial pieces of ontological information in which the parties probe the psychological limits of their mutual demands for satisfaction.

We know that the "mutually avowed reckoning" by which people commit themselves to a supposedly viable ontology consists of stipulations by which they create or sustain a universe of negotiable objects fit for routine strategies of redistribution. A mimetic perspective suggests that the rivals' chances of reaching a settlement over the available goods are contingent on their ability to deflate the ontologies that sustained their mutual animosity. The opening up of a new perspective on the origin of discord may press social actors into designing more viable strategies of convergence on a more inclusive vision of reality, in which they can see that their goals are ultimately compatible and the extant resources amenable to fair allocation.

This alternative perspective forces us to look into the minds of the rivals; it helps us identify the actual springs of their mutual animosity. But the major innovation effected by this perspective in the field of conflict resolution is that it shifts the attention from the demands of satisfaction of the rivals to the ways they rationalize their mutual hostility. Girard helps us see that those demands are mimetic in nature, so that there is no given measure of satisfaction to be filled to appease the rivals. The scene in which the "interpreting and acting on signals" takes place is the mirror of their biased perceptions and stipulations and not a reliable source of information on their egocentric needs. From this perspective we can see that if the rivalry has genuinely mimetic springs any effort to *satisfy* the rivals is hardly likely to succeed. For this reason our attention should be focused instead on tensions occurring within the "public cognitive scene" where the rivals formulate their (mimetically biased) demands for satisfaction.[54] This scene is often plagued by phobic images of the other and by recurring memories of persecution that loom in the successive rationalization scene, when the rivals quarrel over the distribution of the available goods. A Girardian perspective on conflict resolution must therefore concern itself with making the rivals *reflectively aware* of their mimetic plight.

## Mimesis, Identity, Conflict

The most direct ontological implication of Girard's theory is that items valued and pursued by more than one person are likely to become stakes in a mimetic game in which the persons interested in the thing become, by (mimetic) default, rivals. The implication is ontological inasmuch as the *construal* of the thing is contingent on commitments that are prior to the psychological act of surveying what is there.

The rivals' psychologies are shaped by experiences of rivalry or, more important, *recollections* of such experiences. Social groups identify themselves by means of practices of recollection, in the sense that they form a number of basic notions about who they are, their place in the world, and the demarcating barrier between them and the others, and all these notions guide their psychological reactions to external stimuli. Discord entails the manufacturing of new patterns of reality, the drawing of new ontological inventories that guide people's commitments and allegiances. Emphasis on culture and group-psychology may help uncover the subliminal trends whereby the group's perception of what "there is" deviates from possibly shared ontological standards.

"Social identity theory" has offered important insights into both the biased cognitive appreciation of the differences *between* groups (that each group tends to exaggerate) and the differences *within* groups (that group members are inclined to minimize). Phenomena such as in-group bias, stereotyping, and out-group discrimination are operations of "categorization" that play a critical role in the formation of individual and social identity.[55]

In his attempt to draw a genealogy of hatred, Jan Assmann has shown how memories of discrimination and persecution might worm their way into the habits and rituals of a group and work at a subliminal level. Assmann maintains that the construal of the enemy is often the result of a "pathology of memory." The century just behind us bore witness to the worst excesses of collective psychosis, and therefore we need "to trace this history [of psychosis] back to its origin, with the hope that this anamnesis and 'working-through' may contribute to a better understanding and an overcoming of the dynamics behind the development of cultural or religious abomination."[56] Assmann's analysis of the subliminal causes of hatred is supported both by a powerful genetic account of anti-Semitism and by the insight that it is in this intimacy with myths and memories that conflict compounds itself. On a similar vein, Jacques Sémelin has described the psychological attitude of people responsible for ethnic massacres (such as Germans, Serbs, and Hutus), stressing its primitivist and archaic outlook, and its being rooted in a social imaginary of omnipotence and self-glorification that ignites adversarial attitudes against a duly fabricated image of the enemy.[57] "Murderous animosities, fuelled by memories of injustice and vengeance" can take over a group of people or a whole nation.[58] Such animosities are especially difficult to eradicate when group identity is grounded on ingrained adversarial attitudes: "collective memories are imprinted by events related to the conflict; . . . beliefs related to the conflict become societal beliefs and are incorporated into the ethos; and at least one generation is socialized in the conflict climate, not knowing another reality."[59] When it escalates, human discord opens up a space for the return of other knowledges, other untimely pasts, and it is by intervening in this space that discord might be effectively neutralized.

The work of Jayne Docherty on worldview conflicts has shown that groups with fundamentally different worldviews must first deal with reality and engage in a particular kind of activity that she calls "world-naming" and that seems to resemble my own claim for "shared" ontological commitments. But according to Docherty worldviews seem perfectly structured *already before* groups come to clash because of fundamental differences in "naming" and "framing" the world. I contend that mimetic impulses are fundamentally prior to the rivalry between the groups and that world-naming is instrumental to rationalizing ex post mimetic hostility.[60]

Interventions aimed at solving conflict should be directed to the scene in which impulses to inflict harm "without a reason" are likely to arise. The emphasis on unconscious processes challenges assumptions about agency and responsibility, but explanations based on assumptions of transparent motivations and thoughtful deliberation fail to comprehend the complexities of the human impulse to war. We sense that conflictive mimesis is more likely to arise in conditions where identity cleavages favor mimetic polarizations between groups, but the mimetic explanation is not the only possible explanation of conflict from unconscious sources.

I am not at all clear about affirming or denying an ostensibly Jungian approach to the psychology of hatred. Jung, though, offered important insights, as when he wrote that

> the tide that rose in the unconscious after the first World War was reflected in individual dreams, in the form of collective, mythological symbols which expressed primitivity, violence, cruelty: in short, all the powers of darkness. When such symbols occur in a large number of individuals and are not understood, they begin to draw these individuals together as if by magnetic force, and thus a mob is formed.[61]

If we push this argument to the extreme, a coherent mimetic perspective on the sources of human hostility would lead us to the claim that the formation of mimetic opposites precedes the emergence of identity cleavages, in the sense that people "have a feeling" of their diversity, and so form elementary notions about their identity, *after* having experienced hostility towards a group that often shares the same language and morphology. In other words, conflictive mimesis between individuals and groups is not the upshot of prior identity-cleavages, but rather the rivals become identity-aware as a consequence of mimetic impulses that cause them to conflict.

Ole Wæver also challenges the view that conflicts in which identity is used by the parties to rationalize hostility are actually *caused* by identity issues.

How problematic this approach is becomes immediately visible in the case of the conflicts in the former Yugoslavia. The underlying assumption of much identity/culture based thinking about conflict is that the propensity for conflict correlates with differences and cultural distance. However, Croats, Serbs and Bosnians are quite close for most purposes, including language. And this closeness is actually part of the reason for the conflict.[62]

If we accept that conflictual mimesis is *prior* to people's engagement in adversarial behavior, we have made a significant step toward the identification of the specific area where our attempts at conflict resolution should be directed. The *cognitive* scene where people formulate their satisfaction-claims needs to be exposed to a reflective insight *from within,* an insight that shows that the rationalization procedures initiated by the parties suffer from a cognitive bias that is likely to lie unacknowledged. Narratives of scarcity—which get their rationale from the assumption of egocentric desire—serve typically to conceal the genuinely mimetic structure of the attendant hostility.

A reappraisal of the classical approach that lays bare its functional limitations would reveal that discord cannot be easily removed by recourse to a rational neutralizer, and that the use of arbiters and negotiators to find some platform for nonpartisan cooperation is a logical consequence of a persistent theoretical delusion. The classical approach looms not only behind the speeches of the mouthpieces of states and international agencies but also in the widespread metaphor of the fireman running to put out a fire.[63] This is not to say that this approach can be simply dismissed, or that mimetic dynamics can be detected whenever human beings show conflictive dispositions. And the overall picture I have outlined offers only an embryonic clue as to how a certain perspective on human discord can become, through more extensive research, a valuable underpinning of more effective strategies of peacemaking. In place of, or in addition to, the classical question, "Are there outside incentives for pursuing these acts leading to conflict?" we should ask, "Are there psychological facts by which people or groups feel repelled from other people or groups keenly identified as enemies?"[64] By focusing on the *limitations* of the classical approach one can glean a different understanding of how conflicts among humans might be handled.

The shift towards a mimetic perspective entails a further shift from justice-centered strategies of peacemaking to reflective practices consisting in making explicit deep-rooted psychological habits that feed on culture, the group's self-image, representations of its history, and so on. The altero-centric approach to conflict resolution psychologizes the causes of discord and thereby relocates them from the external space of the facts of the world to the internal space inhabited by inimical images of the other. The process of acknowledging the mimetic structure of one's ontological commitments depends on the ability to develop special perceptions about oneself. Through becoming reflective about our impulses and animosities we recognize in the first place that mimetic rivalry is inextinguishable. From this perspective we begin to see that the talk of "satisfaction" that lies beneath the discourse of so-called contact groups is actually instrumental to the aim of discord, which is to conceal its mimetic roots and perpetuate itself.[65] This talk is therefore biased by a blind acceptance of the classical approach so that a new perspective on conflict resolution should address the egocentric construal of the very notion of satisfaction.

A mimetic perspective would lead us in the direction of a full recognition of the fact that satisfaction has primarily *normative* implications, inasmuch as the rivals will be satisfied only after receiving a treatment and a compensation that they deem *fair*. But failures to acknowledge the mimetic sources of desire are likely to lead to solutions that will come consistently short of the "measure of satisfaction" indicated, time and again, by the rivals themselves. If the conflict hides a genuinely mimetic strain, the very act of either distributing shares of land or redrawing boundaries is hardly likely to satisfy the rivals.

Where a "mimetic strain" is at work, recourse to "social identity" is of little use to explain the attendant conflict. Radicalization of identity is, again, the *upshot* of the mimetic crisis, not what sets it off. In conflicts in which animosity is explained in terms of territorialization of identities, a mimetic dynamic is arguably at work. It pushes the rivals against each other and forces people who socialized in an environment with weak identity ties and possessing unclear identity marks (e.g., children of interethnic marriages and, in Bosnia, Muslims who are not ethnically Bosnian) to take on a clearly perceptible identity and thereby engage in the ongoing polarization. Claims of exclusive possession of a given portion of land often take place in environments in which identity issues become politically sensitive only *after* individual and group rivalries set in. Nevertheless, identity is used by both rivals and third parties to rationalize the ensuing conflict, thereby contributing to concealing the mimetic activity that polarizes the scene. Thus identity was blamed as the *cause* of the myriad civil wars—fought at the micro-level in towns and villages with an ethnically mixed population—that punctuated the blurred map of what was left, in the early 1990s, of the former Yugoslavia. In Bosnia, in the early 1990s, towns and villages with a very high concentration (up to 40 percent) of ethnically and confessionally mixed marriages bore witness to a shocking escalation of violence between ethnic-based factions, and people caught in the mimetic thrall of the mounting civil war were understandably losing their bearings. And the many who had married across ethnic lines realized that the world that had once been indifferent to their marriage had "changed so profoundly that what had been accepted and even treasured only a few years ago has suddenly been rendered vestigial and taboo."[66]

## Reflective Justice

Running contrary to the "liberal assumption" that people always fight over the possession of goods—either material or immaterial—an account mindful of the mimetic implications of human agency will recognize that the sources of human discord have been looked for in the wrong place and that mimetic theory—the main psychological underpinning of a radically alternative account—contains the simple suggestion that conflict arises not so much because people are bad negotiators but, rather, because they are poor introspectors.

Reflection, to be sure, involves "cognitive functions, information processing and image building" and enables people to convene on a scene of "mutual reckoning" where the mimetic springs of discord are fully exposed.[67] The reckoning is successful if the mimetic doubles eventually yield to self-reflective *agents* capable of engaging in ontological stipulations whose normative effects will be beneficial to the ensuing peaceful arrangements. Reckoning, exposure, and reflection warrant the genuinely *normative* nature of the arrangements whereby the former rivals seek to refashion their mutual relationships. The normative force of the stipulations regulating such relationships depends on the quality of the reflective commitments they made, on their ability to pin down the possible mimetic departures from genuinely reflective, nonmimetic behavior. The solution to any dilemma in human conflict resolution is, in other words, always normative, never *natural*. The rivals can ultimately make peace *because* they can make themselves subject to stipulations they have freely and reflectively agreed upon.

I have traced two main epistemic domains where talk of conflict resolution occurs, one natural and one normative. One interesting phenomenon of the last decades is the progressive erosion of the normative domain and the rise of natural explanations in areas in which the normative model dictated its epistemic conditions. As I indicated above, the discourse on conflict resolution is difficult to define in terms that naturalize its premises. The rise of naturalistic explanations of human discord has affected such fields as social psychology, sociology, behavioral biology, and psychology, although the recipes usually offered to resolve the discord are normative in nature, being generally grounded on dialogue, persuasion, and redistribution.

The kind of justice underlying the arrangements resulting from these stipulations is not the same justice praised and supported by the classical approach. Rather it is what I would call "reflective justice," a strategy focusing on the active recognition of the mimetic springs of human behavior and conflict.

Barbara Hudson briefly traces this notion to the rather tentative and speculative understanding of justice put forth by the French theorist Jean-François Lyotard. Hudson points out that "discursive justice, relational justice, reflective justice and rights-regarding justice are very much work-in-progress perspectives" still short of the "level of sophistication and influence" of liberal social contract theories. These perspectives, however, are described as viable alternatives or possible complements to a (liberal) discourse that covers our general understanding of justice. However, the "risk society" where we live is challenging the alleged comprehensiveness of the liberal model and stimulates the rise of other "work-in-progress perspectives."[68] This book aims neither to put an end to this work in progress, nor to put forward a full-fledged conception of reflective justice. The book shows that identity claims may be the covert expression of mimetic biases that people rationalize by recourse to fitting narratives of marginality and persecution.[69] It exposes the self-serving agenda of groups committed to conceal historical facts or sanction selective appraisals of the past.

*Reflective* justice typically combines justice and *truth,* and thereby seeks to provide the so-called "virtues of truthfulness" with an appropriate institutional framework, although its scope is not limited to the external world in which the exploits of the rivals take place.[70]

It has been argued that "reconciliation requires a psychological change."[71] Political psychologists, though, have remained vague as to the actual innovations possibly effected by *psychological* insights into the field of conflict resolution. Philosophical work on self-reflection has focused on a typical psychological phenomenon, the case in which "one's actual desires" are left unaltered by "one's deliberative reflection on what's desirable." It is a situation in which two sets of psychological attitudes "are cognitively isolated from each other" and we are no longer capable of playing a clear agentic role with respect to our attitudes and impulses. This peculiar condition, which has been described as "a form of impairment," is particularly effective in those cases when mimetic dynamics gain a momentum of their own and shun agentic control.[72] The challenge for us, and especially for psychologists engaged in conflict resolution, is to bring our own impulses and desires within the locus of agency and control in which they will be subject to the reflective scrutiny and normative authority of reason.

René Girard has focused on a typical form of psychological impairment: the identification of "scapegoats," individuals or groups that attract upon themselves all the mimetic violence. The targeting of scapegoats is a viable and *violent* shortcut to conflict resolution that often eventuates in the restoration of seemingly peaceful arrangements. In these cases memories of violent retribution and successful retaliation do the psychological work that should be done by reflective confrontation with our actual impulses and desires. Scapegoating succeeds, in other words, when people abstain from reflection and yield to the mimetic forces that hold them in their thrall.

Girard has argued that dynamics of scapegoating become "more and more effective as there is less and less knowledge, less awareness of it as a collective delusion."[73] The *political* implications that Girard fails to address concern the role played by institutions in promoting delusion in order to sustain a powerful means of stability. In the same way, "enlightened" institutions may expose scapegoating as a sacrificial strategy that immolates innocent victims for the sake of the stability and continuity of the present arrangements. A perspective on conflict resolution that acknowledges the merits of mimetic theory could help to design arrangements supporting reflective forms of justice, in which people are given psychological incentives for recognizing and exposing mimetic attitudes and polarizations.

Human discord scrupulously conceals its mimetic roots, and the only chance we have to break loose from its grip is by fulfilling the nature of human rationality, namely, its open-endedness, the idea that we have "thoughts about our thoughts, and thoughts about our thoughts about our thoughts."[74] By thinking reflectively on our own thoughts we will get a clearer insight into the highly divisive ontological realities that make up the world out there, and may eventually reach a more accomplished sense of possibility about our actual chances to live in peace.

# CHAPTER 5

# A Political Theology of the Empty Tomb

The distinguishing features of mimetic politics—reciprocal imitation as the cause of human discord, spontaneous polarization, and the ever-growing resemblance of the rivals—emerge typically at the crossroad between religion and politics. The forces of religion and politics have most resoundingly clashed in the twentieth century, and the emergence of religious terrorism in recent years has strengthened dynamics of polarization at the global level.

This chapter acknowledges the limits of Girard's theory and offers a new perspective on the current reemergence of *religious* conflicts. It engages critically in particular with one aspect of Girard's theory, his understanding of the "Kingdom of God" as a final reckoning occurring after an eventual apocalyptic climax.

In the following I propose to gather together the psychological premises of mimetic theory and to explore tentatively how they could be tied up to *actual* demands for peace and reconciliation made by *real* people and not potential candidates for final citizenship in the forthcoming Kingdom. The chapter introduces the important notion of "political theology," a term that resonates with a variety of meanings. This notion was introduced, or at least made famous, by the German legal theorist Carl Schmitt to signify the opposite of "divine politics." While divine politics referred to the authority of God's word in this world, and therefore is related with "divine command theories," political theology is concerned with the kind of politics that takes place *in the absence* of direct and intelligible indications from a transcendent God. This is not to say that political theology is the same as immanent politics, for God is not simply disqualified from playing a role; it rather relates with a phenomenon, in Harald Wydra's apt definition, of "sacralization of world-immanent categories."[1]

In *Twilight of the Idols* Nietzsche wrote that "we cannot get rid of God because we still believe in grammar."[2] The Christian God was, according to Nietzsche, so persistent in the discourse and practices of modernity because of the linguistic conventions stipulated in order to articulate such fundamental notions as authority and subjectivity. Political theology, thus, indicates the resilience of a legacy, not the *hic and nunc* of a theological substance.

The theme of political theology has been introduced in the second chapter, where I described a powerful cleavage line in global politics. A gap opened up at the outset of the modern age, with the destruction of the unity of Christianity brought about by the Reformation. New "world-immanent categories" were introduced by philosophers and scientists to make up for the loss of status of a category that for centuries had been a unique source of causal explanation of all things, both natural and spiritual. God had withdrawn from the world by repeating the act performed by his son, by ascending into the distant and unintelligible heaven of both deists and non-believers. The new categories, though, were part of a structured grammar, of a language that the intellectual authorities of the time worked out to supply a new meaning-making framework for a world that had imploded in the void left by religious skepticism.

The momentous separation of earth and heaven entailed a desacralization of both life and politics, no longer amenable to the dictates and instructions coming from an all-providing divine entity. Political theology is this dimension of distinction and separation; it is the experience of an absence, of a deficiency; it entails the emergence of a new worldview where human beings eventually fill the void left by God. Political theology is politics after God left; it is politics after divine politics. It is not politics without God, as God remains as a problem, a problem that philosophers have tried to resolve.

But political theology is also the context in which Christianity pursues further its age-old project of desacralization. In chapter 1 I explained how Christianity has destroyed the only viable means of neutralization of human conflict: sacrifice becomes ineffectual and vain, and humans lose their most practical means of conflict prevention and resolution. And the long-term effect of this demise is the unleashing of mimetic dynamics now bound to escalate to the extreme.

Interestingly, the mimetic actors that operate within the socially permissive context of desacralized politics build their rationales of persecution and reciprocal aggression by resorting to a language crammed with theological implications. It is in particular the rhetoric of the Kingdom (in all major monotheistic religions) that leads the rivals to articulate their reciprocal offensive in terms and judgments of moral (and theological) finality, and this sense of finality is shored up by the idea of God's presence and active involvement in human history, namely, *by the closing of the earth/heaven gap*.

This chapter picks up and develops a theme in Hobbes's *Leviathan* and introduces the notion of Christ's Ascension (i.e., the emptying of the tomb) as a powerful representation of God's withdrawal from human history. Ascension is a critical feature of Christian theology, despite the many attempts made by commentators over the centuries to conflate it with the theologically more graphic (and startling) doctrine of Christ's Resurrection. Interestingly, Ascension was used by Hobbes as the *terminus a quo* of the so-called "time of regeneration," namely, the time comprised between the Ascension of Jesus Christ and his second coming. It marks the end of the *old* political theology, in which people designed their institutions and social arrangements according to the dictates of God. It was *after* Christ's Ascension—namely, after his exile from the world—that such distinctively modern notions as freedom and responsibility started making full sense.

To be sure, the doctrine of Christ's Ascension has lost its theological lure. For many centuries, and Hobbes notwithstanding, the narrative of Christ's relationship with human history pivoted around his Resurrection, an act with glorious, charismatic, and theologico-political resonances. Emphasis on Resurrection seems indeed to favor the drift towards resacralization (of nature, life, and politics) that Christianity was meant to counter. For Resurrection entailed the refilling of the world with the Word (and Flesh) of God. It is, instead, the acknowledgment of the exit of God from human history that, in a world emptied of the sacred, puts us in charge of our political destiny.

This neo-Hobbesian perspective combines the kind of "reflective justice" described in the previous chapter with the idea that God's exit from human history warrants the autonomy of human agency. Reflective justice is the collective recognition of the mimetic springs of human behavior. It thrives in the reflective space opened up by the desacralization of politics. The "political theology of the empty tomb" put forth in this chapter aims to counter the effects of mimetic politics, a fatal configuration of religion and politics in a world at war with itself, and to open up new possibilities for the future. It is the normative context in which the desacralization of politics has taken place; it is a secular dimension in which people have accepted both the exit of God from the world and the end of his claim to guide and direct his own people, but the stakes involved in the political contest are nonetheless still theological: both parties engage in a mimetic battle each guided by their own eschatology. Both at the time of the English civil wars of religion and today, in the age of a global struggle that can be disaggregated in its basic mimetic lineups, the mimetic twins lay claims of theological finality.

Political theology of the empty tomb may sound like a fancy term, in contrast with the more viable quasi synonym of "secular politics." It is, one could say, secular politics with a further qualification, for the people inhabiting this dimension reflectively acknowledge that freedom and responsibility are fragile items in the political ontology delivered by modernity. The English writer John Fowles wrote once that "God and freedom are totally antipathetic concepts," and I believe this to be true.[3] In the present political circumstances I prefer "political theology of the empty tomb" to the more mundane secular politics for an obvious reason, that the same political goal—keeping politics secular, and defending freedom from incumbent sacrificial threats—would be pursued more effectively if we considered God an "absentee" instead of a metaphysical illusion. It should not matter whether this is a principled, or rather a practical, assumption. I just believe that God is too big of a problem to rule out divine existence from the political realm.

The closing of the earth/heaven gap, the resacralization of life and politics, the colonization of the modern political space (a space opened up by the French Revolution) by new forms of divine politics, are different aspects of the process of globalization. I have stated in the introduction that mimetic politics is both the acknowledgment of the mimetic dimension of politics and the *fact* of mimesis in political processes. The resacralization of the political sphere is the eventual configuration of a kind of politics that fails to acknowledge its mimetic sources, in which the forces of reciprocal imitation are unleashed and not contained by an external "revelation" intended to mitigate the mechanism generative of violence.[4]

This chapter seeks to amend the mimetic perspective put forth by Girard by proposing a nonapocalyptic solution to the escalation of mimetic violence. The chapter refers consistently to a phenomenon called "the sacred," meaning the current dynamic of resacralization of politics, the dynamic described in the third chapter of this volume in terms of a closure of the earth/heaven cleavage.

The sacred has become more and more pervasive over the last few decades in our Western secularized societies.[5] Books, stem cells, land, animals, images, embryos, wars, and so on, are occasionally referred to as "sacred." Their sacredness, however, is less a natural property than a marker of the status of those things within a given language or framework of reference. So sacred is not the thing itself but, rather, the *construal* of the thing. The problem is not that such things have gained sacredness out of their languages of reference but, rather, that those very languages have achieved a different status in our secular worlds, for they have become more pervasive and authoritative in the everyday life of millions of human beings. Daniel Dennett has painted a bleak, but not entirely imaginary, scenario for the role that religion may be playing in the near future: "*The Enlightenment is long gone; the creeping 'secularization' of modern societies that has been anticipated for two centuries is evaporating before our eyes. The tide is turning and religion is becoming more important than ever.*"[6]

But this new religious fervor has little to do with the creed and doctrine of a given faith: the religion "that is on the increase today is . . . chaotic, chiliastic, intuitive, pathological, and for the most part utterly devoid of any theological content."[7]

Consistent with this appreciation of modernity as the logical continuation of Christianity, this chapter argues for a strong continuity between the theological implications of Christ's Ascension and the making of Western modernity.[8] I do not believe that modernity was the result of a sort of lottery of history, and the kind of secular politics that brought about a vast number of things we cherish, a deviation from a course leading purposely to a fatal closure of the earth-heaven gap.[9] The graphic tale of exile and desertion of a God who by ascending to heaven abandons his creatures preys on the Western imaginary and justifies the tales and theories of emancipation from authority that constituted the initial blueprint of the political revolutions that took place after the Reformation. State-of-nature stories made sense so long as all other narratives of normative origins had been disbanded.

The first section will present very much in outline the views of a number of writers on the meaning of secularization. In the second and third sections, I shall focus attention in particular on René Girard's views on both the sacred and the nature of religion. In the fourth section I shall argue that Girard's mimetic theory culminates in a radical rejection of theology, in particular of its claims to articulate a final and comprehensive discourse on the apocalyptic institution of the Kingdom of Christ. This denial of theology's epistemic claims matches well with Girard's attempt to defend a more straightforward access to the Gospel, on the assumption that what the Gospels have to offer is less a theory of God—that is, a *theology*—than a "theory of man." I shall look at the current emergence of the sacred in light of Girard's theory, in particular of his understanding of secularization, but I shall also try to show that his inherent critique of theology blunts the hermeneutical edge of his theory. By doing away with theology, Girard rejects a critical underpinning of a notion of secularization he seems to endorse, namely, the Christian doctrine of Jesus's Ascension.

The cornerstone of my thesis is the notion of "empty tomb," which refers to the sepulcher that Christ exited after his Resurrection and eventual Ascension. The narrative of Jesus's Ascension, which Christian theology seems to have conflated with his Resurrection, played a major role in early modern political theory, as it was considered to signal Christ's eventual departure, his decision to leave human beings alone in the face of the task of building a secular polity in which natural laws were bound to replace the dictates of God. In the kind of "Christian state" envisioned by Thomas Hobbes, the sacred, disguised in the "relics of the ancient religion of the Gentiles," was to be faced by purely rational means, namely, by instituting a perfectly rational polity bearing, and aptly disguising, the mark of its theological origins.

In the following, instead of arguing the case "no secularization out of Christianity" I will argue "no secularization out of Christian theology."

Or, better, *no secularization without a comprehensive and radical doctrine of God's Ascension.* I shall conclude by taking up, in part 5, a distinctively neo-Hobbesian stance: Hobbes is the author who put forward a *political theology* grounded on a strong notion of individual freedom and responsibility. I shall argue that only the notion of an "empty tomb," implying Christ's Ascension, could support the radically modern idea of self-deliverance from the burden of divine direction.

## Two Concepts of Secularization

Secularization—I take this to be common ground among modern interpreters—is responsible for diminishing the authority of both religion and the sacred in our lives. The notion of secularization is tightly entwined with the notion of *modernity,* for modernity is the time frame in which secularization has unfolded in these "Western parts." Institutions, habits, and arrangements are said to be modern inasmuch as they have lost their aura of sacredness and are no longer construed by the languages of the sacred. But next to this standard designation of secularization there is another one. The Catholic theologian Peter Henrici argued that "out of Christianity there has been, until recently at least, no modernity whatsoever."[10] René Girard argued a similar case, pointing out that the modern world, with its institutions, technology, scientific exploits, and even weapons was brought about by a radical desacralization of nature "of the type indicated in the Gospels." So according to Girard "only after the gods were driven out was it possible to steel oneself to treat all of nature as objects obeying *natural* laws."[11]

Girard has argued elsewhere that the scientific mentality, as a distinctive hallmark of modernity,

> presupposes the renunciation of a former preference for the magical causality of persecution so well defined by the ethnologists. Instead of natural, distant, and inaccessible causes, humanity has always preferred causes that are *significant from a social perspective and permit of corrective interventions*—victims. In order to lead men to the patient exploration of natural causes, men must first be turned away from their victims. This can only be done by showing them that from now on persecutors "hate without a

cause" and without any appreciable result. In order to achieve this miracle
. . . there is need of the extraordinary combination of intellectual, moral,
and religious factors found in the Gospel text.[12]

The philosopher Gianni Vattimo has pushed the argument of the emancipation inherent in secularization as far as it goes, arguing that humankind's
chances of emancipation rest in the eventuality of a final weakening of the
Western metaphysical self-understanding, of what Vattimo calls "postmodern nihilism." Hence, the weakening of some sacralized aspects of the
world may favor a more relaxed and resourceful relationship between man
and world.[13] Girard, Henrici, and Vattimo hold views on secularization that
markedly contrast with the standard designation that "everybody is familiar
with," namely, "a long-term process by which a disappearance of religious ties,
attitudes to transcendence, expectations of an afterlife, ritual performances,
and firmly established turns of speech is driven onward in both private and
daily public life."[14]

Canonical views on secularization consider the return of the sacred as
the attempt to compensate a loss, and supply new workable sources of meaning in a world that has lost its religious and moral bearings. Secularization,
according to this classical account, gives rise to the victory of the "nonreligious man—that is, to a man who rejects the sacrality of the world, who
accepts only a profane existence, divested of all religious presuppositions."[15]
According to this view, life in contemporary Western democracies is said to
be stripped of all those elements and properties that made it subject to a cos-
mology in which the barrier between nature and the gods was rather blurred.

Secularization has affected all aspects of human life in Western societies;
the Christian framework of learning gave way to a new secularized curriculum; the relationships between man and woman or among family members
lost their aura; and this loss ended up by weakening the hold of traditional
languages of reference.[16]

According to the approach to secularization that "everybody is familiar
with," secularization is the overcoming of a previous condition in which religion controlled and dominated public life. Secularization, therefore, is not
an event that has been completed once and for all, but a sort of unfinished
project, an occurrence that is always underway. According to this view we
have a quasi coincidence between the "sacred" and "religion," and the only

viable response to their untimely return is to show people that their claims of control are epistemically untenable.

It has been pointed out that "religion as a control-structure overseeing the cognitive processes bred by a science-oriented world-view is simply no longer effective in our world."[17] The same view is being advocated, among others, by such writers as Daniel Dennett and Richard Dawkins, though their attempts to undermine the emergence of the sacred seem to fall short of their objective.[18] Dennett in particular mistakes the "sacred" with "God," and his natural history of religion, which is meant to build a case against the existence of God, fails to address the issue of the *survival* and *return* of the sacred within Western societies. The problem with Dennett's diagnosis is that it fails to distinguish between the two things, God and religion, and seems also quite overconfident as to the effectiveness of his own recipe, that is, solving the *problem* of God by simply *making a case against* the existence of God. Dennett's diagnosis rests on a notion of secularization as the one "everybody is familiar with," namely, secularization as progressive relinquishing of the presence of God in the world.

In a similar vein Steven Pinker has rehearsed a quite classical reading of the biblical text: myths and Bible conspire in handling violence by means of violence, and therefore they have always filled the world with wars and conflicts that only the modern world (e.g., the foundation of the Royal Society, the Enlightenment, and the dwindling of religious beliefs) could bring to a halt. But still, people "in these Western parts" have not relinquished their ideas, to the extent that "sensibilities toward violence have changed so much that religious people today compartmentalize their attitude to the Bible."[19]

Although Dennett's position (and, for that matter, Dawkins's) is representative of a rather established way of articulating and contrasting the emergence of the sacred—namely, by enlightening people's minds and showing that their religious beliefs amount to mistakes—I shall, in the following, pursue a different route, trying to carve out a proposal to counter the emergence of the sacred *within* the conceptual framework offered by the writers mentioned above, in particular by Girard. These writers believe that any effective response to the emergence of the sacred must be articulated *within* the theological framework of Christianity. In their view secularization is threatened by its very incompleteness, so that the final task of Christianity is to *fulfill* the secularization process and work out the means to dispel the extant traces of the sacred. For these writers secularization is not so much the *denial* of some theological assumptions concerning God's agency in the world, as it is a *radicalization* of those assumptions.[20] Secularization, in other words, is somehow consistent with the soteriological plan laid out in the New Testament. It is, in a way, a further stage in the progress made by the word of God in the world.

Accordingly, this current return of the sacred is understood in terms of a *malfunction* in the logic of secularization, therefore requiring a further supplement of secularization that only a radical understanding of God's word could bring about. To put it more succinctly, writers committed to an alternative understanding of secularization are also committed to preempting theology within the framework of Christianity; and achieving a new, possibly more effective, understanding of the sacred.

These two opposite views—secularization as a process aimed at *enhancing* the emancipatory thrust of Christianity, and secularization as a process aimed at *dissolving* Christianity and religion—convey two distinct approaches to the problem of the current reemergence of the sacred. In the following I will try to detail Girard's theory of the sacred. I will try to expose its merits and limits, in particular its attempt at building a nontheological discourse about the fate of humankind along pseudo-Christian, pseudo-apocalyptic lines.

## Girard's Pseudotheology of the Kingdom

Girard's theory of "mimetic desire" involves a powerful conceptual shift of perspective in current theorizing about the springs of human discord. To Girard, the notion of desire that we use when we describe conflictive dynamics has a clear egocentric bias. In effect we are bound to an "egocentric model" based on the mistaken assumption that human discord arises for the mere appropriation of *goods*.

While the classical approach claims that solitary agents have to deal with a limited set of goods, and have to face conflicts arising from the desire to take possession of them, the mimetic model stresses the existence of *rivals*. It is important to stress the unconscious element implicated in the story of how mimetic rivalries come about. The story is bound to remain untold, for it would disclose something that the rivals do not seem prepared to tackle, namely, the *futility* of their claims. Such claims are made in order to give a ring of rationality to actions that on closer scrutiny were executed without a reason.

By pushing the mimetic theory as far as it goes one comes to the conclusion that the claims made by the rivals become more effective when they take the form of *accusations* of those who are deemed responsible for the evils befalling the community. As soon as mimetic conflicts intensify, the excuses that the people give in order to rationalize their hate are *accusations*. In other words, the real cause is replaced by the accusation: this is the motive to which "the *ad causam,* the accusation" holds.[21]

We have seen that this dynamic of scapegoating helps the community to find a way out of the chaos of the mimetic conflict and to replace the missing *cause* of discord with the *person* accused. Scapegoat and mimesis are the two inextricable poles of Girard's theory of the origins of culture. But while mimesis is a natural fact, a psychological feature of humans, scapegoating is a sort of rite of passage to the human condition, a practice that is not encoded in our genes and yet figures in the process of hominization as a critical step, a luminal passage that defines the new dimension of language and ritual. Interestingly this practice thrives in conditions of very limited cognition and awareness: scapegoating dynamics have beneficial effects over the community as long as there is "less awareness" of it as a collective delusion.

Girard's next move—after describing a psychological disposition and a primal social practice—consisted in playing the Scriptures, particularly the Gospels, against that dynamic of collective delusion. The Bible is a set of revelatory texts in which what is revealed is less the reticent talk of the Judeo-Christian God than a fundamental truth about *us.* The Gospels in particular are read by Girard as texts that could disclose what has long remained unrevealed, namely, the actual origins of human discord. But Girard reads the Gospels on the assumption that violence—the kind of violence that the Scriptures seek to expose and deactivate—*is* the sacred, for the most original and pervasive form of violence is *sacrificial* violence, namely a violence fueled by the mistaken assumption that the accused is *always* the actual cause of a cultural and religious crisis that, on closer scrutiny, turns out to be "without a reason."

In *Violence and the Sacred* Girard had not yet fully worked out the *theological* implications of the mimetic theory. His anthropology, in fact, was not yet part of the pseudotheological architectonics he was to develop from 1977. In his book *Things Hidden since the Foundation of the World* the mimesis of human relationships is articulated within a pseudotheological framework: the fate of mimetic desire is the same as the fate of God's word in the world, that is, to be overlooked, disguised, and ultimately expelled. Here, the bad reputation of the mimetic understanding of human relationships, namely, the fact that the word that would jeopardize the machinery of mimesis "is never mentioned," is easy to explain: that word, in fact, would strip violence of its inherent self-absolving rhetoric.[22]

Girard believes that violence is the most distinctive mark of the human condition, and in order to keep going it needs a suitable ideological apparatus to effectively disguise its sources. Disclosures of the machinery of mimesis jeopardize the very existence of this apparatus and undermine violence's chances of fully and comfortably operating within human societies. However, the edifice of violence is not without cracks, as it relies basically on people's "natural" inclination to delude themselves into believing that a certain event that befell the community has a clearly detectable cause. The cause that the perpetrators say they have traced, the *ad causam* of violence and havoc within the community, becomes explicit in the *accusation* they direct against those deemed responsible for the present evils. This "system of violence" works pretty effectively so long as it manages to keep any alternative account about the violent deed from spreading outside the circle in which violence was perpetrated. Rumors about the real *status* of the victims, that is to say, rumors concerning their being actually *innocent,* may generate qualms about the avowed motives of the perpetrators. But according to Girard, God's word is precisely meant to support those "rumors," and unveil the hidden sources of violence, the "things hidden since the foundation of the world." One can push this argument as far as it goes and see that the case for the victim's innocence *is* indeed the word of God.

To Girard, Christ himself is the eternal testimony of what is doomed to remain, in the eyes of the perpetrators, utterly indemonstrable, namely, the innocence of their victims. The Gospels play a key role in this process of demystification of the perpetrators' accusation, for they clearly show the identity relationship between the word of God and the case for the victim's innocence, and tell how both ultimately share the same fate of expulsion and exile.[23] Girard writes that "a non-violent deity can only signal his existence to mankind by having himself driven out by violence—by demonstrating that he is not able to establish himself in the Kingdom of Violence."[24] Therefore, mimesis is the main obstacle, or "stumbling block," on the way to the ultimate realization of God's Kingdom. Hence, knowing the truth does not make us wiser or psychologically more intuitive, for truth plays in this context a truly destabilizing role and becomes the key that is expected to open the doors of this kingdom of nonviolence. It shows to those embedded in the kingdom of violence that there is indeed a way out, that the stability of social orders comes from a hideous deed.

But what exactly is this kingdom of nonviolence? Girard maintains that "the Kingdom of God means the complete and definitive elimination of every form of vengeance and every form of reprisal in relations between men."[25] It is this curious claim that introduces us into Girard's theology of the kingdom. He draws, in the first place, a distinction between "theology of the kingdom" and "apocalyptic theology," and makes the claim that the logic of the Old Testament is still biased by a residue of apocalyptic theology in which traces of the old notion of the sacred loom through. In the Old Testament, indeed, the promise of the end of times is construed as a final epiphany of godly violence. This promise, admittedly, is still internal to the sacrificial logic that the Old Testament was committed to overcome. And it is because of this remnant of apocalyptic understanding of human history, which stresses the eventual explosion of a demanding and violent God, that the Old Testament, according to Girard, "never tips over into the complete rationality that would dispense with this hope of a purgation by violence and would give up requiring God to take the apocalyptic solution by completely liquidating the 'evil' in order to ensure the happiness of the chosen."[26]

The most important point in these pages is the distinction between "the great adventure of the Kingdom" and Apocalypse, which is presented as an eminently human fact, or fate, and not as the product of divine initiative. Girard points out that if the recipients of the message conveyed through the New Testament "had accepted the invitation unreservedly, there would have been no Apocalypse announced and no Crucifixion."[27] In the following page we find this passage:

> we now have in our hands all the threads of the logic that transforms the announcement of the Kingdom into an announcement of the Apocalypse:

if men turn down the peace Jesus offers them—a peace which is not derived from violence and that, by virtue of this fact, *passes human understanding,* the effect of the gospel revelation will be made manifest through violence, through a sacrificial and cultural crisis whose radical effect must be unprecedented since there is no longer any sacralized victim to stand in the way of its consequences. The failure of the Kingdom, from the viewpoint of the Gospels, does not amount to the failure of the mission Jesus undertakes; but it does amount to the inevitable abandonment of the direct and easy way, which would be for all to accept the principles of conduct that he has stated. It is now necessary to turn to the indirect way, the one that has to by-pass the consent of all mankind and instead pass through the Crucifixion and the Apocalypse.[28]

What is remarkable in this passage is the designation of the non-Apocalyptic route to the Kingdom of God—namely, the annihilation, by purely human means, of the realm of violence—as an "easy way."[29] Girard's pseudotheology advocates the final restitution of God's word to the world through the annihilation of all obstacles that hamper its eventual disclosure. What is disconcerting about this pseudotheology is the *proximity* of the Kingdom and the *easiness* of its eventual establishment. Girard's destruction of the claims of theology leads to a revolutionary rearticulation of the notion of *novissima.* Apocalypse in fact is no longer the effect of divine initiative but rather the last and most destructive of all sacrificial crises. Girard pulls the apocalyptic event out of the theological framework in which it was interwoven with God's judgment and agency, namely, with a purely divine initiative, and obliterates its inherently redemptive nature. Apocalypse, construed within a purely anthropological framework, is seen as a final and destructive disclosure of mimetic violence feeding on a climax of collective delusion.

Girard, however, does not seem to consider the fact that secularization, namely, the radical desacralization "of the type indicated in the Gospels," is a *historical* fact and that it is possible to trace in *history* the ideas and debates that contributed to make the so-called "enlightenment project" effective. In other words, the secularization of the premodern worldview and the resulting modernization of institutions and social arrangements have contributed to mitigate the thrust of sacrificial violence and to expose the absurdity of the practice of scapegoating. This secularization of culture led to a dramatic loss of influence of the frameworks of reference of the sacred. In those early modern debates such notions as tolerance and freedom of conscience, combined with the political principle of *cuius regio, eius religio,* were put to work, but the *political* problem at the bottom of those debates was how to clear the world of the remnants of "ancient religions." The most significant theoretical novelty introduced in those debates consisted in a peculiar combination of epistemic claims, something I would call "political theology," a perspective best represented by such writers as Hobbes and Spinoza. The political theology of the early modern age combined the aspiration to build a new secular polity with a general adherence to the framework of classical Christian theology. It is this combination of politics and theology that triggered the process of secularization as Girard, among others, understands it, but it is the very epistemic status of political theology in connection with the notion of kingdom that, as I shall show in the following, has been called into question by Girard himself.

## In Munere Alieno

On several occasions Girard has emphasized that his hermeneutics of the Gospels is *not* a theology. His frequent statements to this effect seem, however, like gestures of *munus efficere,* namely, warnings to hold on to one's duties.[30] But the construal of such issues as Kingdom, Resurrection, and Apocalypse is inherently theological, as it would be difficult to articulate their meaning without taking into account God's agency in history. A discourse concerning the very nature of God's final Kingdom, or Christ's Resurrection, or the Apocalypse is theological in a deep sense, and any attempt to bring such notions to bear on a purely anthropological reading of the Gospels would inevitably dissolve them.

The *mimetic* construal of the Apocalypse put forth by Girard can hardly afford the simplest confrontation with a *theology* of the Apocalypse, that is to say, with a discourse concerning the eventual coming of God. The theological construal of the Apocalypse entails that the apocalyptic event, namely, the final intervention of God in human history, has a distinctive *redemptive* character. Mimetic theory, therefore, seems to be modeled on a typical early modern attitude towards theology, well represented by the expression "silete teologi in munere alieno" ("Be silent, theologians, about matters that do not fall within your domain"), coined by the Italian jurist Alberico Gentili. Here the *munus* (domain, office) of theology is demarcated from the *munus* of other worldly affairs, such as those pertaining to the domains of politics and jurisprudence. Mimetic theory seems to disregard this boundary and takes over the domain of theology by deconstructing the *theological* understanding of the Apocalypse. From the mimetic perspective the event, which is said to pave the way to the eventual establishment of the Kingdom of God, appears as a major sacrificial crisis in which mimetic drives are no longer constrained by age-old sacrificial means. Apocalypse and such cognate concepts as Kingdom of God are just workable metaphors with no reference to the agency of the Christian God in history.

Christian theology played a major role in representing the Kingdom as the final upshot of God's initiative, and not as a metaphor of the human inability to live in peace. The apocalyptic construal of the Kingdom helped postpone its final installation in a dimension that was utterly inaccessible to human initiative. As has been argued, the historical backdrop against which a new basis of justification for a secular polity emerged were the religious wars of early modernity,[31] but a final political and *theological* settlement of those conflicts was brought about not so much by a workable hybridization among different *munia,* such as theology and politics, as by their strategic alliance, by a "political theology of the empty tomb" such as the one envisioned by Thomas Hobbes, a political theology centered on the theological notion of *ascension.*

Ascension lived a quite minor existence within earlier Christian theology, and it was Hobbes who turned it into a crucial theological as well as *political* tenet. If one looks at the theological statements concerning ascension, one sees that it is always mentioned together with resurrection, for ascension is hardly given an autonomous theological standing within the narrative of Christ's coming back to life after crucifixion. There has been, indeed, a widespread "tendency to conflate resurrection, ascension and *parousia*" in Christian theology as witnessed, for example, in the pastoral tradition of the Catholic Church.[32] The thing is that the ascension scene in Luke 24—the only author who in the Gospels offers a detailed account of Jesus's departure—has always been difficult to match with a theology that stresses the eucharistic presence of God. To be sure "this remarkable scene first provides a dramatic closure to the story of Jesus and then a hermeneutical key to the new history to the people of God."[33] But the history of the people of God in terms of abandonment and anticipation of the next coming of Christ became politically influential at a time, as I shall show in the following section, when Jesus's departure was intended to mark the beginning of what Hobbes calls the "regeneration," namely, the time of hope and anticipation when human beings were left alone with their projects of building, *in absentia,* a polity emptied of any aspiration whatsoever of *easily* instituting the Kingdom of Christ.

The theme of ascension is virtually absent in Girard's system of thought, for a number of reasons. It is interesting that the other text in the Gospel containing a powerful ascension scene, the Epistle to the Hebrews, has been amended by Girard (and literally expunged from the canon) on the ground of its sacrificial understanding of the death of Jesus. Girard has argued that the death of Jesus on the cross is *not* sacrificial, at least not in a classical sense, for the whole crucifixion scene lacks the most basic condition required by sacrificial violence, namely, the kind of "collective delusion" allowing all participants to mistake the *cause* for the *accused.* Christ's innocence is *apparent,* whereas the victims of the Greek myths (Oedipus is a case in point) are *never* portrayed as innocent. But Hebrews is also one of the most significant documents of the New Testament concerning Jesus's departure; indeed, "for the author of Hebrews . . . the ascension is that which determines both the shape and the content of his great epistle."[34] Hence Girard strips the Gospels of one of their fundamental theological tenets, consistent with his "purely" anthropological understanding of Christianity. Ascension becomes more or less a workable fiction to indicate the expulsion of God's word from the world. But this final withdrawal is brought about by *human* initiative. If the *verbum* of God *is* the truth—a truth that men failed to acknowledge—humans strive now to eliminate all the clues that might hint at the condition of "collective delusion" in which violence and the sacred have thrived.[35]

Girard has always supported a substantial notion of truth against the poststructuralist vogue of the 1980s. He believes that truth, namely, the truth of human relationships, is the only workable antidote against theological delusions. Here, a political theology of secularization and desacralization has been turned into an anthropology of secularization, a system that fails to acknowledge the grand tradition of modern political theology, from Hobbes to contemporary Christian theology.

In the next section I shall expand on Hobbes's attempt to stress the distance between the secular world of human institutions and the Kingdom to come, following on the second coming of Christ.

## A Neo-Hobbesian Perspective

The time of "regeneration"—as Hobbes calls the time frame "between the ascension and the general resurrection"—is marked by the silence of God's word.[36] The risk, for the community of believers, consisted in taking "for His law whatsoever is propounded by every man in His name."[37] And to avoid this fate of juridical fragmentation, in which the world resonates of myriad and differing perspectives, during this time of regeneration there are no prophets authorized to put God's intentions into words. During the regeneration human beings are bound to obey the laws promulgated by their earthly sovereign. Rejecting the direct rule of God caused his creatures to provide for enduring institutions in the absence of his commandments. It is the institution of a secular polity in which people are accountable for their own decisions as to how to conduct their own lives.[38]

The Hobbesian narrative of withdrawal of God from the world echoes the story told by Paul in the synagogue of Antiochia (Acts 13:16–41), in which the apostle expounded a narrative of biblical history starting from the exile of the people of God in Egypt through the announcement of the second coming of Christ. This grandiose narrative of the fading presence of God in the world has the underlying moral and *political* purpose of cautioning people against the foolishness of the belief in a substantial and eucharistic presence of God in the world. This is the actual challenge posed to the stability of a polity grounded on a rational agreement between free individuals. It is the challenge of what, in a language foreign to Hobbes, one would be tempted to call the "sacred."

Hobbes pins down and names the concept of the sacred in chapter XLV of *Leviathan: Of Demonology and Other Relics of the Religion of the Gentiles.* Hobbes was convinced that such "relics" had survived within Christianity as a genetic flaw capable eventually of corrupting the body politic. But Hobbes also realized that the only way to remove these residues was to affirm the impressive antimythical power of Christianity, expressed in the belief that the "last prophecy" heard in the world referred to Christ's *next* coming. Hobbes understood that the residue that posed a threat to the *pax christiana,* and which had never been fully neutralized and removed, reemerged in the form of indirect powers or counterforces, whose only objective was to destroy the great Leviathan.

Hobbes's understanding of these relics is quite vague, though the whole book IV of *Leviathan* seems to be aimed at better articulating this elusive notion. Hobbes details such things as the "demons of the ancients," the phantasms and other idols that were left in the Church and that continued to operate under disguise. But Hobbes here pushes his argument as far as it goes, and suggests that "the religious rites of the Greeks and Romans" have survived in a number of religious and *social* practices.[39] The chapter ends with a hint at the "old empty bottles of Gentilism," in a passage that seems to pave the way to the next chapter, *Of Darkness from Vain Philosophy and Fabulous Traditions,* where Hobbes argues that the relics of "Gentilism," consisting in a mistaken understanding of the relationship between God and the world, have filtered through the myriad ways people in "these Western parts" articulate the ideas and beliefs underlying their social habits and institutions. The final upshot of the working of Gentilism within human institutions is an ultimate "suppression of Reason" that will lead to that condition of crisis of the State which is a recurrent theme in Leviathan and that in chapter 46 is called "rebellion and sedition."[40] For Hobbes "rebellion and sedition" were mainly the outcome of idolatry and of the false worship of God, the outcome of the need to fill the temporal void, the *interim* interrupting the history of salvation, defeating the expectations of the final fulfillment of the Kingdom. The achievement of a time frame emptied of the idols of the pagans is indeed an *effect* of Christianity: as Hobbes points out, "in the planting of Christian Religion, the oracles ceased in all parts of the Roman empire, and the number of Christians increased wonderfully every day and in every place, by the preaching of the Apostles and Evangelists."[41]

The objective of the third book of *Leviathan* is to work out a viable strategy for placating the war among factions during the temporary absence of God by neutralizing, in Carl Schmitt's words, "Christ's effectiveness" (*Wirkung Christi*), namely the actual and efficient presence of Christ in the *interim* of "regeneration."[42] Hobbes's theological enemies, for whom the Kingdom of Christ had already begun and "was a political entity liable to trigger a civil war," strongly supported the idea of a mystical and "eucharistic" presence of Christ "even in this world." They failed to acknowledge that in the time in which they lived—the time after Christ's ascension—human beings had to take their bearings within a world emptied of the indications and constraints of a substantially present deity.

Hobbes stresses that it is Jesus's Ascension and *not* his Resurrection that marks the beginning of regeneration. The basic theological underpinning of the Hobbesian realm of secular politics, in which peace and social stability depend on the rational soundness of the institutions that human beings manage to create, is ascension, namely, the narrative of Christ's *departure* and not his glorious and charismatic rise from the dead. Hobbes distinguishes what the tradition had conflated in order to better demarcate the domain of human *responsibility*, that is to say, of the human ability to be responsive to the dictates of reason only. But quite surprisingly, Hobbes's project remains confined within the mainstream tradition of Christian theology, for the most audacious intellectual move he performs could be performed within a Christian theological framework only. By stressing God's departure in a way that was unheard-of, Hobbes builds up the edifice of modern political theology and ensures that modern history makes the kind of turn that we call "secularization."

Seen through this Hobbesian lens, Girard's pseudotheology of the kingdom apparently fails to provide an equally solid underpinning to the notion of human responsibility, namely, the quality of a person who has freed herself from the rules and constraints of a God-dominated world. Girard's unfortunate carrier of secondhand desires is hardly *responsible* for actions and beliefs that originate from distant and inaccessible universes, from the minds of those *rivals* whose capacity for agency is never original, but always dependent on the desires of other rivals.

## Conclusion

A political theology of the empty tomb supports a particular kind of skepticism as to our capacity to discern the charismatic glow of the resurrected body of Christ. No longer capable of seeing his resurrected body, we fail to appreciate his direction and guidance.

Hobbes's political theology was meant to make all the possible individual political purposes unavailable to men. Individual projects of moral accomplishment, the pursuit of a happy life, individual attempts to gain special reputation among one's fellow citizens are options no longer available *within* the state, for now "the State claims for itself the monopoly of definition on what should count as history."[43] And the definition on what should count as history could be extended to include *what is left* of history, that is to say, the time left *before* the end of history and the ensuing inception of the "happy life." Hobbes's state is in fact the *sole* carrier of a fundamental entitlement to legislate, in the historical interim of "regeneration," how one should behave if one wished to be accepted in the final Kingdom of God. The *Leviathan* collapses theology and politics in a new project of neutralization of religion in which people are bound to lose their moral agency and insight and are no longer in a position to negotiate *directly* their individual claims to perfection and moral rectitude.

Hobbes states that no eventual suspension of mimetic conflict, and no final messianic revelation, can be achieved by purely human means, and all attempts to present the final Kingdom as immediately available is a relic of "ancient religions," a residue "of Gentilism," a ladder in the fabric of *true* Christianity. Proclaiming the closeness and availability of the final Kingdom of God has been indeed a very common temptation, and the modern tradition of political theology has insisted on the risk inherent in an earthly pursuit of the Kingdom.

A politics, or political theology, of the empty tomb must be prepared to address a number of questions, as, for example, whether politics needs a theological component. It has been argued that

> the philosopher of the Enlightenment could deny this. But a post-Enlightenment tradition of political theology could assert the need for this kind of legitimation. It is the consequence of modern nihilism. The rational evidence for a God and his orders failed; therefore politics needs a new mythology.[44]

A political theology of the empty tomb may endorse Girard's understanding of secularization and the sacred, but it will also be aware that his general epistemic stance is unfit to meet the challenge posed by current returns of the sacred. Girard's theory appears to be epistemologically too charged and demanding, and his attempt to preempt theology from playing any role whatsoever suggests that theology itself is for Girard a vehicle of the sacred. Hobbes's abstinence, on the contrary, is mainly instrumental to the preservation of peace. Hobbes's perspective, however, is inside Christianity. Despite the common allegations, from Hobbes's contemporaries as well as from his critics, that Hobbes's views on religion were utterly instrumental to avoiding charges of atheism, the recent reevaluation of the theological aspects of Hobbes's work has thrown light on its relationship with Christianity.

The present conditions of fear, hope, and anticipation resemble the conditions in which Hobbes was writing. These are ideal psychological conditions for the thriving of those attitudes that feed the emergence of the sacred. But any attempt to restore God's word to the world—the refilling of the empty tomb—cannot, in principle, exclude the possibility of its eventual resacralization.

# A Genealogy of
# "Planetary Reciprocity"

M y aim in this book was not to propose a general theory of globalization from a mimetic standpoint, or to repair, or depart from, existing variants of mimetic theory. Other writers (notably Giuseppe Fornari) have tried to restructure mimetic theory from within, to show that its theoretical potential is held back by its confinement within the bounds of the Girardian scholastic. My goal was different, for I have tried to use the mimetic approach less as a comprehensive and eponymous theory than as a particular perspective on things.

What I saw from this remarkable viewpoint, as I pointed out in chapter 1, was a different ontological setting, not the Platonic one pullulating with objects, but a rather thin ontological landscape where a variety of pseudo-objects emerged as fabricated by human rivalries. It seemed to me that a number of phenomena that we had considered from a more conventional viewpoint emerged as the result of polar tensions, of radically dyadic patterns. The book is an attempt to explore these patterns and to give an account of the ontological configurations that structure our global world.

The focus of my analysis is not on conventional political actors like states or international organizations, but rather on dyads and twin-like configurations, where the dialectic between reciprocal imitation and rivalry

suggests that a mimetic dynamic is at work. Mimetic dynamics, which are
no longer contained by sacrificial devices, have exploded in a myriad of
micro-conflicts that tend to coalesce into macro-configurations (chapter 2).
Girard has contended that it is "not surprising that in the era of globalization . . . when wars are increasing, mimetism has gained ground since 1945
and is taking over the world."[1] But mimetism has gained ground not only
where micro-conflicts can be detected; mimetism is taking over the political
process of democratic nations too. The arch-conflict of our time, the Israel-
Palestinian conflict, spills over into the political system of those nations,
and the radicalization of the left/right polarization (chapter 3) is the upshot
of major mimetic cleavages.

"Reciprocal action is so amplified by globalization, the planetary reciprocity in which the slightest event can have repercussions on the other side
of the globe, that violence is always a length ahead of our movements."[2] In
chapter 3 I have described the way democratic systems track the moves "of
either Israelis or Palestinians, as part of a more general 'scorekeeping' attitude." Here the repercussions of "the slightest event" show up not so much
"on the other side of the globe" but at the core of the system of globalization.
Political adjustments along the left/right axis are caused by the "slightest
event" occurring in the Middle East.

For a little less than two centuries the left/right cleavage centered on
issues of equality and class. It is along this axis that modern politics managed
to sublimate mimetic tensions coming from society and to suspend the sacrificial drift that had ruled since early sacrificial societies. The new principle
of equality reflected the attempt to react to the old arrangement, based on
what Girard has called "degree," namely, a hierarchical ordering of the social
structures with the objective of preempting their ever-menacing sacrificial
drift. Theories of the social contract were designed to provide a new kind
of normativity after the collapse of the old degree. The political space was
cleared from its age-old ritual encrustations and made amenable to new
possibilities. The loss of the sacrificial protections granted by the old degree
unleashed a spiral of mimetic relations between equals. Displaced from their
once revered social niches, and no longer protected by the boundary of status
and degree, people found themselves exposed to an unprecedented level of
mimetic attention. *Before* the collapse of the degree, social relations were
only to a very limited extent "reciprocal," and reciprocity was allowed only

within the same social niche: by structuring human relationships in hierar-chical (i.e., nonreciprocal) patterns, degree prevented exposure and mimesis.

The new dogma of equality underpinned the new concept of citizenship, a marker of equal status that stripped people of age-old sacrificial privileges and protections. However, the normative and political order brought about by these political developments was a *weak* order, deprived of traditional means of containing violence. Girard has pointed out that "in the West, we have something special: we have . . . a society that can be stable with-out strict internal hierarchical structure."[3] The fragile mimetic equilibrium of Western societies is based on a nonsacrificial mechanism of stabilization consisting in a structured ability to displace mimetic tensions into an insti-tutional setting that absorbs and neutralizes them. If in the past it was the "degree" that stabilized social orders, namely, the tight fabric of sacrificial arrangements grounded on hierarchy and authority, modernity has dissolved those arrangements by letting the notion of equality gnaw its way into the venerable institutions of the West. Girard uses Ulysses's speech about Troy besieged by the Greeks in *Troilus and Cressida* to illustrate this structure and elaborate on its fragility and exposure,

> *How could communities,*
> *. . . . . . . . . . . . . . . .*
> *Prerogative of age, crowns, scepters, laurels,*
> *But by degree, stand in authentic place?*
> *Take but one degree away, untune that string,*
> *And hark what discord follows! Everything meets*
> *In mere oppugnancy.*
> (1.3.115–23)

I don't think I need to elaborate further on Girard's genealogy of moder-nity, grounded on the rather exclusive agency of Christianity in the process of desacralization that brought about the post-Revolution political arrange-ments. I rather see a mechanism based on the modern notion of "representa-tion," a system that manages to include and socialize an astonishingly larger number of people, and part of the legitimacy of the system is certainly based on this element of success, on its inherent ability to warrant inclusion and keep reciprocal violence at bay.

However, equality turned out to be a phenomenal breeding ground for the explosion of mimetic fluxes. The intimate nexus between the rise of equality as a key feature of the modern world and the return of unbound mimetic tensions, no longer contained within an age-old sacrificial order, has been investigated by Wolfgang Palaver, who has shown that the intellectual lineage that runs through Hobbes and Rousseau all the way to Tocqueville provides a theoretical justification for the progressive flattening of a residual "degree" in Western societies.[4]

Progressive concepts of equality remained the spur of political mobilization—a mobilization dense with mimetic implications—for a very long time, until at least the late 1970s, when a mechanism of polarization emerged that focused more on identity issues. Nowadays, especially in international politics, talk of identity becomes especially heated in the discourse that opposes East to West, and in chapter 2 I expanded on the mimetic rationale behind this new global discourse of identity. It is the need to mark oneself as different that pushes the rivals to don new and showy identity clothes, although on closer scrutiny (we are still looking at the scene from our mimetic perspective) the rivals look more and more like twins.

However, identity remains the new grammar of social diversity in a world made homogeneous by globalization. In chapter 3 I showed that the global appeal of this notion of identity reveals a slight adjustment in the political discourse of the West. Here the notion of equality, reminiscent of a discourse of class and social justice, has been slightly pushed aside by a discourse centered on such notions as inclusion and representation. Identity (and identity markers, such as East and West) is a force that structures and aggregates consensus along the political spectrum. This force, though, is catalyzed by those international issues in which the East/West divide has become a reference and a blueprint (e.g., the Israeli-Palestinian conflict) and that are able to mobilize opinions along the left-right continuum.

In chapter 2 I focused on one "international" issue that spurs polarization and pushes the two sides "to the extreme" (and even beyond) of the democratic spectrum. The Israeli-Palestinian schism rebounds on the global public sphere by placing strain on a space that was created at the time of the French Revolution, a space structured along a left-right axis.

The escalation of what Girard calls "planetary reciprocity" is precisely this collapsing of critical cleavage lines: left/right, East/West and earth/

heaven. Chapter 5 in particular contends that contemporary forms of "divine politics" have challenged the fragile arrangements that underpinned the modern political space, the space created by the French Revolution. The epistemic and political warrants of this space consisted in the suspension of all sacrificial solutions to the problem of the escalation of conflict, and the structuring of the political exchange along an horizontal axis. The age-old (vertical) degree had fallen apart and a new (horizontal) dimension for life and politics had been created. Social conflicts could be embedded in a "normal" political exchange, and new normative standards for this "normality" were adopted. The new order has been doing its job in quite a satisfactory way since its inception a little more than two hundred years ago, although it did collapse a few times, notably in the twentieth century, when it was destroyed by a major resurgence of sacrificial politics, only to resurface along the very same juridical as well as philosophical tenets after 1945.

I want to devote a few words to that resurgence, and to a powerful mimetic interpretation given by a professional historian. In the following pages I will dabble in what Girard himself has called "mimetic history."[5] Twenty-five years ago the German newspaper *Frankfurter Allgemeine Zeitung* hosted two articles by, respectively, Ernst Nolte and Michael Sturmer, that triggered a debate that came to be known as the *Historikerstreit*. The stakes involved were admittedly highly political, as they concerned the moral (and thereby political) standing of Germany as a nation, and affected several important issues very high on the agenda of both German intellectuals and policymakers, such as multiculturalism and citizenship.

In order to shore up his case for revisiting recent German history from a revisionist perspective, Nolte started with a full appraisal of the ideological and political contexts in which Nazi Germany operated. Nolte basically contested the epistemic value of any explanation based on the singular "process of individuation" of *one* polity. He placed Germany in a context of mimetic mirroring in which it is difficult to track an original agentic intention. State-agency is hardly original, and Nazi Germany was no exception. In an article for the Italian newspaper *Corriere della Sera,* published on July 3, 1989, Nolte wrote, "I believe that European history *cannot be written as the history of individual states* and also not as the history of a destructive ideology which only emerged in Germany. Throughout Europe there existed a fear of Communism."

Nolte contested the "ontology of originals" that supported the earlier discourse about *unique* historical actors *uniquely* responsible for their deeds. He argued that Nazi politics was dictated by a careful and obsessive monitoring of Germany's ideological rival, communism, and this monitoring led to a full-fledged mimetic attitude, a consistent imitative outlook that prompted a number of initiatives that were not therefore "original." This mimetic interpretation of a central event of World War II has remained confined within the limits of a discussion about the extent and resilience of German guilt.

The idea of mimetic mirroring between two empires, the German Reich and the Soviet empire, was never a serious topic on the agenda of professional historians.[6] Only recently, a powerful genealogy of the collapse of communism in terms that acknowledge the mimetic mirroring between Russia and Europe has been put forth by Harald Wydra:

> Besides the messianic horizon of expectation, Russia's geo-political competition with Europe was symbolically creative in its own right. For centuries, the dominating strata in Russian society had lived under the spell of Europe. The symbol of Europe was a spiritual fact but also had a social, economic, and political dimension. The admiration for Europe's economic and technological superiority turned into a mimetic competition for imitating Europe in order to overcome it. The aristocratic elites in Tsarist Russia celebrated their self-image of being European in court rituals and symbols, rooting their own power in the imagery of foreign and "transcendental" origin.[7]

Mimetic history opens up new scenarios; it helps us "understand what is at stake in our own times," and what is at stake is the transposition of the same cleavage line on a different, much larger, scale.[8] The "non-European other" is no longer the Russian empire, and the line that separates East and West has been pushed farther east.[9] It is as if the former East was contaminated and mimetized by an all-encompassing West, as if it became part of the West; and this more comprehensive West is preparing for a new battle, a battle to the end, with a new comprehensive East.

After World War II, and after a relatively long period of stability and remission of mimetic tensions, a one-world system is being strained by a

new challenge, that is, by the compounding and collapsing of three different cleavage lines, each animated by a deep-seated mimetic thrust. Girard
maintains that "there is no totality that does not run the risk of being
affected by the doubling that used to be contained by sacrifice," and the risk
of an escalating doubling in global politics would meet little resistance in
our postsacrificial times.[10] The closing of the earth/heaven gap is aggravat-
ing the current crisis to an unbearable extreme, and the reception of the
tension between East and West is barely endurable in "these Western parts."
It is on this East/West division that I would like to elaborate a bit further
in the pages that follow.

◆   ◆   ◆

The borderline limit that has separated East from West has been constantly
renegotiated since the Greek historian Herodotus drew a tentative version
of it some twenty-five hundred years ago.[11] The political East/West fault line
was displaced from its original setting between Asia and Europe and pushed
back and forth by the imperial agendas of both Spain and Turkey. A new
dyad had taken over all the other dyads, and a new tension emerged in the
West to determine which nation, or empire, was entitled to engage in the
mimetic confrontation with the Eastern rival. Fuchs provides an account of
how the new dyadic pattern set in.

> Spain was beleaguered not only by rival European powers but by the forces
> of Islam in the Western Mediterranean. After the defeat of the Ottoman
> navy at Lepanto in 1571, corsairs from Tunis and Algiers, client states to the
> Turks, posed the primary threat to Spanish coastal settlements.[12]

Geopolitical tension between East and West reached an unprecedented
scale in the sixteenth century. There were no longer two peoples or nations
facing one another as the two extremes of a global spectrum, but rather two
*empires* were now confronting each other. However, the predominance of the
individuation model in explaining the emergence of either Turkey or Spain
as a global imperial actor has eclipsed the mimetic moment in the structuring
of the dyad. What we have is an interesting anecdotic that is difficult to frame
in a coherent discourse. The most remarkable effect of academic speculations
on the mimetic intercourse between East and West was the discourse on

"Orientalism." This discourse has discarded genuinely mimetic explanations of the tensions within the dyad by interpreting the Western interest in the East as a consistent attempt to caricature and ultimately diminish it, *never* as a way to imitate it.[13]

If this notion of Orientalism entails mimesis and fascination, the origins of this attitude towards the Eastern "other" are difficult to track down. Anthony Pagden has traced these origins to a single event, that is, to Napoleon's siege of Alexandria, when "the Islamic world's long isolation from its western neighbors had come brusquely to an end."[14]

Zachary Lockman has described the "Orientalist" cultural frenzy of the early nineteenth century in terms of a general attempt to make up for a loss, or dissatisfaction for, the landmark cultural and intellectual products of the West: "rejecting the rationalism of the Enlightenment . . . some of the Romantic poets, novelists, dramatists and philosophers saw the Orient as the repository of a hitherto inaccessible source of wisdom on which they might draw in order to revive and redeem a spiritually exhausted and increasingly materialistic West."[15]

Bernard Lewis extends the origins of the Orientalist idea back in time, but still in the context of the reciprocal mirroring between East and West. Lewis considers the cultural fascination of both East and West for one another as an age-old affair that exploded after the French Revolution:

> the long association, sometimes in coexistence, more often in confrontation, with Christendom, led to the acceptance, in the later Islamic monarchies in Iran and Turkey and their successor states, of patterns of religious organization that might suggest a probably unconscious imitation of Christian ecclesiastical usage. These Western influences became more powerful and more important after the French Revolution.[16]

The single case of Egypt shows how the impulse to imitate the *success* of the West (more than an internal, autochthonous impulse towards emancipation in the East), was the critical spur of modernization in Egypt after it gained independence from British tutelage. In Anthony Pagden's words,

> if the Western infidel enemy had triumphed so decisively and incontrovertibly over God's peoples, clearly something must be wrong. But what? As in

nearly all such situations, the possible replies were limited to two: defeat was due to either the skill or virtues of the victor, or it could be blamed on some internal weakness of the vanquished. If the former were the case, the obvious thing to do was to find what it was that had made the enemy successful and then imitate it.[17]

While the process of modernization was pursued as a mimetic reaction to Western military success, some of the *concepts* involved in the process were also of Western coinage. As for Egyptian nationalism, the attempt "to link an Islamic present and future back to the past of the pharaohs" was made possible through a form of nationalism "*in imitation* of the European concepts of national rebuilding."[18]

♦   ♦   ♦

How does all this bear with the question of the mimetic status of globalization? A mimetic history of the global emergence of deep-seated cleavage lines can help break down the processes that lead to the current "planetary reciprocity" into stages in which the actors developed a mutually threatening mimetic outlook. We are faced with the challenge of an escalating "planetary reciprocity," the global emergence of cleavage lines that are compounding themselves in new powerful configurations, new "cumulative cleavages."[19] A genealogy of bipolarity is meant to unveil this process, these multiple stages "in the emergence of a planetary principle of reciprocity."[20] But what is remarkable in this process is that it is difficult to track an original actor, a primal source of mimetic appeal.

Again, genealogy proceeds backward; it explains present social arrangements by giving an account of how they have come about. Genealogy detects discontinuities and fractures in the historical continuum and challenges pleasing just-so stories. The present global battle to the end has distant roots, and my investigation into early modern dynamics of reciprocal imitation aims at explaining the present situation.

If we were to track a sort of initial situation when early modern imperial polities started negotiating their way in Europe, we would see that historians would hardly agree on *which* would be the first empire to show up on Europe's political scene, namely, what would be the "vanguard" polity to lay avowedly imperial claims. Fuchs points out that the English experience of piracy has usually been glorified as the proleptic wanderings of a future imperial power—pirates as the vanguard of the empire. Under Elizabeth, England pursued a highly aggressive para-naval policy towards Spain: in the 1570s and 1580s, piracy became England's belated answer to Spain's imperial expansion. Long before war became open in 1588, the queen was giving her not-so-tacit approval to privateering expeditions that ostensibly sought new channels for English trade but in fact consisted mainly of attacks on Spanish colonies in the New World. Elizabeth espoused piracy as a kind of imperial mimesis—if England had not yet managed to acquire its own empire, it could at least imitate Spain in exploiting the riches of the New World.[21]

Here we have two principal actors, England and Spain, involved in a struggle for both political domination and mimetic recognition. England is modeling its agency on another political entity, and by doing so it behaves like the imitator in Girard's example, who turns to another person "to inform him of what he should desire." England turns to Spain, which suggests that Spain was the original, the arch-model of modern empire. But on a closer look it is difficult to determine which came first, and each historical deed that one may take as the actual "vanguard" seems to lead to an ever earlier start on the side of the rival. That Spain was the original has become commonplace, although in terms of strict chronology the Portuguese came first. By describing the mimetic dynamics involved in the rush for empire, Anthony Pagden has pointed out that "as with conquest, the first objectives of all the European powers in the Atlantic had been simply to imitate the Spaniards."[22] Here, though, imitation is restricted to the action of conquering land, and does not concern the complex practice of building an empire.[23] In other words, when Pagden introduces the notion of the "rush for empire" he uses the word "empire" in a way that explains the effects of choices made by the elites, but does not account for what these elites were up to.[24] To be sure, the political elites involved in the rush did not have an articulate sense of what they were doing. For them, the word "empire" was less a technical term, or the cipher of a prospective political experience, than a workable catchword with fancy resonances. We can see the self-conscious involvement of proto-imperial elites in a predatory venture that fell short, until the early sixteenth century, of the articulate normative discourses worked out by the first ideologues of the empire. And it is difficult to determine at which point the rush *for conquest* turned into a self-conscious rush *for empire.*[25]

Spain, to be sure, led the rush for conquest, in the sense that one can track the actual beginnings of this rush, but the *mimetic* rush for empire has less clear origins, as more actors seem to develop an imperial outlook by using the rival as a model. It might be argued that the arch-model was *literary,* and that the first mimetic deed was committed by looking at the "Roman model" as the model of all imperial models.[26]

Our backward genetic investigation seems to stop in 1494, when the Treaty of Tordesillas sanctioned the division of the globe in two hemispheres under the influence of Spain and Portugal. But the Spanish geographic discoveries were spurred by the race of exploration engaged with Portugal at the end of the fifteenth century. Again, once we seem to have reached the end of the process, and pinned down the "original," our attention is deflected to an earlier phase, so that the original turns out to be the mimetic clone of an older original.

I do not intend to detail the process whereby the dyad Portugal/Spain evolved into an eventual struggle between two mimetic doubles. The process, though, was complicated by a number of pushes and challenges from other actors that struggled to enter the mimetic fray. England, for one thing, at the very end of the sixteenth century was looking for someone to tell her "what she should desire." And it was by following the successes of both Portugal and Spain that England developed its typical imperial outlook.

We could gesture, very much in outline, at a mimetic account of the emergence of the "Spain-England" dyad through five phases. In phase 1 England, envious of the wealth of Spain, attempts simple imitation: as Arthur Young pointed out in 1772, "we, at present, have her example to guide her reckoning; she had none by which to frame her conduct."[27] England's imperial musings took the form of a quest for lands to conquer and exploit, preferably lands with precious metals: here we see the "imitation of a model who becomes a rival." Phase 2 is the stage of reckoning and disillusion. The initial ventures are a failure: no Aztecs or Incas in Newfoundland, no god or silver either. Now the British settlers make virtue out of necessity, and phase 3 bears witness to a shift to agriculture and trade that will result, in the end, in a different imperial base. Phase 4 consists in the repudiation of the initial goals as inhuman, and a new imperial ideology was bound to develop out of this ideological refutation. The British Empire thrives and supersedes Spain. Spain (phase 5) goes into decline and looks back to the now far more successful rival/model: at this stage what we see is the imitation "of a rival who becomes a model." Spain initiates reforms to imitate Britain and adopts the English critique of empire (aided by Montesquieu). The circle is now complete, and both polities lose their empires.

Mimetic patterns are often entrenched in age-old military and diplomatic mores, and shape the mimetic performance of nations in different ways. In Fuchs's words, "how did the English reliance on outmoded aristocratic models of virile conquest and plunder complicate England's actual colonial ventures, as it attempted to imitate Spain in the Americas?"[28]

It could be argued that the rise of the British Empire can be explained in terms of the emergence of a new, powerful mimetic model, a pseudo-original that "suggested" to other imperial actors what to do. The British Empire will play the role of the mimetic partner in a number of dyads for two centuries, until the American Revolution and the Napoleonic wars altered the pattern. But the same empire will continue to operate and inspire mimetic awe, although the nineteenth century bore witness to the emergence of a new imperial polity born out of the fabric of the British Empire: the United States of America. A new pattern emerged, and powerful dynamics of reciprocal imitation wove invisible threads between Europe and America.

As I said before, "global political lineups" were woven back in time, when early modern empires were engaged in endless mimetic confrontations.[29] The ideological cement of their action, the strategy of rationalization of this early clash of civilizations, was religion.

Ideologically the struggle against Islam offered a descriptive language that allowed the generally shabby ventures in America to be vested with a seemingly eschatological significance.[30]

Religion, in other words, was the "text" in which early modern empires framed their political claims. In Fuchs's words,

> Once Islam and England have been equated as threats, the old analogy between the Reconquista of Spanish territory from the Moors and the Conquista of the New World plays itself out in reverse: because both Spain and America are newly threatened by infidels and heretics, they now merit

equal protection as strongholds of the Faith. Religious discourse cloaks imperial competition in the borrowed dignity of a crusade, much as the talk of conversions had dignified Spain's original New World conquests.[31]

And religion remains a critical strategy of rationalization of today's global mimetic lineups.

The mimetic explanation of the pattern has several advantages. Discourse of elite groups, strategy, and decision-making is so steeped with assumptions concerning the actors' capacity for (original) agency that the mimetic explanation seems to debunk the very premises of the individuation model. A discourse of imitation and "mimetic mirroring" challenges the epistemic self-sufficiency of the model and opens up different scenarios. It relativizes the role played by individual actors and their *reasons*. England had reasons to fight Spain, and Spain, in turn, had reasons to counter the push of the Ottoman Empire. The causal narratives invoked by historians hinge on the reasons of the actors involved. Imitation complicates these stories of individuation by challenging one of their conceptual tenets, namely, the underlying notion of agency. Only *originals* are full-fledged agents, possessing the capacity of fully appreciating the causal implications of their actions. Mimetic clones are only accidental actors in history.

◆   ◆   ◆

Historians are keen on attributing original intentions to historical actors, so that whatever is *not* original is said to be derivative and clichéd. Mimetic dynamics *are* political processes that find their place in the thin interstice between original and nonoriginal, an interstice in which nothing interesting, or historically relevant, is said to happen. Fuchs has pointed out that "in our post-romantic era, we still assign disproportionate value to originals."[32] Failure to acknowledge the mimetic mirroring occurring in the reciprocal dealing between different polities has the effect of biasing our perceptions and obscuring the dyadic dynamics that compound historical processes.

Exposing mimesis in historical processes, however, is not an attempt at relativizing the moral responsibility of historical actors. Moral responsibility is not diminished by the fact that either state or individual agency is compounded by mimetic drives, and that some historical outcomes are not distinctively original. What we miss is, possibly, a different conception of

agency, one that does not fully rely on the myth of an individual actor imper-
meable to external influences.

Our obsession with originals seems even more compelling as soon as our
discourse discloses normative implications, as when we concern ourselves
with those supranational polities to which some people attach undisputed
imperial properties. It is in particular the United States that seems nowadays
especially amenable to a discourse about imperialism, and any reference to
mimetic mirroring sounds like an attempt to relativize, and therefore minimize, the responsibility of the U.S. administration.

Interestingly, Fuchs herself is cautious in pushing forth an account of
historical processes where mimetic dynamics take over agency and develop a
logic and momentum of their own. Fuchs argues instead for a "revaluation"
of imitation as a "cultural and political practice" that actors stage self-con-
sciously. The contexts that she explores show that the actors involved remain
in charge of their actions; mimesis is a strategic option that they choose, and
"a calculated deployment of similarity" is the outcome of a thoughtful decision that eliminates the other option, "the defense of difference."[33] Similarly,
a "deliberate enactment of imitation" is what historians have failed to see as
they have succumbed to the myth of ontological primacy of originals over
facsimiles.[34]

When Fuchs talks about "ideologies of differences" she refers to something that historians have fabricated despite historical evidence. The actors
who feature in her narrative, in other words, *knew* they were imitating originals, and did nothing to conceal their dabbling in mimetic exchanges. It is
the assumption of exceptionalism that biases our understanding of imperial
narratives, and Fuchs's Lacanian approach to historical truths is designed
to redress a bias embedded in the ways we look at the past. She argues that
"where ideologies of difference seek to solidify distinctions, mimesis recalls
underlying likenesses."[35] But these likenesses, in Fuchs's analysis, were *inten-
tionally* enacted; they were generated by mimetic attitudes that brought
strategic advantages to their authors.

Fuchs's book is an interesting insight into the different ontological
perspective implied by mimetic theory. She tries to take facsimiles away
from the minor ontology in which they have been confined and show that
the traces they left suggest a crucial historical role. Not every actor claiming a "singular entitlement" to a given course of action turns out to be an

original, and the search for a historical matrix may turn into a frustrating infinity regression.

Speaking of actors claiming a singular entitlement to action, mimetic theory shows that not only European history but world history too "cannot be written as the history of individual states." The dyadic patterns that operate in history leave barely visible traces, and we rely on models that fail to detect those traces. Mimetic explanations dissolve the lines of responsibility that we try to trace, to single original actors, carriers of a singular entitlement to action. For *only originals are responsible.* Interestingly, all attempts to deconstruct the lexicon of authority and responsibility that dominates the study of ethics, let alone politics and international relations, was done by borrowing from such authors as Foucault, Lacan, Kristeva, and, more recently, Butler, on the assumption that in order to liberate the discourse on human morals from its authoritarian structure one needed to revisit and critique its subjectivist underpinnings. These new insights, though, seem difficult to match "with the discipline of International Relations whose defining moment is sovereignty, statehood, and an international system variously defined as anarchic or state societal. Despite inroads made by normative theory, questions of ethics remain in the margins of the discipline."[36]

And it is within the realm of ethics that the classical discourse of agency and responsibility has been subject to radical challenges. However, this book is not crediting a poststructuralist type of revision of such notion. The brand of mimetic theory put forth in this book acknowledges agency as a process, not as a quality that humans possess as a given, but as a transient condition of suspension of mimetic reciprocity. The attempt to bring mimetic theory to bear, and replace a classical conception of responsibility with a more nuanced understanding of agency, has the advantage of explaining a penumbra of phenomena that are hard to acknowledge and difficult to explain through the canonical discourse of agency.

The epistemology supported by mimetic theory acknowledges the working of dyads, not individual originals. Globalization does not per se challenge the individuation model, although "a globalized environment" makes the epistemic warrants of the model look more and more suspect. It is true that it is becoming "difficult if not impossible to understand one system in isolation," but our normative models bias our understanding of the complicated patterns that structure global politics.

We consistently apply such (normative) terms as justice and democracy to international politics on the assumption that all actors possess a distinctive capacity for agency, that is, they are "originals" engaged in actions to which they are (normatively) entitled. The normative lexicon of responsibility, if applied consistently and comprehensively, rules out all facts and phenomena that fall short of the standard of agency. The mimetic approach suspends this lexicon and favors a meta-normative language in which the principal actors are not primarily "subjects of responsibility" but *forces* operating in a mimetic scenario dominated by dyadic patterns.

In chapter 4 I have suggested that the forces that struggle and "battle to the end" have a chance of becoming subjects of freedom and responsibility through "reflective justice." The problem is that Girard's theory sets standards of subjectivity that are almost impossible to reach: the becoming-subject of the individual occurs only on occasion of the final establishment of the Kingdom, when the subject-of-desire is fully individualized. Individuation, the making of fully-fledged subjectivities, of full-grown subjects of responsibilities, is granted instead by the reflective acknowledgment that the violence that sets us apart "operates without a reason." Sacred, in this context, is the residual belief that the ultimate sources of moral edification on which we would want to rely reside within ourselves, in the dealings and stipulations that constitute the fabric of a reflective society. The temptation to seek assistance and solace from an external divinity, from a simulacrum of deity operating in this world, is therefore "sacred."

The mimetic solution to the normative dilemmas posed by IR theory rejects the standard account of the actors' demand for "satisfaction." The classical normative solution applies to the thick ontology of the individuationist model, and supports systems of distributive justice as the classical normative means to appease rivalries and establish durable institutions. In contrast, the reflective justice put forth in chapter 4 acknowledges the mimetic sources of (most) human conflicts. It challenges the kind of bad reciprocity that forces conflicts to escalate. Mimetic antagonism compounds itself in a cumulative structure that strains the institutional configuration of democracies. Spirals of violence reverberate in the political spectrum of Western nations and polarize opinions and views to the extreme.

Girard believes that "we have entered an era in which anthropology will become a more suitable tool than political science."[37] Seen from a mimetic perspective, globalization breeds the formation of a number of "Siamese twins," states, para-states, and transnational actors that operate without the bounds of age-old juridical ties. Their fluid nature makes them vulnerable to the mimetic fluxes that straddle the unified world of globalization.

One of the major intuitions of the late Girard is that in global politics the mimetic dynamic is the same as the one that operates in early sacrificial societies: mimetic desire generates rivalries, and unless the whole process is stopped by ad hoc interventions, it is bound to produce doubles that tend to aggregate in ever larger symmetrical configurations. "In the beginning the mimetic rivalries may be separated centers of attention, but then they tend to contaminate each other more and more, becoming more mimetically attractive as they include more rivals, since mimesis is cumulative."[38]

This cumulative process of progressive compounding of cleavages terminates when all these mimetic "centers" have collapsed into one single mimetic struggle, comprehending all others. It is a situation that corresponds to the Girardian "extreme," an apocalyptic climax in which mimesis, and humanity, consume themselves "to the end."

I believe that reflection, our ability to think "recursively" about things and about ourselves, and not sacrifice, is the very last protection of which we can avail, after the eventual exhaustion of earlier sacrificial strategies.[39] Protecting the life and politics of "he that wants protection" is a difficult task, in times where the temptation to relapse into the *easy* way, the sacrificial way of handling conflicts, looms on the horizon. The concluding chapter of the volume envisions a situation of absolute desacralization, a final emptying of the last residues of the sacred. It would be a radical cultural development, similar to the kind of "purgation from pity and fears" that Aristotle called *catharsis,* a clarification, a disclosure, a special insight into things human delivered by exposure to truth. A political theology of the empty tomb would be the foundation of a new politics, in which the mimetic sources of human conflicts were reflectively acknowledged and the demands of "he that wants protection" were finally met.

# Notes

## Introduction

1. This is the description of a large-scale photograph shown at the exhibition *Post-Modernism: Style and Subversion 1970–1990* held at the MART Museum of Rovereto, in northern Italy, in May 2012.

2. Slavoj Žižek, *How to Read Lacan* (London: Granta, 2006), 38ff.

3. The expression "animal spirits" is from John M. Keynes, *The General Theory of Employment, Interest and Money* (London: Macmillan, 1936), 162.

4. René Girard, *Evolution and Conversion: Dialogues on the Origins of Culture,* ed. P. Antonello and J.C. de Castro Rocha (London: Continuum, 2008), viii.

5. A strong case for the persistence of forms of sacrifice in modern politics, contrary to the common understanding that proclaims sacrifice a relic of premodern times, was made by Paul Kahn: "modernity does not end the link of sovereignty to sacrifice." *Sacred Violence: Torture, Terror, and Sovereignty* (Ann Arbor: University of Michigan Press, 2008), 35.

6. Thomas Hobbes, *Leviathan,* ed. E. Curley (Indianapolis: Hackett, 1994), 243.

7. I have always been wary of the several definitions of politics involving struggle or competition for power. Unlike a number of animal collectives in which significant strains of cooperation and competition suggest similarities with human forms of aggregation, *political* units are distinctively and exclusively human so long as their foremost concern is to exercise some sort of protection for at least some of their members. This attempt at definition could be challenged in different ways. However, from a mimetic perspective, the political element that characterizes human societies is not struggle per se (which is not distinctively human) but the ability to practice sacrifice as a means of protection against mimetic drifts.

8. Hobbes, *Leviathan,* 219.

9. Girard, *Evolution and Conversion,* 219.

10. On the "escalation to extremes," see René Girard, *Battling to the End: Conversations with Benoît Chantre* (East Lansing: Michigan State University Press, 2010), chapter 1.

11. Martha C. Nussbaum and Amartya Sen, eds., *The Quality of Life* (Oxford: Clarendon, 1989), 317.

12. "Normative International Relations discourse is largely modeled on debates in moral philosophy, with ontological foundations based on a Kantian conception of autonomous individuality." Vivienne Jabri, "Restyling the Subject of Responsibility in International Relations," *Millennium Journal of International Studies* 27, no. 3 (1998): 593.

13. Herfried Münkler, *Die neuen Kriege* (Reinbeck: Rowohlt, 2003).

14. Harald Wydra, *Communism and the Emergence of Democracy* (Cambridge: Cambridge University Press, 2007), 59.

## Chapter 1. A New (Mimetic) Paradigm for Our Postsacrificial Times

1. Girard, *Battling to the End,* 2.

2. It all started with the discovery of a cluster of neurons that do not belong to the purely perceptual and cognitive functions of the brain. Mirror neurons fire when one observes and captures the intention of someone performing an action, as if the action were processed imitatively by a specific part of the brain. For an overview see Cowdell, "Hard Evidence," 219–26.

3. René Girard, *I See Satan Fall Like Lightning,* trans. James G. Williams (Maryknoll, NY: Orbis Books, 2001), 11.

4. Necati Polat's is a most recent attempt to revisit a number of issues and concepts in IR theory from a noncanonical perspective that acknowledges the significance of mimesis in politics. *International Relations: Meaning and Mimesis* (London and New York: Routledge 2012).

5. Daniele Caramani, ed. *Comparative Politics* (Oxford: Oxford University Press, 2008), 55.

6. Mark Juergensmeyer, *Terror in the Mind of God: The Global Rise of Religious Violence,* 3rd ed. (Berkeley: University of California Press, 2003), 169.

7. "Girard's point is that humans are first competitive before they are aggressive." Peter Stork, "Human Rights: Controlling the Uncontrollable?" in Cowdell, Fleming, and Hodge, *Violence, Desire, and the Sacred,* 206.

8. Stork, "Human Rights," 206.

9. John Keane, *Violence and Democracy* (Cambridge: Cambridge University Press, 2004), 8.

10. Keane, *Violence and Democracy,* 11. This is, to be sure, a fundamental misunderstanding of Girard on violence. Mark Anspach puts the point strikingly: "People are not fundamentally violent, they are fundamentally social. Once they have satisfied their material instincts—eating and reproducing—they still sense a lack. They desire something more, but what?" Mark Anspach, "Global Markets, Anonymous Victims," *The UNESCO Courier,* May 2001.

11. Keane, *Violence and Democracy,* 8.

12. Wydra, *Communism,* 16.

13. Wydra, *Communism,* 16.

14. Jean-Pierre Dupuy and Paul Dumouchel, *L'enfer des choses* (Paris: Seuil, 1979). *The Ambivalence of Scarcity and Other Essays* (East Lansing: Michigan State University Press, 2014) contains an English translation of Dumouchel's section of *L'Enfer des choses*.

15. Barbara Fuchs, *Mimesis and Empires: The New World, Islam, and European Identities* (Cambridge: Cambridge University Press, 2001), 4.

16. Fuchs, *Mimesis and Empires*, 5.

17. René Girard, *Violence and the Sacred*, trans. Patrick Gregory (Baltimore: Johns Hopkins University Press, 1977), 146.

18. Girard, *Violence and the Sacred*, 145.

19. Girard, *Violence and the Sacred*, 79.

20. Girard, *Battling to the End*, 41.

21. Girard, *Battling to the End*, 56.

22. Girard, *Battling to the End*, 11.

23. Girard, *Battling to the End*, 183.

24. Girard, *Battling to the End*, 14.

25. Girard, *Battling to the End*, xiv.

26. Girard, *Battling to the End*, 62.

27. "The mimetic nature of this process is particularly obvious in rituals, where all these stages of development are re-enacted. Why does the ritual so often begin with concocted disorder, with a deliberate simulated cultural crisis, and end with a victim who is expelled or ritually killed? The purpose is simply to re-enact the mimetic crisis which leads to the scapegoat mechanism. The hope is that the re-enactment of this mechanism will reactivate its power of reconciliation." Girard, *Evolution and Conversion*, 65.

28. Girard fails to be specific about this point, and always presents the sacred as a cultural practice, namely, as "sacrifice" and its ritualization in ever less violent forms. However, the principal condition for the sacred to operate in human communities is a "collective delusion." The sacred configuration (and the attendant cultural practices) of human sociality hold so long as humans are prey of this collective (and highly instrumental) misunderstanding of the actual motives of social aggregation.

29. René Girard, "Generative Scapegoating," in *Violent Origins: Walter Burkert, René Girard, and Jonathan Z. Smith on Ritual Killing and Cultural Formation*, ed. R. G. Hamerton-Kelly (Stanford, CA: Stanford University Press, 1987), 84.

30. See Walter Burkert, *Homo Necans: The Anthropology of Ancient Greek Sacrificial Ritual and Myth* (Berkeley: University of California Press, 1986).

31. Kahn, *Sacred Violence*, 120.

32. Communities exist so long as people share a common experience of the sacred, and it is through this experience that such terms as torture and terror are framed by a community; "when the community is no longer felt to bear a sacred meaning . . . we will be done with torture and terror except as a problem of individual pathology to be met with the twin institutions of therapy and criminal law." Kahn, *Sacred Violence*, 178.

33. "There is a structural difference between archaic religion and Christianity. Within an archaic

framework, one doesn't realize that the scapegoat is only a scapegoat. One believes that the victim is guilty, because everybody says so. In the Gospel there is also a moment of unanimity when all the disciples run away from Jesus and go with the crowd. Then the unanimity is destroyed by the Resurrection, and the disciples, who are (directly or indirectly) responsible for the Gospels, denounce the crowd and the scapegoat system as well." Girard, *Evolution and Conversion,* 218.

34. Girard, *Battling to the End,* 19.

35. "Mimesis is cumulative." Girard, *Evolution and Conversion,* 66.

36. Girard, *Violence and the Sacred,* 231.

37. Girard, *Violence and the Sacred,* 24 and 231.

38. "The more there is an opening in a world where ritual is dead, the more dangerous this world becomes. It has both positive aspects, in the sense that there is less sacrifice, and negative aspects, in that there is an unleashing of mimetic rivalry." Girard, *Evolution and Conversion,* 254.

39. Girard, *Evolution and Conversion,* 21.

40. R. Brandon, *Making It Explicit: Reasoning, Representing, and Discursive Commitment* (Cambridge: Harvard University Press, 1994), 8.

41. Steven Pinker, *The Better Angels of Our Nature: Why Violence Has Declined* (New York: Penguin, 2011), 583.

42. Joseph Raz, *Engaging Reason: On the Theory of Value and Action* (Oxford: Oxford University Press, 1999), 73. Raz has expanded on "the reason-dependent character of desires" in *The Morality of Freedom* (Oxford: Clarendon, 1986), 140–43.

43. Akeel Bilgrami, *Self-Knowledge and Resentment* (Cambridge: Harvard University Press, 2006), 99.

44. John von Neumann and Oskar Morgenstern, *Theory of Games and Economic Behavior,* ed. A. Rubinstein (Princeton: Princeton University Press, 2007), 224.

45. Harold W. Kuhn and Sylvia Nasar, eds., *The Essential John Nash* (Princeton: Princeton University Press, 2001), xiii.

46. Kuhn and Nasar, *The Essential John Nash,* xix.

47. J. Henrich, R. Boyd, S. Bowles, C. Camerer, E. Fehr, and H. Gintis, *Foundations of Human Sociality: Economic Experiments and Ethnographic Evidence from Fifteen Small-Scale Societies* (Oxford: Oxford University Press, 2004), 8.

48. Bernard Williams, "Internal and External Reasons," in *Rational Action,* ed. Ross Harrison (Cambridge: Cambridge University Press, 1980), 17–28. This issue had been one of the centerpieces of Williams's philosophical agenda since the early 1970s.

49. Pinker, *Better Angels,* 585.

50. Plutarch, "Life of Pelopidas," in *The Age of Alexander: Nine Greek Lives,* trans. Ian Scott-Kilvert (New York: Penguin, 2012), 52.

51. Charles Larmore, *Les pratiques du moi* (Paris: PUF, 2004), 61 (italics added).

## Chapter 2. The Mimetic Context of the "New Wars"

1. Richard N. Haas, "The Age of Nonpolarity," *Foreign Affairs,* May–June 2008, 44–56.

2. Allen Feldman, "Deterritorialized Wars of Public Safety," in *State, Sovereignty, War: Civil Violence in Emerging Global Realities,* ed. Bruce Kapferer (Oxford: Berghahn Books, 2004), 17.

3. Readers may object that this attempt to generalize the individuationist model is a nice exercise in straw man construction. I use the term "individuationist" *largissimo sensu* to indicate that such "units" as individuals, groups, states, etc. remain, if not a locus of agency, the ultimate realities in IR theory. It is tempting to universalize the critique of Alexander Wendt to Kenneth Waltz, that despite his "professed structuralism, ultimately he is an individualist" (Alexander Wendt, *Social Theory of International Politics* [Cambridge: Cambridge University Press, 1999], 15). I am not denying some actual differences, but I believe that mimetic theory offers a new vantage point from where the distinctions negotiated by scholars in IR theory (mainly along the agency-structure axis) seem to vanish. Individual units, whether their capacity for agency is localized or dissolved, are *not* the ultimate realities in the IRs. One of the aims of this chapter (the general aim) is to credit the mimetic perspective with special epistemological value, and present it as a valuable resource for IR theorists.

4. Douglas Lemke and William Reed, "The Relevance of Politically Relevant Dyads," *Journal of Conflict Resolution* 45, no. 1 (2001): 126–44.

5. John A. Vasquez, *The War Puzzle* (Cambridge: Cambridge University Press, 1993), 75.

6. "Wars of rivalry are wars between equals." Vasquez, *The War Puzzle,* 64.

7. Retrospectively, the British Empire and the Spanish Empire can be considered members of a mimetic dyad—as illustrated by Barbara Fuchs—whereas the United States and Vietnam are definitely not. Girard himself puts the point strikingly when he discusses envy as a specific form of rivalry. Fuchs, *Mimesis and Empires.* To Girard "all envy is mimetic, but not all mimetic desire is envious." *A Theater of Envy: William Shakespeare* (New York: Oxford University Press, 1991), 5.

8. Girard's incursion into IR theory is limited to parts of *Battling to the End.*

9. Girard, *Violence and the Sacred,* 46.

10. Kalevi J. Holsti, *The State, War, and the State of War* (Cambridge: Cambridge University Press, 1996), 12.

11. For this notion of *Asymmetrisierung* see Münkler, *Die neuen Kriege.* I shall use (very sparingly) such notions as "asymmetry" and "asymmetrization" in ways that are consistent with Münkler's use of the terms.

12. Girard, *Battling to the End,* 57.

13. Girard, *Battling to the End,* 56.

14. Herfried Münkler, *The New Wars* (London: Polity, 2004), 144.

15. Mary Kaldor, *New and Old Wars* (London: Blackwell, 1999), 109.

16. Vasquez, *The War Puzzle,* 75.

17. John A. Vasquez, ed., *What Do We Know about War?* (Lanham, MD: Rowman & Littlefield, 2012)—notably chapters 4 and 5—revisits the concept of rivalry by testing its applicability in the field of IR. Brandon Valeriano seeks to determine "what the field knows about the origins of rivalry" to explain the process of rivalry development. Brandon Valeriano, "Becoming Rivals: The Process of Rivalry Development" in Vasquez, *What Do We Know about War?* 81.

18. There are minor internal fractures within the same paradigm. An interesting contribution to the discussion is an article by Goertz, Jones, and Diehl that challenges the "repeated conflicts"

literature (which focuses on the impact of recent disputes), and argues for the primacy of the longer term history of the rivalry in explaining recurring conflicts. Gary Goertz, Bradford Jones, and Paul F. Diehl, "Maintenance Processes in International Rivalries," *Journal of Conflict Resolution* 49 (2005): 742–69.

19. The most widely used data set on international rivalries was offered in Paul Diehl and Gary Goertz, *War and Peace in International Rivalry* (Ann Arbor: University of Michigan Press, 2000). More recently Klein, Goertz, and Diehl introduced new conceptual criteria, like "rivalry symmetry," to amend an earlier collection strategy. James P. Klein, Gary Goertz, and Paul F. Diehl, "The New Rivalry Dataset: Procedures and Patterns," *Journal of Peace Research* 43 (2006): 331–48. However, it does not challenge the genetic story of how rivalries come about but it rather tackles *other* rivalry collections.

20. Girard, *Evolution and Conversion*, 57.

21. This passage has been synthesized by Girard in his conversations with Pierpaolo Antonello and João de Castro Rocha, in the section "Scapegoating and Social Order," *Evolution and Conversion*, 64ff.

22. Bernard Wasserstein, *Israelis and Palestinians: Why Do They Fight? Can They Stop?* (New Haven, CT: Yale University Press, 2001), 3.

23. David Hare, *Via Dolorosa & When Shall We Live* (London: Faber & Faber, 1998), 7.

24. Benny Morris, *Righteous Victims: A History of the Zionist-Arab Conflict, 1881–2001* (New York: Knopf, 2001), 635.

25. Morris, *Righteous Victims*, 612.

26. Hallward shows how scholarly discourse and methods of analysis in IR theory bias the representation of the Israeli-Palestinian conflict, and not merely in academic forums. It is the very notion of "conflict" that is fraught with assumptions that bias the argument towards one set of conclusions. Maia Hallward, "International Relations Scholarship, Academic Institutions, and the Israeli-Palestinian Conflict," *Cambridge Review of International Affairs* 2 (2010): 259–80.

27. See http://cdsweb.cern.ch/record/1054838.

28. See http://www.focus.de/politik/ausland/nahost/jugendtreffen_aid_113064.html.

29. Similarities between Israelis and Palestinians, though, are not registered only at the boutique level. Stanley Fish, "Boutique Multiculturalism, or Why Liberals Are Incapable of Thinking about Hate Speech," *Critical Inquiry* 1 (1997): 378–95.

> "After a colloquium on the narrative of creation, a deputy representative of a league of mosques confessed: 'I didn't know that we had so many religious traits in common' (*Ich wusste gar nicht, dass wir so viele religiöse Gemeinsamkeiten haben*)." Brigitte Jähnigen, "Miteinender Reden," *Jüdische Allgemeine*, January 28, 2010, 10.

30. Livia Manera, "Multiculturalismo, un'invenzione," *Corriere della Sera*, October 5, 2008, 35; italics added.

31. Stressing similarities is indeed the strategy pursued by *all* multiculturalists, not only the naive ones. If one looks at the discourse of the women peace activists on both sides of the Israeli-Palestinian divide, one can see that "the underlying assumption has been that successful alliances should be based on similarities, and therefore that Palestinian women had to change and become more like Israeli-Jewish women." Simona Sharoni, *Gender and the Israeli-Palestinian Conflict: The Politics of Women's Resistance* (Syracuse, NY: Syracuse University Press, 1995), 143.

32. There is, to be sure, no "authentic" Israeli or Arab cuisine: "The cuisine of the Levant—Syria, Lebanon and Israel—is a blend of Persian, Arabic, Turkish, and Sephardic influences." Gil Marks, *Olive Trees and Honey: A Treasury of Vegetarian Recipes from Jewish Communities around the World* (Hoboken, NJ: Wiley, 2004), 10.

33. Think of the seeming paradoxical reading proposed by Katja Lüthge in a brilliant review of this film in the German newspaper *Berliner Zeitung:* "Does the solution of the Middle East problem lie in the temporary resettlement [*Umsiedlung*] of the whole population of the Middle East in New York?" Katja Lüthge, "Bis in die Spitzen: 'Leg dich nicht mit Zohan an': Adam Sandler in einer Frisöragentenkomödie," *Berliner Zeitung,* August 14, 2008.

34. Girard, *Battling to the End,* 10.

35. Girard, *Battling to the End,* 42.

36. This last paragraph may sound controversial, as the process of undifferentiation remains ambiguous in Girard, and one can distinguish a long-term, *cultural* undifferentiation, and a short-term, *tactical* indifferentiation, which is the one examined in the book on Clausewitz.

37. Kaldor, *New and Old Wars,* 110.

38. Surveying all these variants of a broader genus is not within the scope of this chapter. For an overview and a critique see Errol Henderson and David J. Singer, "'New Wars' and Rumors of 'New Wars,'" *International Interactions* 28, no. 2 (2002): 165–90.

39. Thomas X. Hammes, "War Evolves into the Fourth Generation," in *Global Insurgency and the Future of Armed Conflict: Debating Fourth-Generation Warfare,* ed. Terry Terriff, Aaron Karp, and Regina Karp (New York: Routledge, 2008), 21–44; and William S. Lind, Keith Nightengale, John F. Schmitt, Joseph W. Sutton, and Gary I. Wilson, "The Changing Face of War: Into the Fourth Generation," in Terriff, Karp, and Karp, *Global Insurgency,* 13–20.

40. Henderson and Singer, "New Wars," 165ff.

41. Kaldor's approach to both NWs and cosmopolitan democracy, for one thing, has been criticized by authors of both neorealist and constructivist persuasion.

42. Pippa Norris and Ronald Inglehart, *Sacred and Secular: Religion and Politics Worldwide* (Cambridge: Cambridge University Press, 2004), 241.

43. Girard, *Battling to the End,* 47.

44. Holsti, *State, War,* 195.

45. Kaldor, *New and Old Wars,* 109. Kaldor continues by saying that "the new wars have political goals. The aim is political mobilization on the basis of identity. The military strategy for achieving this aim is population displacement and destabilization so as to get rid of those whose identity is different and to foment hatred and fear" (110).

46. "The impenetrable web of motives and causes, which often leaves no prospect of lasting peace, is a direct consequence of the fact that it is not states but para-state players that confront one another in the new wars." Münkler, *The New Wars,* 8.

47. Idean Salehyan, *Rebels without Borders: Transnational Insurgencies in World Politics* (Ithaca: Cornell University Press, 2011), 171.

48. Holsti, *State, War,* xii.

49. Girard himself puts the point strikingly, implying that identity claims help rationalize the difference from one's mimetic rival, especially when this rivalry reaches a climax of

undifferentiation and conflict. "Everyone now knows that the looming conflict between the United States and China, for example, has nothing to do with a 'clash of civilizations,' despite what some might try to tell us. *We always try to see differences where in fact there are none*" (Girard, *Battling to the End,* 42; italics added).

50. Julie Flint and Alex De Waal, *Darfur: A Short History of a Long War* (New York: Zed Books, 2005), 3. See the TV documentary *Darfour: Autopsie d'une Tragédie,* by Christoph Ayad and Vincent De Cointet, broadcast on December 6, 2007, by ARTE France.

51. Daoud Hari, *The Translator: A Memoir* (New York: Random House, 2008), 187. Hagan and Rymond-Richmond found that the creation of an Arab/black African divide especially in Darfur dated back twenty years before the escalation of the civil war. John Hagan and Wenona Rymond-Richmond, *Darfur and the Crime of Genocide* (New York: Cambridge University Press, 2009), 111.

52. Sumantra Bose, *Contested Lands: Israel-Palestine, Kashmir, Bosnia, Cyprus, and Sri Lanka.* (Cambridge: Harvard University Press, 2010), 122.

53. Kaldor, *New and Old Wars,* 6. What for Kaldor is a "paradigm case" is described by Holsti as "the Bosnia prototype." Holsti, *State, War,* 192.

54. Kaldor, *New and Old Wars,* 35.

55. Stevan M. Weine, *When History Is a Nightmare: Lives and Memories of Ethnic Cleansing in Bosnia-Herzegovina* (New Brunswick, NJ: Rutgers University Press, 1999), 19. "Far from seeing the violence as evidence of ethnic ties . . . one could argue that Bosnia shows how weak and how fluid political identity really is." John E. Mueller, *The Remnants of War* (Ithaca: Cornell University Press, 2004), 197. Mueller was reporting the views of Cheryl Bernard, who worked with Muslim refugees early in the Bosnia war.

56. Girard, *Battling to the End,* 62.

57. Girard, *Battling to the End,* 103.

58. Girard, *Battling to the End,* 47.

59. Girard, *Battling to the End,* 42.

60. Girard, *Battling to the End,* 57.

61. Girard, *Battling to the End,* 183.

62. For a rich and sweeping account of the East/West contest, see Anthony Pagden, *Worlds at War* (Oxford: Oxford University Press, 2008).

63. Girard suggests that the escalation of inimical reciprocity may take place between Arab nations and the Western world. "Note that it has already begun: the exchange of attacks and American 'interventions' can only accelerate, as each side responds to the other. Violence will continue on its way" (Girard, *Evolution and Conversion,* 20).

64. Girard, *Evolution and Conversion,* 24 and 18.

65. Pagden, *Worlds at War,* 517; Girard, *Battling to the End,* 20.

66. Girard, *Violence and the Sacred,* 231.

67. The Peace Research Institute in the Middle East founded by scholars from both sides at the Ben-Gurion University in Israel is working on a handbook of the history of the Israeli/Palestinian conflict that seeks to accommodate both perspectives. Similarly, scholars at the University of

Skopje in Macedonia are working on an Albanian/Macedonian history book. A. Schenk, "Die Geschichte der Anderen," *Die Zeit,* June 10, 2009, 65. These handbooks are designed to provide an external insight into a mimetic scenario in which each member of the dyad "from the inside" always believes in its difference, whereas the two members, from the outside, would look like what they actually are: "simple doubles" (Girard, *Battling to the End,* 14). Here the external insight into the Israeli/Palestinian conflict is provided by the Georg-Eckert-Institut für internationale Schulbuchforschung in Braunschweig, Germany, which sponsors the project.

68. On the critical, reciprocal implication between the discourse of victimhood and mimetic theory, I wish to redirect the reader to Wydra, "Victims and New Wars," *Cambridge Review of International Affairs* 26, no. 1 (2013): 159–60.

69. Girard, *Battling to the End,* 10.

## Chapter 3. Cleavage Lines in Global Politics

1. Elias Canetti, *Masse und Macht* (Frankfurt, Germany am Main: Fischer Verlag, 1994), 188.

2. Cass Sunstein, *Going to Extremes: How Like Minds Unite and Divide* (New York: Oxford University Press, 2009). The notion of "cumulative cleavage positions" is in G. Bingham Powell, "Political Cleavage Structure, Cross-Pressure Processes, and Partisanship: An Empirical Test of the Theory," *American Political Science Review* 1 (1976): 1–23.

3. Norberto Bobbio argues that the debate on the left/right cleavage is "still very much alive, in spite of constant references to its demise." *Left and Right: The Significance of a Political Distinction* (Chicago: University of Chicago Press, 1996), 84.

4. Giovanni Sartori, *Teoria dei partiti e caso italiano* (Milan: SugarCo, 1982), 255. However, the filling of either left or right with new content does not build on a complete vacuum. In a way, the original imprinting of the dichotomy, its being designed to host polar approaches to equality, is constitutive of the ways the dichotomy has been construed over the course of its history.

5. Equality still plays a major role in polarizing the political spectrum: "the contemporary opposition between the left and the right is thus a conflict over the meaning of equality in a modern, predominantly liberal society." Alain Noël and Jean-Philippe Thérien, *Left and Right in Global Politics* (Cambridge: Cambridge University Press, 2008), 19. On equality as the discriminating criterion to distinguish between left and right, see Bobbio, *Left and Right.* For an overview, and a thoughtful critique of Bobbio, see Ambrogio Santambrogio, *Destra e sinistra: Un'analisi sociologica* (Rome: Laterza, 1998).

6. For the notion of "polarization" see Giacomo Sani and Giovanni Sartori, "Polarization, Fragmentation and Competition in Western Democracies," in *West European Party Systems: Continuity and Change,* ed. Hans Daalder and Peter Mair (London: Sage, 1983), 307–40.

7. It might be argued that a clearer distinction needs to be made between "international" and "global." To be sure, the two are not the same. This is particularly true of the principal case dealt with in this chapter, for Israel is an example of an international issue that turned global. Other international issues remain international and never turn global. Sometimes, however, the two notions are interchangeable, and international and global are two different "levels of address." In other cases, the difference is mainly rhetorical, such as when international terrorism (a correct phrasing in my view) becomes "global terror."

8. Noël and Thérien, *Left and Right,* 198.

9. Marco Revelli, *Sinistra Destra. L'identità smarrita* (Roma-Bari: Laterza, 2007), 203.

10. International actors can "manipulate the U.S. domestic political system directly, by *penetrating* the American body politic." Stephen M. Walt, *Taming American Power: The Global Response to U.S. Primacy* (New York: Norton, 2005), 25.

11. Robin Shepherd, *A State beyond the Pale: Europe's Problem with Israel* (London: Weidenfeld & Nicolson, 2009), 9. I agree, and this is the point of this chapter, that the Israel-Palestine conflict is taking place over a major ideological fault line. I disagree with Shepherd that the fault line is civilizational. I believe that Shepherd has a point when he argues that "as Frenchmen, Germans, Britons, Dutchmen, Italians, Spaniards, Swedes, Poles or indeed Americans, we come to the question of Israel and the Middle East with assumptions that are quintessentially Western. And, as anyone who follows this conflict in even the most cursory way knows, mere mention of Israel opens up a schism in the mind of the West like no other."

12. Noël and Thérien, *Left and Right*, 8.

13. One of the reasons why Israel is polarizing the global political spectrum is possibly "the more or less conscious identification of Israel with 'the West.'" A. Levi, "Prefazione all'edizione italiana," in W. D. Rubinstein, *La sinistra, la destra e gli ebrei* (Bologna: Il Mulino, 1986), xii. Arrigo Levi, in his introduction to the Italian edition of Rubinstein's book, stressed the "anti-Occidentalism" of the Western lefts: "for a curious turn of their fate, the Zionist Jews—the Israelis who created the Jewish state to escape the persecution of the West—are suffering the same extreme consequences of the kind of anti-Occidentalist masochism that the West, its historical triumphs and successes notwithstanding, has nourished within itself."

14. Andrei S. Markovits, "The European and American Left since 1945," *Dissent,* Winter (2005), 12.

15. Stefano Bartolini, *The Political Mobilization of the European Left, 1860–1980: The Class Cleavage* (Cambridge: Cambridge University Press, 2000).

16. See Sunstein, *Going to Extremes;* Bill Bishop, *The Big Sort: Why the Clustering of Like-Minded America is Tearing Us Apart* (Boston: Mariner Books, 2009); Marc J. Hetherington and Jonathan D. Weiler, *Authoritarianism and Polarization in American Politics* (Cambridge: Cambridge University Press, 2009).

17. See chapter 4 ("Class Dismissed") of Geoff Nunberg, *Talking Right: How Conservatives Turned Liberalism into a Tax-Raising, Latte-Drinking, Sushi-Eating, Volvo-Driving, New York Times–Reading, Body-Piercing, Hollywood-Loving, Left-Wing Freak Show* (New York: PublicAffairs, 2007). J. P. Diggins has offered a sweeping account of the ideological transformations of the left in America. "The first stirrings of the post-war Left originated in the civil rights movement." John Patrick Diggins, *The Rise and Fall of the American Left* (New York: Norton, 1992), 238.

18. Anthony Giddens, *Beyond Left and Right: The Future of Radical Politics* (Stanford: Stanford University Press, 1994), 18.

19. Bartolini, *Political Mobilization,* 554.

20. The process is not as smooth as it may appear, and the shift from class to identity is subject to spasms and recoil. Writing in the immediate aftermath of the 2008 American elections, Bradley R. Schiller argued that "the preferred ploy of Democrats these days is the 'class' card. Democrats have increasingly tried to redefine the 'them vs. us' struggle in terms of class rather than color." Bradley Schiller, "The Futility of Class Warfare: Why 'Us' versus 'Them' Doesn't Sell," *Policy Review,* October and November 2008.

21. See Pagden, *Worlds at War,* 9ff.

22. Niall Ferguson, *The War of the World: Twentieth-Century Conflict and the Descent of the West* (New York: Penguin, 2006), 645.

23. Noël and Thérien, *Left and Right,* 108.

24. Noël and Thérien, *Left and Right,* 152.

25. The Italian elections of 2008 have challenged the "strong correlation between left-right self-placement and voting behavior" (Noël and Thérien, *Left and Right,* 40). See A. Di Virgilio, "Le promesse del voto," *Il Mulino* 4 (2008): 629–38.

26. Umberto Eco, "Al diavolo la classe operaia," *L'Espresso,* July 16, 2009.

27. On the necessity of extending bonds of "civic solidarity" across European borders, see chapter 6 of Jürgen Habermas, *The Divided West* (Cambridge: Polity, 2006).

28. Manfred B. Steger, *The Rise of the Global Imaginary: Political Ideologies from the French Revolution to the Global War on Terror* (Oxford: Oxford University Press, 2008), 199.

29. Tony Judt, *Postwar: A History of Europe since 1945* (New York: Penguin, 2006), 819.

30. "EU/Israel Action Plan," http://ec.europa.eu/world/enp/pdf/action_plans/israel_enp_ap_final_en.pdf.

31. Mary Douglas, *How Institutions Think* (Syracuse, NY: Syracuse University Press, 1986), 80.

32. Peter Berkowitz, "The European Left and Ours," *Policy Review* 152 (December 2008–January 2009). Berkowitz's piece is a long review article of Bernard-Henri Lévy, *Left in Dark Times: A Stand against the New Barbarism* (New York: Random House, 2008).

33. See Efraim Karsh, "What's behind Western Condemnation of Israel's War against Hamas," http://jcpa.org/article/whats-behind-western-condemnation-of-israels-war-against-hamas/.

34. W. D. Rubinstein, *The Left, the Right and the Jews* (London: Croom Helm, 1982), 157.

35. On New Labour's discourse of orientation and justification beyond right and left, see Torben Bech Dyrberg, "What Is beyond Right/Left? The Case of New Labour," *Journal of Political Ideologies* 2 (2009): 133–53.

36. Ben Cohen, "The Persistence of Anti-Semitism on the British Left," *Jewish Political Studies Review* 3–4 (2004), 157–69.

37. On Blair's Britain having emerged as the closest ally of Bush's war on terrorism "in marked contrast to increasing European reservations over American policy in general, and towards Iraq and Israel in particular" see Bill Coxall, Lynton Robins, and Robert Leach, *Contemporary British Politics* (London: Macmillan, 2003), 276.

38. It is especially in academia that anti-Zionist feelings have thrived. An open letter by neurobiologist Steve Rose to *The Guardian* on April 6, 2002, was subscribed by several academics.

39. An AMW study on the 7:00 P.M. Channel 4 news surveying six items on Palestine, stated that the Palestinian sources were given an average of airtime "more than twice as long as the non-Palestinian sources." See http://www.arabmediawatch.com/amw/Portals/0/documents/media/20080530AMW.Channel4Study.pdf. On the other hand, the popular 6:30 P.M. ITV news is reported to be highly selective and biased, with Palestinians "rarely given the opportunity to speak for themselves" (http://www.arabmediawatch.com/amw/Portals/0/documents/media/20080529AMW.ITVstudy.pdf ). In an interview to the Italian newspaper *Corriere della Sera,* Sharif Nashashibi, chair and founder of AMW, maintained that "in Great Britain, over the

last nine years, the pro-Arab lobby has raised its voice and gained influence." V. Mazza, "Adesso i media americani hanno un tono meno pro-Israele," *Corriere della Sera,* January 12, 2009.

40. Http://www.arabmediawatch.com/amw/Portals/0/documents/media/20080522AMW. LanguageStudy.pdf.

41. Ludger Volmer, *Die Grünen und die Außenpolitik—ein schwieriges Verhältnis. Eine Ideen-, Programm- und Ereignisgeschichte grüner Außenpolitik* (Münster: Verlag Westfälisches Dampfboot, 1998), 458 (cited in Andrea Humphreys, "Die Grünen and the Israeli-Palestinian Conflict," *Australian Journal of Politics and History* 3 [2008]: 407–19).

42. Joschka Fischer, "Das dünne Eis der Geschichte: Israel und die deutsche Neue Linke," in *Die deutsche "Linke" und der Staat Israel,* ed. Reinhard Ranger (Leipzig: Forum Verlag, 1994), 159–65. Artist and Green Party politician Claudia Roth wondered whether Germans could "criticize Israel without being called anti-Semites." Claudia Roth, "Politische Rede auf der Landesdelegiertenkonferenz Nordrhein-Westfalen," Landesdelegiertenkonferenz Unna, May 25–26, 2002.

43. The CDU-led majority at the Bundestag pronounced a parliamentary *Erklärung* without involving Die Linke, because of its apparently unclear standing on Israel. See C. Seils, "Gysi, die Linke und der Antisemitismus," *Die Zeit,* November 4, 2008.

44. "Die Haltung der deutschen Linken zum Staat Israel," posted by Gysi on April 14, 2008. See http://die-linke.de/die_linke/nachrichten/detail/zurueck/aktuell/artikel/die-haltung-der-deutschen-linken-zum-staat-israel/.

45. A. Panebianco, "Un conflitto nuovo," *Il Corriere della Sera,* January 12, 2009.

46. "Within the E[uropean] P[arliament], traditional divisions are apparent, such as the division between the left (European Socialist Party) and the right (European Popular Party). However, the structural division in the EP . . . is not between left and right. It is a division between member states which favor more integration and member-states which favor less integration, or between mobile alliances of member-states with highly developed and less developed economies." Sergio Fabbrini, *Compound Democracies: Why the United States and Europe Are Becoming Similar* (Cambridge: Cambridge University Press, 2007), 137.

47. Habermas, *The Divided West,* 81.

48. The Plan stresses that "the EU and Israel share the common values of democracy, respect for human rights and the rule of law and basic freedoms. Both parties are committed to the struggle against all form of anti-Semitism, racism and xenophobia. Historically and culturally, there exist great natural affinity and common heritage." "EU/Israel Action Plan," 1.

49. "EU/Israel Action Plan," 6.

50. "At the present time and at the light of the events of these last days, we estimate that this measure constitutes a defensive action and non-offensive." J. Putuznik, spokesman for the Czech presidency of the EU at a press conference following Israel's land attacks on Gaza of January 2, 2009.

51. Paul Pennings and Christine Arnold, "Is Constitutional Politics like Politics 'at Home'? The Case of the EU Constitution," *Political Studies* 4 (2008): 789.

52. Judt, *Postwar,* 764.

53. "Almost every comparative study of political cultures concludes that ideology plays a smaller role in American political culture than in many others, with only handfuls of Americans supporting

such classically European ideologies as socialism, communism, or fascism." Austin Ranney, "Politics in the United States," in *Comparative Politics Today: A World View,* ed. Gabriel A. Almond, G. Bingham Powell, Russell J. Dalton, and Kaare Strom (New York: Longman, 2004), 754.

54. Norman G. Finkelstein, *Beyond Chutzpah: On the Misuse of Anti-Semitism and the Abuse of History* (Berkeley: University of California Press, 2005), 22.

55. Berkowitz, "The European Left and Ours." Nunberg, *Talking Right,* 17. In a footnote to this passage Nunberg states that "those criticisms don't extend to Fox News, where those phrases have been uttered 799 times over the past five years."

56. Lisa McGirr sees the roots of the political success of the religious right in its ability to speak "to the concerns over the autonomy of communities, the erosion of individualism, the authority of the family, and the place of religion in national life." *Suburban Warriors: The Origins of the New American Right* (Princeton: Princeton University Press, 2001), 272. It was precisely over these concerns that a schism had opened up in America during the 1960s and 1970s, and a new evangelical-oriented religious right was good at providing *representation* to individuals and groups that thought they had lost political *recognition.*

57. Pagden, *Worlds at War,* 459.

58. Wydra, *Communism,* 59.

59. Pagden, *Worlds at War,* 459.

60. Howard Fineman, "Bush and God," *Newsweek,* March 10, 2003.

61. Remarks by the president for "Humanity Event" at Waco, Texas, on August 8, 2001.

62. "National outliers and anomalies to the general cultural patterns we have established are worth examining in detail. It is clear that the United States *is* exceptionally religious for its level of development, but it remains unclear why." Norris and Inglehart, *Sacred and Secular,* 240.

63. Norris and Inglehart, *Sacred and Secular,* 83.

64. Norris and Inglehart, *Sacred and Secular,* 26.

65. James Madison, *To the Baptist Churches in Neal's Creek and on Black Creek, North Carolina* (June 3, 1811), in *Letters and Other Writings of James Madison, Fourth President of the United States, Published by the Order of Congress,* vol. 2 (Philadelphia: J. B. Lippincott, 1865), 511–12.

66. Naomi Wolf, "God Crashes the Tea Party," *Huffington Post,* posted on August 3, 2010.

67. Peter Singer, *A Darwinian Left: Politics, Evolution and Cooperation* (New Haven: Yale University Press, 2000), 6.

68. See Loet Leydesdorff and Janelle Ward, "Science Shops: A Kaleidoscope of Science-Society Collaborations in Europe," *Public Understanding of Science* 14 (2005): 353–72.

69. In an attempt to survey the damage effected by G. W. Bush in the field of scientific research and development, the Washington correspondent for *Seed* magazine, Chris Mooney, wrote that "under the Bush Administration we have seen scientists suppressed, scientific reports forcefully edited or censored, scientific advisory committees politically tilted, and widespread distortion and misrepresentation of scientific knowledge." "Undoing Bush," *Harper's Magazine,* June 2007, 50.

70. It is precisely the democratic outlook of America that is at stake in the battles currently fought along such cleavages as the gender divide, the "digital divide" (Pippa Norris, *Digital Divide: Civic Engagement, Information Poverty, and the Internet Worldwide* [Cambridge: Cambridge University

Press, 2001], and the "stem-cell divide" (Michael Bellomo, *The Stem Cell Divide: The Facts, the Fiction, and the Fear Driving the Greatest Scientific, Political, and Religious Debate of Our Time* [New York: Amacom, 2006]).

71. For Israel's use of religion in constructing its political identity I am indebted to Emanuel Gutmann for helpful insights.

72. See Donald Wagner, "Evangelicals and Israel: Theological Roots of a Political Alliance," *Christian Century*, November 4, 1998, 1020–26.

73. And, one could add, to help identify Shimon Peres, a major sponsor of the Oslo Accords, "with a peace process that had engendered massive terrorism and loss of security." Morris, *Righteous Victims*, 640. For an extensive, overall sympathetic, and at times amusing account of the "theological convergence" between the Likud and the Evangelist right in America—and the meeting between Netanyahu and Falwell—see Zef Chafets, *A Match Made in Heaven: American Jews, Christian Zionists, and One Man's Exploration of the Weird and Wonderful Judeo-Evangelical Alliance* (New York: Harper, 2008).

74. More generally, the original shift of the "American Jewry to the right" (Rubinstein, *The Left, the Right*, 145) can be traced back to Nixon, who managed to detach "Jewish voters from the Democratic tradition" (Chafets, *Match Made in Heaven*, 25).

75. It would be a mistake to overlook the universal character of the French Revolution, and see the development of the American polity as following a separate course. On the huge influence of the French Revolution on the early American Republic, see Stanley Elkins and Eric McKitrick, *The Age of Federalism: The Early American Republic* (Oxford: Oxford University Press, 1995).

76. Philip Roth, *American Pastoral* (London: Jonathan Cape, 1997), 122 and 85.

77. On "cumulative cleavages" see Powell, "Political Cleavage Structure," which was an attempt to test empirically the theory of cleavage structures put forth in Seymour M. Lipset and Stein Rokkan, *Party Systems and Voter Alignments: Cross-National Perspectives* (Glencoe, IL: Free Press, 1967).

78. Manfred B. Steger depicts a possible scenario resulting from the open-ended structure of globalization, a final clash between the two species of "Imperial Globalism" and "Jihadist Globalism" (Steger, *Rise of the Global Imaginary*, 213ff).

79. "Unless there is a genuine and universally accepted peace treaty in the Middle East, and should the stalemate there continue, most mainstream socialist parties in the Western world will have adopted explicitly anti-Zionist platforms by 1990." Rubinstein, *The Left, the Right*, 227.

## Chapter 4. A Mimetic Perspective on Conflict Resolution

1. Arguably, primates do make peace without resorting to normative concepts. Christopher Boehm's work is an attempt at exploring the exemplary character of *natural* conflict resolution among primates. "Global Conflict Resolution: An Anthropological Diagnosis of Problems with World Governance," in *Evolutionary Psychology and Violence: A Primer for Policymakers and Public Policy Advocates*, ed. Richard W. Bloom and Nancy Kimberly Dess (Westport, CO: Praeger, 2003).

2. Boehm, "Global Conflict Resolution," 203.

3. Filippo Aureli and Frans B. M. de Waal, eds., *Natural Conflict Resolution* (Berkeley: University of California Press, 2000).

4. In this chapter I often use reconciliation and conflict resolution as mutually entailing notions, and not in the sense that reconciliation concerns the formation of new societal beliefs and a

peaceful ethos whereas conflict resolution would be the "formal" aspect of the process (as in Daniel Bar-Tal, "From Intractable Conflict through Conflict Resolution to Reconciliation: Psychological Analysis," *Political Psychology* 2 ([2000)]: 351–65). I think the two expressions refer to two different ways of looking at the same phenomenon, and stressing the distinction has, in my view, the sole effect of suggesting a separation between form and content that does not seem epistemically promising.

5. John Rawls, *The Law of Peoples* (Cambridge: Harvard University Press, 1999), 47.

6. Korsgaard makes clear this mutual relationship between reflexivity and normativity: we, indeed, have normative problems inasmuch as we are reflective beings, in the sense that we have "to figure out what to believe and what to do." Christine Korsgaard, *The Sources of Normativity* (Cambridge: Cambridge University Press, 1996), 46. If we were not capable of reflection we would not have normative problems.

7. Peter Wallensteen, *Understanding Conflict Resolution: War, Peace and the Global System* (London: Sage, 2002), 16.

8. The word "distribution" may sound misleading; it stands at the center of a semantic area identified by various cognate terms such as restitution, restoration, reparation, etc.

9. Carrie J. Menkel-Meadow, ed., *Dispute Resolution: Beyond the Adversarial Model* (New York: Aspen Publishers, 2005), 27.

10. Georg W. Hegel, *Encyclopedia of the Philosophical Sciences in Outline* (New York: Continuum, 1990), § 413; italics added.

11. Cecilia Albin and Daniel Druckman, "Equality Matters: Negotiating an End to Civil Wars," *Journal of Conflict Resolution* 56, no. 2 (2012): 156.

12. M. Van der Stoel, "The Role of the CSCE High Commissioner on National Minorities in CSCE Preventive Diplomacy," in *The Challenge of Preventive Diplomacy* (Stockholm: Ministry for Foreign Affairs, 1994), 37.

13. John Heil, *From an Ontological Point of View* (Oxford: Clarendon Press, 2003).

14. Willard Quine, "On What There Is," in *From a Logical Point of View* (Cambridge: Harvard University Press, 1953).

15. Milbank and Kirkpatrick address the ontological implications of conflict resolution: John Milbank, *Being Reconciled: Ontology and Pardon* (London: Routledge, 2003); Frank G. Kirkpatrick, *A Moral Ontology for a Theistic Ethics: Gathering the Nations in Love and Justice* (Aldershot: Ashgate, 2003).

16. I am following Raz, *Practical Reason and Norms,* 2nd ed. (Princeton: Princeton University Press, 1990) in positing that reasons are *facts,* so that responsiveness to reasons can be explained in terms of a thoughtful adjustment to a given fact or state of affairs. People act in light of a particular purpose, and a reason for someone to φ requires that he "has some motive which will be served or furthered by his φ-ing," Bernard Williams, *Moral Luck* (Cambridge: Cambridge University Press, 1981), 103.

17. Joseph Raz, "Agency, Reason, and the Good," in *Engaging Reason,* 23.

18. W. J. Long and P. Brecke, *War and Reconciliation: Reason and Emotion in Conflict Resolution* (Cambridge, MA: The MIT Press, 2003), 69; italics added.

19. Handbooks on conflict resolution indicate, among the roots of human discord, poverty, overpopulation, incompatibility of goals, environmental degradation, and lack of legitimate

political institutions. See for an overview in S. J. Stedman, "Alchemy for a New World Order: Overselling Preventive Diplomacy," *Foreign Affairs,* May–June (1995).

20. Hobbes, though, does not say that the classical case is universally applicable, as one of the principled "causes of quarrel" that he cites is actually *vainglory*. Hobbes, *Leviathan* vi. 39.

21. Plato, "Phaedo," in *Five Dialogues: Euthyphro, Apology, Crito, Meno, Phaedo,* ed. G. M. A. Grube (Indianapolis: Hackett Publishing Co., 2012), 66d.

22. Canetti, *Masse und Macht,* 107.

23. See Ho-Wan Jeong, "Research on Conflict Resolution," in *Conflict Resolution: Dynamics, Process, and Structure* (Aldershot: Ashgate, 1999), 3–34.

24. Wallensteen, *Understanding Conflict Resolution,* 38.

25. Rawls, *The Law of Peoples,* 127.

26. "Now, between life thus refined and humanized, and that life of savagery, nothing marks the difference so clearly as law and violence [*ius atque vis*]. Whichever of the two we are unwilling to use, we must use the other. If we would have violence abolished, law must prevail, that is, the administration of justice, on which the law wholly depends; if we dislike the administration of justice, or if there is none, force must rule [*vis dominetur necesse est*]." Cicero, "Pro Sestio," in *Pro Sestio and in Vatinium,* trans. R. Gardner (Cambridge: Harvard University Press, 1966), XLII, 91.

27. Think of Hannah Arendt's idea that "only when our sense of justice is offended do we react with rage." Hannah Arendt, *On Violence* (London: Allen Lane, 1970), 64.

28. Diogenes Laertius, *Lives of Eminent Philosophers,* ed. R. D. Hicks (Cambridge: Harvard University Press, 1989), X.150.31. The tradition, though, is much older. Epicurus stated that "justice is nothing on its own, but whenever and wherever people interact with one another it is a kind of compact not to harm or be harmed." *Kuriai Doxai* 33; cf. 31, 32, and 36, and Plato, *Republic* 2.358e3–359b5; cited in Kinch Hoekstra, "Hobbes on the Natural Condition of Mankind," in *The Cambridge Companion to Hobbes' Leviathan,* ed. Patricia Springborg (Cambridge: Cambridge University Press, 2007), 124. See also Lucretius, *On the Nature of Things,* ed. W. H. D. Rouse (Cambridge: Harvard University Press, 1989), 5.1019–27.

29. John Stuart Mill, *On Liberty* (Harmondsworth: Penguin, 1982), 163.

30. See Renato Ruggiero, "Managing a World of Free Trade and Deep Interdependence," press release, World Trade Organization, September 10, 1996, http://www.wto.org/english/news_e/pres96_e/pr055_e.htm.

31. Christian Davenport, *State Repression and the Domestic Democratic Peace* (New York: Cambridge University Press, 2007), 89.

32. Fish, "Boutique Multiculturalism," 392.

33. Rawls stresses the significance of practices of giving and acknowledging reasons in the formation of social consensus. According to Rawls, people "give reasons for their beliefs and conduct before one another confident that *this avowed reckoning itself will strengthen and not weaken public understanding.*" John Rawls, *Political Liberalism* (New York: Columbia University Press, 1993), 68 (italics added).

34. Bernard Williams, *Truth and Truthfulness: An Essay in Genealogy* (Princeton: Princeton University Press, 2002), 220.

35. Long and Brecke, *War and Reconciliation,* 158.

36. In other words human beings, if rational, have the ability to act *on reasons,* but they are also capable of acting *reflectively* in virtue of their ability to have an insight into the reasons they adopt to structure agency. On reflexivity as a critical attribute of rationality see Larmore, *Les pratiques du moi.*

37. René Girard, *Things Hidden since the Foundation of the World,* trans. Stephen Bann and Michael Metteer (Stanford: Stanford University Press, 1987), 203.

38. Girard, *A Theater of Envy,* 219.

39. Girard, *Violence and the Sacred,* 180.

40. "This weakness of individual desire—of single and unsupported desire, celibate desire—reappears constantly in Shakespeare." Girard, *A Theater of Envy,* 133.

41. Here mimetic desire needs to be distinguished from the mere notion of envy: according to Girard "all envy is mimetic, but not all mimetic desire is envious. Envy suggests a single static phenomenon, not the prodigious matrix of forms that conflictual imitation becomes in the hand of Shakespeare." Girard, *A Theater of Envy,* 18.

42. Girard, *Violence and the Sacred,* 145.

43. Raz, "Explaining Normativity: On Rationality and the Justification of Reason," in *Engaging Reason,* 73. Raz has expanded on "the reason-dependent character of desires" in *The Morality of Freedom,* 140–43.

44. Girard, *A Theater of Envy,* 101.

45. Girard, *A Theater of Envy,* 18.

46. Girard, *Things Hidden,* 90 (italics added).

47. Girard, *Violence and the Sacred,* 46.

48. Postindependence Zimbabwe has been haunted by serious ethnic polarization that never eventuated in "open" ethnic warfare. See Kriger for very useful insights into the postwar settlement in Zimbabwe from the perspective of the social integration programs of former guerrilla combatants. Kriger demonstrates convincingly that the process of state-building in Zimbabwe "despite its much heralded success, did not mark an identifiable break between war and peace." Norma Kriger, *Guerrilla Veterans in Post-war Zimbabwe: Symbolic and Violent Politics, 1980–1987* (Cambridge: Cambridge University Press, 2006), 5.

49. The work of Carl Schmitt seems particularly useful in the area of global conflict developments, where such phenomena as coups d'états and terrorist attacks are indicators of the radical polemicity of politics, that is, the irreducibility of the dyad friend and foe. Schmitt, however, remains difficult to engage in the present discussion given that the very idea of conflict *resolution* seems foreign to his intellectual universe. Indeed *solving* conflict by normative (e.g., redistributive) means is for Schmitt one of the chimerical objectives that liberalism set to politics. If politics is inherently polemical any commitments to "solve" conflict, and therefore rid the world of politics itself, are the effect of a characteristic inability to grasp the actual nature of the political. Schmitt calls "liberalism" precisely this failure to acknowledge the inherently conflictual and polemical nature of politics. A Girardian perspective on conflict and conflict resolution accepts the fact that conflict and risk are inherent to politics, but it grants a reflective, i.e., normative, way out of the theorem of the irreducibility of conflict. If, for Schmitt, it is the "decision" that does all the reconciliatory work, in a Girardian perspective it is self-reflection that acknowledges, and therefore preempts, the sources of human discord.

50. Arundathi Roy, "The Algebra of Infinite Justice," *The Guardian,* September 29, 2001, 29.

51. David Weissman, *Social Ontology* (New Haven: Yale University Press, 2000), 25.

52. R. Jay Wallace, *Responsibility and Moral Sentiments* (Cambridge: Harvard University Press, 1998), 54.

53. Long and Brecke, *War and Reconciliation,* 3.

54. Aryeh Neier, "What Should Be Done about the Guilty?" *The New York Review of Books* 37 (1990): 32–34.

55. See Henry Tajfel and John C. Turner, "The Social Identity Theory of Inter-group Behavior," in *Psychology of Intergroup Relations,* ed. S. Worchel and L. William G. Austin (Chicago: Nelson-Hall, 1986), 7–24.

56. Jan Assmann, *Moses the Egyptian: The Memory of Egypt in Western Monotheism* (Cambridge: Harvard University Press, 1997), 44.

57. Sémelin traces the clearest formulation of this phobic imaginary to Melanie Klein's analysis of ultraaggressive fantasies of hate and greed in the child, arguing that the manipulation of this "elementary psychic nucleus" in a context fraught with social and ethnic divisions is likely to lead to a phobic construal of the enemy. Jacques Sémeline, *Purifier et détruire: Usages politiques des massacres et genocides* (Paris: Éditions du Seuil, 2005).

58. Judt, *Postwar,* 666.

59. Bar-Tal, "Intractable Conflict," 355.

60. See Jayne Docherty, *Learning Lessons from Waco: When the Parties Bring Their Gods to the Negotiation Table* (Syracuse, NY: Syracuse University Press, 2001).

61. Carl Gustav Jung, "The Fight with the Shadow," in *Collected Works,* vol. 10 (London: Routledge & Kegan Paul, 1970), 220.

62. Ole Wæver, "Peace and Security: Two Concepts and Their Relationship," in *Conceptual Innovation and Contemporary Security Analysis: Essays in Honour of Haakan Wiberg* (Copenhagen: Copenhagen Peace Research Institute, 2002), 43.

63. Pleas for a "third party" hinge on the assumption that a very different type of world order depends on the possibility "to readily and reliably police those who would wage war." Christopher Boehm, "Global Conflict Resolution: An Anthropological Diagnosis of Problems with World Governance," in Bloom and Dess, *Evolutionary Psychology and Violence,* 204.

64. Wallensteen, *Understanding Conflict Resolution,* 44.

65. A striking, and paradoxical, unintended consequence of the Oslo contact talks of the mid-1990s was one of the most destructive waves of terrorist violence in Israel. More nuanced are the attempts at interpretation and political analysis of why that was the case. See, for an overview, Davis Makovsky, *Making Peace with the PLO: The Rabin Government's Road to the Oslo Accord* (Boulder, CO: Westview Press, 1996). Kriger suggests that NGOs and contact groups in Zimbabwe claimed political success for their mediation by cheating on language: they described as "peace" a condition of actual "war" (even if not open warfare, but still war). Kriger, *Guerrilla Veterans.*

66. Weine, *When History Is a Nightmare,* 19.

67. Jeong, "Research on Conflict Resolution," 19.

68. See Barbara Hudson, *Justice in the Risk Society: Challenging and Reaffirming Justice in Late Modernity* (London: Sage, 2003), xv and 199.

69. Mary Douglas has focused on "hidden groups" invoking "a history of persecution and resistance." *How Institutions Think,* 80.

70. Here I am referring to Williams, *Truth and Truthfulness.*

71. Bar-Tal, "Intractable Conflict," 356.

72. Richard Moran, *Authority and Estrangement: An Essay on Self-Knowledge* (Princeton: Princeton University Press, 2001), 60.

73. Girard, "Generative Scapegoating," 84.

74. Steven Pinker, *The Blank Slate: The Modern Denial of Human Nature* (New York: Viking, 2002), 336.

## Chapter 5. A Political Theology of the Empty Tomb

1. Harald Wydra, "Violence, Peace, and the Symbolism of the Victim," paper presented at the conference "Between Animal and Human," University of Cambridge, October 16–17, 2009.

2. Friedrich Nietzsche, *Twilight of the Idols,* trans. Duncan Lange (Oxford: Oxford University Press, 1998), 19.

3. John Fowles, "Foreword," *The Magus* (London: Vintage, 2004), 10.

4. One could argue that mimetic theory provides this kind of revelation, for it stresses the mimetic dimension of human nature and shows that our understanding of political phenomena is grounded on a number of "impostures."

5. Interestingly, Jürgen Habermas identified the years 1989–1990 as the turning point for the "*political* revitalization" of religion in America. Habermas, *The Divided West,* 119 (italics added).

6. Daniel Dennett, *Breaking the Spell: Religion as a Natural Phenomenon* (London: Allen Lane, 2006), 35.

7. Anthony Pagden, *The Enlightenment: And Why It Still Matters* (New York: Random House, 2013), 405.

8. This passage, from the theology of ascension to the type of secular politics supported by Western modernity, may look unwarranted. See Roberto Farneti, *Il canone moderno: Filosofia politica e genealogia* (Turin: Bollati Boringhieri, 2002), where I have tried to detail the intellectual passages that marked this eventful process.

9. Jürgen Habermas has reported the view of a scholar from Tehran, according to whom "the comparative study of cultures and religious sociology surely suggests that European secularization was the odd one out among the various developments." Cited in Pagden, *The Enlightenment,* 404.

10. Peter Henrici, "Die Modernität und das Christentum," *Internationale Katholische Zeitschrift Communio* 4 (1990): 296.

11. Girard, *Things Hidden,* 259.

12. René Girard, *The Scapegoat,* trans. Yvonne Freccero (Baltimore: Johns Hopkins University Press, 1989), 204.

13. Secularization, according to Gianni Vattimo, "comprises all the forms of dissolution of the sacred

characteristic of the modern process of civilization." *After Christianity* (New York: Columbia University Press, 2002), 24. However, this same modern process of civilization, according to Vattimo, is a consequence of *kenosis,* namely, of the "incarnation as God's renunciation of his own sovereign transcendence." "The Age of Interpretation," in *The Future of Religion,* ed. Santiago Zabala (New York: Columbia University Press, 2005), 51.

14. Hans Blumenberg, *The Legitimacy of the Modern Age* (Cambridge: MIT Press, 1985), 3.

15. Mircea Eliade, *The Sacred and Profane: The Nature of Religion* (Ft. Washington, PA: Harvest Books, 1968), 5.

16. "For nonreligious man, all vital experiences—whether sex or eating, work or play—have been desacralized." Eliade, *The Sacred and Profane,* 150.

17. Hermann Lübbe, "Heilsmythen nach der Aufklärung. Geschichtsphilosophie als Selbstermächtigungsideologie," in *Religionstheorie und Politische Theologie. Theokratie,* ed. J. Taubes (München: Wilhelm Fink Verlag, 1987), 279.

18. Daniel Dennett, *Breaking the Spell: Religion as a Natural Phenomenon* (London: Allen Lane, 2006); Richard Dawkins, *The God Delusion* (New York: Houghton Mifflin, 2006).

19. Pinker, *Better Angels,* 11.

20. See Marcel Gauchet, *The Disenchantment of the World: A Political History of Religion* (Princeton: Princeton University Press, 1993), xiii. According to Charles Taylor, in his foreword to Gauchet's book, it is part of the book's central point that "Christianity was the religion that first produced exit from religion, and so the postreligious world exists only in ex-Christendom." A similar view, from the perspective of the sociology of religion, has been expounded in Rodney Stark, *The Victory of Reason: How Christianity Led to Freedom, Capitalism, and Western Success* (New York: Random House, 2006).

21. Girard, *The Scapegoat,* 109.

22. Girard, *Things Hidden,* 206.

23. "The Christ can no longer continue to sojourn in a world in which the word is either never mentioned or, even worse, derided and devalued by those who take it in vain—those who claim to be faithful to it but in reality are far from being so. Jesus' destiny in the world is inseparable from that of the Word of God." Girard, *Things Hidden,* 206.

24. Girard, *Things Hidden,* 219.

25. Girard, *Things Hidden,* 197.

26. Girard, *Things Hidden,* 200.

27. Girard, *Things Hidden,* 201 and 202.

28. Girard, *Things Hidden,* 203.

29. In an interview with Robert Harrison for the radio station of Stanford University, on October 4, 2005, Girard was asked to elaborate on the salvific dimension of his theology of the kingdom, that is, on how the Passion of Jesus determines salvation. Girard did not really reply to the question, claiming that the same question should be asked to theologians, and not to anthropologists. Theologians, though, have failed to say anything definitive on this matter.

30. In an interview with Giuseppe Fornari, Girard claimed that his "mimetic approach transforms dramatically the usual meaning of 'anthropology' as well as the meaning of 'theology.'" Giuseppe Fornari, *La vittima e la folla* (Treviso: Santi Quaranta, 1998), 161.

31. Habermas, *The Divided West,* 125.

32. Douglas Farrow, *Ascension and Ecclesia* (Edinburgh: T&T Clark, 1999), 216. More emphasis on the theological theme of ascension was given by the Ecumenical Council II. See Heinrich Denzinger, *Enchiridion symbolorum definitionum et declarationum de rebus fidei et morum,* ed. P. Hünermann (Bologna: Dehoniane, 1995), §§ 4005, 4204, and 4224.

33. Farrow, *Ascension and Ecclesia,* 16.

34. Farrow, *Ascension and Ecclesia,* 33.

35. Von Harnack "regarded the ascension myth as one of the 'semi-doctrinal legends' developed by second generation believers in the interchange between Jewish and Hellenic ideas" (quoted in Farrow, *Ascension and Ecclesia,* 16).

36. Hobbes, *Leviathan,* 337.

37. Hobbes, *Leviathan,* 357.

38. See Peter Henrici, "Vernunftreich und Staat-Kirche: Das Reich Gottes im neuzeitlichen Denken," *Internationale Katholische Zeitschrift Communio* 2 (1986): 131–41.

39. Hobbes, *Leviathan,* 453.

40. Hobbes, *Leviathan,* 468.

41. Hobbes, *Leviathan,* 73.

42. Hobbes's objective, according to Schmitt, was "to make Christ's effectiveness undamaging in the social and political domain." Carl Schmitt, *Glossarium: Aufzeichnungen der Jahre 1947–1951* (Berlin: Duncker & Humblot, 1991), 243.

43. Mathias Eichorn, *Es wird regiert! Der Staat im Denken Karl Barths und Carl Schmitts in den Jahren 1919 bis 1938* (Berlin: Duncker & Humblot, 1994), 268.

44. Christofer Frey, "The Biblical Tradition in the Perspective of Political Theology and Political Ethics," in *Politics and Theopolitics in the Bible and Postbiblical Literature,* ed. Henning Graf Reventlow, Yair Hoffmann, and Benjamin Uffenheimer (Sheffield, UK: Academic Press, 1994), 61.

## Epilogue. A Genealogy of "Planetary Reciprocity"

1. Girard, *Battling to the End,* 42.

2. Girard, *Battling to the End,* 18. "What is experienced now is a form of mimetic rivalry on a planetary scale." Girard, *Evolution and Conversion,* 238.

3. Girard, *Evolution and Conversion,* 240.

4. See Wolfgang Palaver, "Gleichheit als Sprengkraft? Zum Einfluß des Christentums auf die Entwicklung der Demokratie," in *Verweigerte Mündigkeit? Politische Kultur und Kirche,* ed. Józef Niewiadomski (Thaur: Kulturverlag, 1989), 195–217.

5. "I am now convinced that mimetic history needs to be written: it would help us understand what is at stake in our own times" (Girard, *Battling to the End,* 40).

6. Several scholars have discussed "the ways in which 'empire' as a category of analysis applies to Germany" or, for that matter, to the Soviet Union. Shelley Baranowski, *Nazi Empire: German Colonialism and Imperialism from Bismarck to Hitler* (Cambridge: Cambridge University Press,

2011), 3. The "imperial" outlook may be considered as a fallout of the totalitarian structure of the state, and the search for a viable living space (Lebensraum) only one aspect of Nazi ideology. The "Third Reich" did after all call itself an empire, and adopted the formal process of *translatio imperii,* whereas the Soviets could hardly do that, not only because of Marx and Lenin's identification of imperialism with capitalism, but because the Romanovs had styled themselves as "emperors." The Third Reich definitely shared with classical empires a striking number of features, including the typical mimetic attitude described above. "German initiatives in Europe became . . . contentious. In addition to encouraging British fears that Germany aspired to continental hegemony in the manner of Napoleon, they multiplied the points of tension with the Russian Empire." Baranowski, *Nazi Empire,* 40.

7. Harald Wydra, "The Power of Symbols: Communism and Beyond," *International Journal of Politics, Culture, and Society* 1 (2012): 57.

8. Girard, *Battling to the End,* 40.

9. For this notion of the "non-European other" see Judt, *Postwar,* 765, and Luisa Passerini, "From the Ironies of Identity to the Identities of Irony," in *The Idea of Europe: From Antiquity to the European Union,* ed. Anthony Pagden (Cambridge: Cambridge University Press, 2002), 200ff.

10. Girard, *Battling to the End,* 103.

11. Pagden, *Worlds at War,* 9ff.

12. Fuchs, *Mimesis and Empires,* 139.

13. Edward Said, *Orientalism* (New York: Vintage, 1979).

14. Pagden, *Worlds at War,* 347.

15. Zachary Lockman, *Contending Visions of the Middle East: The History and Politics of Orientalism* (Cambridge: Cambridge University Press, 2004), 69.

16. Bernard Lewis, *What Went Wrong? Western Impact and Middle Eastern Response* (Oxford: Oxford University Press, 2003), 112.

17. Pagden, *Worlds at War,* 438.

18. Pagden, *Worlds at War,* 415 (italics added).

19. Girard, *Battling to the End,* 18.

20. Girard, *Battling to the End,* 40.

21. Fuchs, *Mimesis and Empires,* 118.

22. Anthony Pagden, *Lords of All the World: Ideologies of Empire in Spain, Britain and France c.1500–c.1800* (New Haven: Yale University Press, 1995), 67.

23. The original prompt of the rush was actually the search for precious metals.

24. Pagden, *Lords of All the World,* 65.

25. Anthony Pagden suggested that what we need here is a definition of empire, or at least an account of what might be thought to be at stake in making a rush for it. The problem in the text is that we are faced with two senses of "empire," one descriptive and one normative. The farther back we go in history, the harder it is to find a consensus among both scholars and policymakers on what polities qualify as empires.

26. Pagden, *Lords of All the World,* 197.

27. Cited in Pagden, *Lords of All the World,* 73.

28. Fuchs, *Mimesis and Empires,* 137.

29. Münkler, *The New Wars,* 144.

30. Pagden, *Lords of All the World,* 74.

31. Fuchs, *Mimesis and Empires,* 145.

32. Fuchs, *Mimesis and Empires,* 164

33. Fuchs, *Mimesis and Empires,* 164.

34. Fuchs, *Mimesis and Empires,* 165

35. Fuchs, *Mimesis and Empires,* 164.

36. Jabri, "Restyling the Subject," 591.

37. Girard, *Battling to the End,* 2.

38. Girard, *Evolution and Conversion,* 66.

39. Michael C. Corballis, *The Recursive Mind: The Origins of Human Language, Thought, and Civilization* (Princeton: Princeton University Press, 2011).

# References

Albin, Cecilia, and Daniel Druckman. "Equality Matters: Negotiating an End to Civil Wars." *Journal of Conflict Resolution* 56, no. 2 (2012): 155–82.

Anspach, Mark. "Global Markets, Anonymous Victims." UNESCO Courier, 2001. Http://www.mimetictheory.org/bios/articles/Anspach_UNESCO.pdf.

Anttonen, Veikko. "Space, Body, and the Notion of Boundary: A Category-Theoretical Approach to Religion." *Temenos* 2 (2005): 185–202.

Arendt, Hannah. *On Violence.* London: Allen Lane, 1970.

Assmann, Jan. *Moses the Egyptian: The Memory of Egypt in Western Monotheism.* Cambridge: Harvard University Press, 1997.

Aureli, Filippo, and Frans B. M. de Waal, eds. *Natural Conflict Resolution.* Berkeley: University of California Press, 2000.

Baranowski, Shelley. *Nazi Empire: German Colonialism and Imperialism from Bismarck to Hitler.* Cambridge: Cambridge University Press, 2011.

Bar-Tal, Daniel. "From Intractable Conflict through Conflict Resolution to Reconciliation: Psychological Analysis." *Political Psychology* 2 (2000): 351–65.

Bartolini, Stefano. *The Political Mobilization of the European Left, 1860–1980: The Class Cleavage.* Cambridge: Cambridge University Press, 2000.

Bellomo, Michael. *The Stem Cell Divide: The Facts, the Fiction, and the Fear Driving the Greatest Scientific, Political, and Religious Debate of Our Time.* New York: Amacom, 2006.

Berkowitz, Peter. "The European Left and Ours." *Policy Review* 152 (December 2008–January 2009). Http://www.hoover.org/publications/policy-review/article/5663.

Bilgrami, Akeel. *Self-Knowledge and Resentment.* Cambridge: Harvard University Press, 2006.

Bishop, Bill. *The Big Sort: Why the Clustering of Like-Minded America Is Tearing Us Apart.* Boston: Mariner Books, 2009.

Blumenberg, Hans. *The Legitimacy of the Modern Age.* Cambridge: MIT Press, 1985.

Bobbio, Norberto. *Left and Right: The Significance of a Political Distinction.* Chicago: University of Chicago Press, 1996.

Boehm, Christopher. "Global Conflict Resolution: An Anthropological Diagnosis of Problems with World Governance." In *Evolutionary Psychology and Violence: A Primer for Policymakers and Public Policy Advocates,* ed. R.W. Bloom and N. Dess, 203–38. Westport, CO: Praeger, 2003.

Bose, Sumantra. *Contested Lands: Israel-Palestine, Kashmir, Bosnia, Cyprus, and Sri Lanka.* Cambridge: Harvard University Press, 2010.

Brandon, Robert. *Making It Explicit: Reasoning, Representing, and Discursive Commitment.* Cambridge: Harvard University Press, 1994.

Burkert, Walter. *Homo Necans: The Anthropology of Ancient Greek Sacrificial Ritual and Myth.* Berkeley: University of California Press, 1986.

Canetti, Elias. *Masse und Macht.* Frankfurt am Main: Fischer Verlag, 1994.

Caramani, Daniele, ed. *Comparative Politics.* Oxford: Oxford University Press, 2008.

Chafets, Zef. *A Match Made in Heaven: American Jews, Christian Zionists, and One Man's Exploration of the Weird and Wonderful Judeo-Evangelical Alliance.* New York: Harper, 2008.

Cicero. "Pro Sestio." In *Pro Sestio and in Vatinium,* trans. R. Gardner. Cambridge: Harvard University Press, 1966.

Cohen, Ben. "The Persistence of Anti-Semitism on the British Left." *Jewish Political Studies Review* 3–4 (2004), 157–69.

Corballis, Michael C. *The Recursive Mind: The Origins of Human Language, Thought, and Civilization.* Princeton: Princeton University Press, 2011.

Cowdell, Scott. "Hard Evidence for Girardian Mimetic Theory? Intersubjectivity and Mirror Neurons." In *Violence, Desire, and the Sacred: Girard's Mimetic Theory across the Disciplines,* ed. Scott Cowdell, Chris Fleming, and Joel Hodge, 219–26. London: Continuum, 2012.

Cowdell, Scott, Chris Fleming, and Joel Hodge, eds. *Violence, Desire, and the Sacred: Girard's Mimetic Theory across the Disciplines.* London: Continuum, 2012.

Coxall, B., L. Robins, and R. Leach. *Contemporary British Politics.* London: Macmillan, 2003.

Davenport, Christian. *State Repression and the Domestic Democratic Peace.* New York: Cambridge University Press, 2007.

Dawkins, Richard. *The God Delusion.* New York: Houghton Mifflin, 2006.

Dennett, Daniel. *Breaking the Spell: Religion as a Natural Phenomenon.* London: Allen Lane, 2006.

Denzinger, Heinrich. *Enchiridion symbolorum definitionum et declarationum de rebus fidei et morum.* Ed. P. Hünermann. Bologna: Dehoniane, 1995.

De Waal, Frans B. M. *Peacemaking among Primates.* Cambridge: Harvard University Press, 1989.

Diehl, Paul, and Gary Goertz. *War and Peace in International Rivalry.* Ann Arbor: University of Michigan Press, 2000.

Diggins, John Patrick. *The Rise and Fall of the American Left.* New York: Norton, 1992.

Di Virgilio, Aldo. "Le promesse del voto." *Il Mulino* 4 (2008): 629–38.

Docherty, Jayne. *Learning Lessons from Waco: When the Parties Bring Their Gods to the Negotiation Table.* Syracuse, NY: Syracuse University Press, 2001.

Douglas, Mary. *How Institutions Think.* Syracuse, NY: Syracuse University Press, 1986.

Dupuy, Jean-Pierre, and Paul Dumouchel. *L'enfer des choses.* Paris: Seuil, 1979.

Dyrberg, Torben Bech. "What Is beyond Right/Left? The Case of New Labour." *Journal of Political Ideologies* 2 (2009): 133–53.

Eichorn, Mathias. *Es wird regiert! Der Staat im Denken Karl Barths und Carl Schmitts in den Jahren 1919 bis 1938.* Berlin: Duncker & Humblot, 1994.

Eliade, Mircea. *The Sacred and Profane: The Nature of Religion.* Ft. Washington, PA: Harvest Books, 1968.

Elkins, Stanley, and Eric McKitrick. *The Age of Federalism: The Early American Republic.* Oxford: Oxford University Press, 1995.

Fabbrini, Sergio. *Compound Democracies: Why the United States and Europe Are Becoming Similar.* Cambridge: Cambridge University Press, 2007.

Farneti, Roberto. *Il canone moderno: Filosofia politica e genealogia.* Turin: Bollati Boringhieri, 2002.

———. "Hobbes on Salvation." In *Cambridge Companion to Hobbes's* Leviathan, ed. Patricia Springborg, 291–308. Cambridge: Cambridge University Press, 2007.

Farrow, Douglas. *Ascension and Ecclesia.* Edinburgh: T&T Clark, 1999.

Feldman, Allen. "Deterritorialized Wars of Public Safety." In *State, Sovereignty, War: Civil Violence in Emerging Global Realities,* ed. Bruce Kapferer, 16–28. Oxford: Berghahn Books, 2004.

Ferguson, Niall. *The War of the World: Twentieth-Century Conflict and the Descent of the West.* New York: Penguin, 2006.

Finkelstein, Norman G. *Beyond Chutzpah: On the Misuse of Anti-Semitism and the Abuse of History.* Berkeley: University of California Press, 2005.

Fischer, Joschka. "Das dünne Eis der Geschichte. Israel und die deutsche Neue Linke." In *Die deutsche "Linke" und der Staat Israel,* ed. Reinhard Ranger, 159–65. Leipzig: Forum Verlag, 1994.

Fish, Stanley. "Boutique Multiculturalism, or Why Liberals Are Incapable of Thinking about Hate Speech." *Critical Inquiry* 23, no. 2 (1997): 378–95.

Flint, Julie, and Alex De Waal. *Darfur: A Short History of a Long War.* New York: Zed Books, 2005.

Fornari, Giuseppe. *Da Dioniso a Cristo: Conoscenza e sacrificio nel mondo greco e nella civiltà occidentale.* Genova: Marietti, 2006.

———. *La vittima e la folla.* Treviso: Santi Quaranta, 1998.

Fowles, John. "Foreword." *The Magus.* London: Vintage, 2004.

Frey, Christofer. "The Biblical Tradition in the Perspective of Political Theology and Political Ethics." In

*Politics and Theopolitics in the Bible and Postbiblical Literature,* ed. Henning Graf Reventlow, Yair Hoffmann, and Benjamin Uffenheimer, 55–65. Sheffield, UK: Academic Press, 1994.

Fuchs, Barbara. *Mimesis and Empires: The New World, Islam, and European Identities.* Cambridge: Cambridge University Press, 2001.

Gauchet, Marcel. *The Disenchantment of the World: A Political History of Religion.* Princeton: Princeton University Press, 1993.

Giddens, Anthony. *Beyond Left and Right: The Future of Radical Politics.* Stanford: Stanford University Press, 1994.

Girard, René. *Battling to the End: Conversations with Benoît Chantre.* Trans. Mary Baker. East Lansing: Michigan State University Press, 2010.

———. *Evolution and Conversion: Dialogues on the Origins of Culture.* Ed. P. Antonello and J. C. de Castro Rocha. London: Continuum, 2008.

———. "Generative Scapegoating." In *Violent Origins: Walter Burkert, René Girard, and Jonathan Z. Smith on Ritual Killing and Cultural Formation,* ed. R. G. Hamerton-Kelly, 73–105. Stanford: Stanford University Press, 1987.

———. *I See Satan Fall Like Lightning.* Trans. James G. Williams. Maryknoll, NY: Orbis Books, 2001.

———. *The Scapegoat.* Trans. Yvonne Freccero. Baltimore: Johns Hopkins University Press, 1989.

———. *A Theater of Envy: William Shakespeare.* New York: Oxford University Press, 1991.

———. *Things Hidden since the Foundation of the World.* Trans. Stephen Bann and Michael Metteer. Stanford: Stanford University Press, 1987.

———. *Violence and the Sacred.* Trans. Patrick Gregory. Baltimore: Johns Hopkins University Press, 1977.

Goertz, Gary, Bradford Jones, and Paul F. Diehl. "Maintenance Processes in International Rivalries." *Journal of Conflict Resolution* 49 (2005): 742–69.

Haas, Richard N. "The Age of Nonpolarity." *Foreign Affairs,* May–June 2008, 44–56.

Habermas, Jürgen. *The Divided West.* Cambridge: Polity, 2006.

———. *Zwischen Naturalismus und Religion: Philosophische Aufsätze.* Frankfurt am Main: Suhrkamp, 2005.

Hagan, John, and Wenona Rymond-Richmond. *Darfur and the Crime of Genocide.* New York: Cambridge University Press, 2009.

Hallward, Maia. "International Relations Scholarship, Academic Institutions, and the Israeli-Palestinian Conflict." *Cambridge Review of International Affairs* 2 (2010): 259–80.

Hamerton-Kelly, Robert G., ed. *Violent Origins: Walter Burkert, René Girard, and Jonathan Z. Smith on Ritual Killing and Cultural Formation.* Stanford: Stanford University Press, 1987.

Hammes, Thomas X. "War Evolves into the Fourth Generation." In *Global Insurgency and the Future of Armed Conflict: Debating Fourth-Generation Warfare,* ed. Terry Terriff, Aaron Karp, and Regina Karp, 21–44. New York: Routledge, 2008.

Hansen, Lene, and Ole Wæver. *European Integration and National Identity: The Challenge of the Nordic States.* London: Routledge, 2002.

Hare, David. *Via Dolorosa & When Shall We Live.* London: Faber & Faber, 1998.

Hari, Daoud. *The Translator: A Memoir.* New York: Random House, 2008.

Hegel, Georg W. *Encyclopedia of the Philosophical Sciences in Outline, and Other Philosophical Writings.* Ed. Ernst Behler. New York: Continuum, 1990.

Heil, John. *From an Ontological Point of View.* Oxford: Clarendon Press, 2003.

Henderson, Errol A., and David J. Singer. "'New Wars' and Rumors of 'New Wars.'" *International Interactions* 28, no. 2 (2002): 165–90.

Henrich, Joseph, Robert Boyd, Samuel Bowles, Colin Camerer, Ernst Fehr, and Herbert Gintis. *Foundations of Human Sociality: Economic Experiments and Ethnographic Evidence from Fifteen Small-Scale Societies.* Oxford: Oxford University Press, 2004.

Henrici, Peter. "Die Modernität und das Christentum." *Internationale Katholische Zeitschrift Communio* 4 (1990): 289–97.

———. "Vernunftreich und Staat-Kirche: Das Reich Gottes im neuzeitlichen Denken." *Internationale Katholische Zeitschrift Communio* 2 (1986): 131–41.

Hetherington, Marc J., and Jonathan D. Weiler. *Authoritarianism and Polarization in American Politics.* Cambridge: Cambridge University Press, 2009.

Hobbes, Thomas. *Leviathan.* Ed. Ed Curley. Indianapolis: Hackett, 1994.

Hoekstra, Kinch. "Hobbes on the Natural Condition of Mankind." In *The Cambridge Companion to Hobbes' Leviathan,* ed. Patricia Springborg, 109–27. Cambridge: Cambridge University Press, 2007.

Holsti, Kalevi J. *The State, War, and the State of War.* Cambridge: Cambridge University Press, 1996.

Hudson, Barbara. *Justice in the Risk Society: Challenging and Reaffirming Justice in Late Modernity.* London: Sage, 2003.

Humphreys, Andrea. "Die Grünen and the Israeli-Palestinian Conflict." *Australian Journal of Politics and History* 3 (2008): 407–19.

Jabri, Vivienne. "Restyling the Subject of Responsibility in International Relations." *Millennium Journal of International Studies* 27, no. 3 (1998): 591–611.

Jeong, Ho-Wan. "Research on Conflict Resolution." In *Conflict Resolution: Dynamics, Process, and Structure,* ed. Ho-Wan Jeong, 3–34. Aldershot: Ashgate, 1999.

Judt, Tony. *Postwar: A History of Europe since 1945.* New York: Penguin, 2006.

Juergensmeyer, Mark. *Terror in the Mind of God: The Global Rise of Religious Violence.* 3rd ed. Berkeley: University of California Press, 2003.

Jung, Carl Gustav. "The Fight with the Shadow." In *Collected Works,* vol. 10: 218–26. London: Routledge & Kegan Paul, 1970.

Jünger, Ernst, and Carl Schmitt. *Briefe: 1930–1983.* Ed. Helmuth Kiesel. Stuttgart: Klett-Cotta, 1999.

Kahn, Paul W. *Sacred Violence: Torture, Terror, and Sovereignty.* Ann Arbor: University of Michigan Press, 2008.

Kaldor, Mary. *New and Old Wars.* London: Blackwell, 1999.

Keane, John. *Violence and Democracy.* Cambridge: Cambridge University Press, 2004.

Keynes, John M. *The General Theory of Employment, Interest and Money.* London: Macmillan, 1936.

Kirkpatrick, Frank G. *A Moral Ontology for a Theistic Ethics: Gathering the Nations in Love and Justice.* Aldershot: Ashgate, 2003.

Klein, James P., Gary Goertz, and Paul F. Diehl. "The New Rivalry Dataset: Procedures and Patterns." *Journal of Peace Research* 43 (2006): 331–48.

Korsgaard, Christine. *The Sources of Normativity.* Cambridge: Cambridge University Press, 1996.

Kriger, Norma. *Guerrilla Veterans in Post-war Zimbabwe: Symbolic and Violent Politics, 1980–1987.* Cambridge: Cambridge University Press, 2006.

Kuhn, Harold W., and Sylvia Nasar, eds. *The Essential John Nash.* Princeton: Princeton University Press, 2001.

Larmore, Charles. *Les pratiques du moi.* Paris: PUF, 2004.

Lemke, Douglas, and William Reed. "The Relevance of Politically Relevant Dyads." *Journal of Conflict Resolution* 45, no. 1 (2001): 126–44.

Levi, Arrigo. "Prefazione all'edizione italiana." In *La sinistra, la destra e gli ebrei,* by W. D. Rubinstein. Bologna: Il Mulino, 1986.

Lévy, Bernard-Henri. *Left in Dark Times: A Stand against the New Barbarism.* New York: Random House, 2008.

Lewis, Bernard. *What Went Wrong? Western Impact and Middle Eastern Response.* Oxford: Oxford University Press, 2003.

Leydesdorff, Loet, and Janelle Ward. "Science Shops: A Kaleidoscope of Science-Society Collaborations in Europe." *Public Understanding of Science* 14 (2005): 353–72.

Lind, William S., Keith Nightengale, John F. Schmitt, Joseph W. Sutton, and Gary I. Wilson. "The Changing Face of War: Into the Fourth Generation." In *Global Insurgency and the Future of Armed Conflict: Debating Fourth-Generation Warfare,* ed. Terry Terriff, Aaron Karp, and Regina Karp, 13–20. New York: Routledge, 2008.

Lipset, Seymour M., and Stein Rokkan. *Party Systems and Voter Alignments: Cross-National Perspectives.* Glencoe, IL: Free Press, 1967.

Lockman, Zachary. *Contending Visions of the Middle East: The History and Politics of Orientalism.* Cambridge: Cambridge University Press, 2004.

Long, W. J., and P. Brecke. *War and Reconciliation: Reason and Emotion in Conflict Resolution.* Cambridge: MIT Press, 2003.

Lübbe, Hermann. "Heilsmythen nach der Aufklärung: Geschichtsphilosophie als Selbstermächtigungsideologie." In *Religionstheorie und Politische Theologie,* vol. 3: *Theokratie,* ed. J. Taubes, 279–92. Munich: Wilhelm Fink Verlag, 1987.

Madison, James. *Letters and Other Writings of James Madison, Fourth President of the United States, Published by the Order of Congress.* Vol. 2. Philadelphia: J. B. Lippincott, 1865.

Makovsky, Davis. *Making Peace with the PLO: The Rabin Government's Road to the Oslo Accord.* Boulder, CO: Westview Press, 1996.

Markovits, Andrei S. "The European and American Left since 1945." *Dissent,* Winter 2005, 5–13.

Marks, Gil. *Olive Trees and Honey: A Treasury of Vegetarian Recipes from Jewish Communities around the World.* Hoboken, NJ: Wiley, 2004.

McGirr, Lisa. *Suburban Warriors: The Origins of the New American Right.* Princeton: Princeton University Press, 2001.

Menkel-Meadow, Carrie J., ed. *Dispute Resolution: Beyond the Adversarial Model.* New York: Aspen, 2005.

Milbank, John. *Being Reconciled: Ontology and Pardon.* London: Routledge, 2003.

Mill, John Stuart. *On Liberty.* Harmondsworth: Penguin, 1982.

Mooney, Chris. "Undoing Bush." *Harper's,* June 2007, 50–52.

Moran, Richard. *Authority and Estrangement: An Essay on Self-Knowledge.* Princeton: Princeton University Press, 2001.

Morris, Benny. *Righteous Victims: A History of the Zionist-Arab Conflict, 1881–2001.* New York: Knopf, 2001.

Mueller, John E. *The Remnants of War.* Ithaca: Cornell University Press, 2004.

Münkler, Herfried. *Die neuen Kriege.* Reinbeck: Rowohlt, 2003.

———. *The New Wars.* Trans. Patrick Camiller. London: Polity, 2004.

Neier, Aryeh. "What Should Be Done about the Guilty?" *New York Review of Books* 37 (1990): 32–34.

Nietzsche, Friedrich. *Twilight of the Idols.* Trans. Duncan Lange. Oxford: Oxford University Press, 1998.

Noël, Alain, and Jean-Philippe Thérien. *Left and Right in Global Politics.* Cambridge: Cambridge University Press, 2008.

Norris, Pippa. *Digital Divide: Civic Engagement, Information Poverty, and the Internet Worldwide.* Cambridge: Cambridge University Press, 2001.

Norris, Pippa, and Ronald Inglehart. *Sacred and Secular: Religion and Politics Worldwide.* Cambridge: Cambridge University Press, 2004.

Nunberg, Geoff. *Talking Right: How Conservatives Turned Liberalism into a Tax-Raising, Latte-Drinking, Sushi-Eating, Volvo-Driving, New York Times–Reading, Body-Piercing, Hollywood-Loving, Left-Wing Freak Show.* New York: PublicAffairs, 2007.

Nussbaum, Martha C., and Amartya Sen, eds. *The Quality of Life.* Oxford: Clarendon, 1989.

Pagden, Anthony. *The Enlightenment: And Why It Still Matters.* New York: Random House, 2013.

———. *Lords of All the World: Ideologies of Empire in Spain, Britain and France c.1500–c.1800.* New Haven: Yale University Press, 1995.

———. *Worlds at War.* Oxford: Oxford University Press, 2008.

Palaver, Wolfgang. "Gleichheit als Sprengkraft? Zum Einfluß des Christentums auf die Entwicklung der Demokratie." In *Verweigerte Mündigkeit? Politische Kultur und Kirche,* ed. Józef Niewiadomski, 195–217. Thaur: Kulturverlag, 1989.

Passerini, Luisa. "From the Ironies of Identity to the Identities of Irony." In *The Idea of Europe: From Antiquity to the European Union,* ed. Anthony Pagden, 191–208. Cambridge: Cambridge University Press, 2002.

Pennings, Paul, and Christine Arnold. "Is Constitutional Politics Like Politics 'At Home'? The Case of the EU Constitution." *Political Studies* 4 (2008): 789–806.

Pinkard, Terry. *German Philosophy 1760–1860: The Legacy of Idealism.* Cambridge: Cambridge University Press, 2002.

Pinker, Steven. *The Better Angels of Our Nature: Why Violence Has Declined.* New York: Penguin, 2011.

———. *The Blank Slate: The Modern Denial of Human Nature.* New York: Viking, 2002.

Plato. "Phaedo." In *Five Dialogues: Euthyphro, Apology, Crito, Meno, Phaedo,* ed. G. M. A. Grube. Indianapolis: Hackett, 2012.

Plutarch. "Life of Pelopidas." In *The Age of Alexander: Nine Greek Lives,* trans. Ian Scott-Kilvert. New York: Penguin, 2012.

Polat, Necati. *International Relations: Meaning and Mimesis.* New York: Routledge 2012.

Powell, G. Bingham. "Political Cleavage Structure, Cross-Pressure Processes, and Partisanship: An Empirical Test of the Theory." *American Political Science Review* 1 (1976): 1–23.

Quine, Willard. "On What There Is." In *From a Logical Point of View.* Cambridge: Harvard University Press, 1953.

Ranney, Austin. "Politics in the United States." In *Comparative Politics Today: A World View,* ed. Gabriel A. Almond, G. Bingham Powell, Russell J. Dalton, and Kaare Strom, 743–86. New York: Longman, 2004.

Rawls, John. *The Law of Peoples.* Cambridge: Harvard University Press, 1999.

———. *Political Liberalism.* New York: Columbia University Press, 1993.

Raz, Joseph. "Agency, Reason, and the Good." In *Engaging Reason: On the Theory of Value and Action,* 22–45. Oxford: Oxford University Press, 1999.

———. "Explaining Normativity: On Rationality and the Justification of Reason." In *Engaging Reason: On the Theory of Value and Action,* 90–117. Oxford: Oxford University Press, 1999.

———. *The Morality of Freedom.* Oxford: Clarendon, 1986.

———. *Practical Reason and Norms.* 2nd ed. Princeton: Princeton University Press, 1990.

Revelli, Marco. *Sinistra Destra: L'identità smarrita.* Rome: Laterza, 2007.

Roth, Philip. *American Pastoral.* London: Jonathan Cape, 1997.

Roy, Arundathi. "The Algebra of Infinite Justice." *The Guardian,* September 29, 2001.

Rubinstein, W.D. *The Left, the Right and the Jews.* London: Croom Helm, 1982.

Said, Edward. *Orientalism.* New York: Vintage, 1979.

Salehyan, Idean. *Rebels without Borders: Transnational Insurgencies in World Politics.* Ithaca: Cornell University Press, 2011.

Sample, Susan G. "Arms Races: A Cause or Symptom." In *What Do We Know about War?* ed. John A. Vasquez, 111–38. Lanham, MD: Rowman & Littlefield, 2012.

Sani, Giacomo, and Giovanni Sartori. "Polarization, Fragmentation and Competition in Western Democracies." In *West European Party Systems: Continuity and Change,* ed. Hans Daalder and Peter Mair, 307–40 London: Sage, 1983.

Santambrogio, Ambrogio. *Destra e sinistra: Un'analisi sociologica.* Rome: Laterza, 1998.

Sartori, Giovanni. *Teoria dei partiti e caso italiano.* Milan: SugarCo, 1982.

Schiller, Bradley. "The Futility of Class Warfare: Why 'Us' versus 'Them' Doesn't Sell." *Policy Review,* October and November 2008. Http://www.hoover.org/research/futility-class-warfare.

Schmitt, Carl. *Glossarium: Aufzeichnungen der Jahre 1947–1951.* Berlin: Duncker & Humblot, 1991.

Sémeline, Jacques. *Purifier et détruire : Usages politiques des massacres et genocides.* Paris: Éditions du Seuil, 2005.

Sharoni, Simona. *Gender and the Israeli-Palestinian Conflict: The Politics of Women's Resistance.* Syracuse, NY: Syracuse University Press, 1995.

Shepherd, Robin. *A State beyond the Pale: Europe's Problem with Israel.* London: Weidenfeld & Nicolson, 2009.

Singer, Peter. *A Darwinian Left: Politics, Evolution and Cooperation.* New Haven: Yale University Press, 2000.

Stark, Rodney. *The Victory of Reason: How Christianity Led to Freedom, Capitalism, and Western Success.* New York: Random House, 2006.

Stedman, Stephen John. "Alchemy for a New World Order: Overselling Preventive Diplomacy." *Foreign Affairs,* May–June 1995, 14–20.

Steger, Manfred B. *The Rise of the Global Imaginary: Political Ideologies from the French Revolution to the Global War on Terror.* Oxford: Oxford University Press, 2008.

Stork, Peter. "Human Rights: Controlling the Uncontrollable?" In *Violence, Desire, and the Sacred: Girard's Mimetic Theory across the Disciplines,* ed. Scott Cowdell, Chris Fleming, and Joel Hodge, 205–17. London: Continuum, 2012.

Sunstein, Cass. *Going to Extremes: How Like Minds Unite and Divide.* New York: Oxford University Press, 2009.

Tajfel, Henry, and John C. Turner. "The Social Identity Theory of Inter-group Behavior." In *Psychology of Intergroup Relations,* ed. Stephen Worchel and William G. Austin, 7–24. Chicago: Nelson-Hall, 1986.

Valeriano, Brandon. "Becoming Rivals: The Process of Rivalry Development." In *What Do We Know about War?* ed. John A. Vasquez, 63–82. Lanham, MD: Rowman & Littlefield, 2012.

Van der Stoel, M. "The Role of the CSCE High Commissioner on National Minorities in CSCE Preventive Diplomacy." In *The Challenge of Preventive Diplomacy,* 33–54. Stockholm: Ministry for Foreign Affairs, 1994.

Vasquez, John A. *The War Puzzle.* Cambridge: Cambridge University Press, 1993.

———, ed. *What Do We Know about War?* Lanham, MD: Rowman & Littlefield, 2012.

Vattimo, Gianni. *After Christianity.* New York: Columbia University Press, 2002.

———. "The Age of Interpretation." In *The Future of Religion,* ed. Santiago Zabala, 43–54. New York: Columbia University Press, 2005.

Volmer, Ludger. *Die Grünen und die Außenpolitik—ein schwieriges Verhältnis. Eine Ideen-, Programm- und Ereignisgeschichte grüner Außenpolitik.* Münster: Verlag Westfälisches Dampfboot, 1998.

von Neumann, John, and Oskar Morgenstern. *Theory of Games and Economic Behavior.* Ed. A. Rubinstein. Princeton: Princeton University Press, 2007.

Wæver, Ole. "Peace and Security: Two Concepts and Their Relationship." In *Conceptual Innovation and Contemporary Security Analysis: Essays in Honour of Haakan Wiberg,* ed. Dietrich Jung and Stefano Guzzini, 43–57. Copenhagen: Copenhagen Peace Research Institute, 2002.

Wagner, Donald. "Evangelicals and Israel: Theological Roots of a Political Alliance." *Christian Century,* November 4, 1998, 1020–26.

Wallace, R. Jay. *Responsibility and Moral Sentiments.* Cambridge: Harvard University Press, 1998.

Wallensteen, Peter. *Understanding Conflict Resolution: War, Peace and the Global System* London: Sage, 2002.

Walt, Stephen M. *Taming American Power: The Global Response to U.S. Primacy.* New York: Norton, 2005.

Wasserstein, Bernard. *Israelis and Palestinians: Why Do They Fight? Can They Stop?* New Haven: Yale University Press, 2001.

Weine, Stevan M. *When History Is a Nightmare: Lives and Memories of Ethnic Cleansing in Bosnia-Herzegovina.* New Brunswick, NJ: Rutgers University Press, 1999.

Weissman, David. *Social Ontology.* New Haven: Yale University Press, 2000.

Wendt, Alexander. *Social Theory of International Politics.* Cambridge: Cambridge University Press, 1999.

Williams, Bernard. "Internal and External Reasons." In *Rational Action,* ed. Ross Harrison, 17–28. Cambridge: Cambridge University Press, 1980.

———. *Moral Luck.* Cambridge: Cambridge University Press, 1981.

———. *Truth and Truthfulness: An Essay in Genealogy.* Princeton: Princeton University Press, 2002.

Wydra, Harald. *Communism and the Emergence of Democracy.* Cambridge: Cambridge University Press, 2007.

———. "The Power of Symbols: Communism and Beyond." *International Journal of Politics, Culture, and Society* 1 (2012): 49–69.

———. "Victims and New Wars." *Cambridge Review of International Affairs* 26, no. 1 (2013): 159–60.

Žižek, Slavoj. *How to Read Lacan.* London: Granta, 2006.

# Index